In *Metanoia*, Alan Hirsch and Rob Kelly recognize the church has reached a turning point. Social unrest, political discord, a life-altering pandemic—all of these are forcing leaders to consider how they move forward in a changed world. Hirsch and Kelly offer insightful answers to important missiological questions: What if, instead of following old models, we turned to God for new ideas? What if, instead of holding onto the past, we sought God's future? *Metanoia* brilliantly explains how repentance realigns our hearts with God's and creates a shift that prepares his people to reach the world in brand-new ways.

DAVE FERGUSON, lead visionary, NewThing; author, *BLESS*

The church needs a course correction! Far beyond the guilt and shame frameworks of repentance we have previously held to, this book beckons us to consider metanoia as the radical paradigm shift we need in order to see with fresh eyes the beauty awaiting us in Christ. Compelling, hopeful, and unflinching, *Metanoia* is a masterful book that every Christian leader should read.

LISA RODRIGUEZ-WATSON, national director, Missio Alliance; contributing author, *Voices of Lament* and *Red Skies*

Every once in a while, I find myself reading a book that I have to close. It's too much, too good. My imagination is captivated, the vision of God is beyond belief, and I need to breathe. It's so overwhelmingly true and hopeful, that it shifts the foundation of my soul. With the WHY linked with the HOW, Alan and Rob plumb the depths of Jesus and emerge with a way forward for all of us, individually and collectively—a force, perhaps like the one that caused the disciples to drop everything and follow.

NANCY ORTBERG, CEO, Transforming the Bay with Christ; author, *Unleashing the Power of Rubber Bands*

In a world awash with peripherals, the message of *Metanoia* is truly and refreshingly radical—striking right at the very radix, the root, of the ways in which we are to think, live, and lead as followers of Jesus Christ. I particularly welcome the blend of provocative thought and pragmatic empowerment, typical as it is of Alan Hirsch's life as both a prophetic intellect and catalytic leader.

PETE GREIG, 24-7 Prayer International and Emmaus Rd, UK

There are very few writers who can take a concept that you have known for a long time and help you rediscover it in a way that helps you see everything anew. Alan Hirsch seems to do this with every book. In *Metanoia*, he and his coauthor, Rob Kelly, reframe a biblical idea that for many has become burdensome and guilt-inducing into a pathway for new energy, creativity, and deep transformation. You'll want to return to this book over and over again, as Hirsch and Kelly demonstrate their ability to be docents of genuine transformation.

TOD BOLSINGER, Fulle~ ʼ   ʼ and *Tempered Resilience*

We are living in days of unprecedented change and cannot afford to ignore the practice and discipline of metanoia. Alan and Rob help us understand how we have got to where we are and show us how to get to where God wants to take us. *Metanoia* is not for the faint of heart but for those who wholeheartedly want to join God in his mission here on earth. This book should be read by every leader, and the concepts integrated into every church, ministry, and organization.

CHRISTINE CAINE, founder, A21 and Propel Women

Coming to terms with, and applying, the grace implicit in discovering and admitting error (our own not others) may be the most important competency of our time. This book is a master class, a philosophical tour de force—a profound, transformative, and luminous work.

BRIAN SANDERS, founder, Underground Network; author, *Microchurches*

Metanoia courageously peels back the wilting ecclesiastical onion and exposes the heart of our problem within the Western church. Alan Hirsch and Rob Kelly challenge us to a fundamental intellectual reorientation of our very selves as a true and fitting worship response before we ever dare to chart a new course. Unlearning before relearning. And mind-blowing metanoia in between. Through personal experience and biblical reflection, Hirsch and Kelly offer us dynamite in a few dangerous pages. Read slowly and carefully. And at your own risk. For what your heart has been craving might be revealed.

JEFF CHRISTOPHERSON, leader and movement catalyst; author, *Once You See*

This book comes at a time when it is deeply needed, as the church continues to recover from a global pandemic, as well as navigating racial unrest, political polarization, and the need for a new awakening within evangelicalism. Within these pages you will gain insights that hopefully lead you as church leaders to rediscover biblical rootedness, reimagine the mission of the church, and re-engage cultures for a greater advancement of the kingdom of God.

DR. EFREM SMITH, co-pastor, Midtown Church; author, *The Post-Black and Post-White Church* and *Killing Us Softly*

This book is like Lady Wisdom crying out in the streets, inviting people to open their minds and soften their hearts to receive the precious, life-altering, beautiful, good news of Jesus. Read it and weep. Your tears will turn to joy as the One who holds our lives and future comes into clearer view.

DANIELLE STRICKLAND, advocate, author, and speaker

The body of Christ is the hope of the world, but is there hope for the church? Hirsch and Kelly have gifted us with eyes to see that we are living in a kairos moment in time, and that if we choose continual metanoia, God can shift the tracks of history through us.

JR WOODWARD, national director, The V3 Movement; author, *The Scandal of Leadership* and *Creating a Missional Culture*

With scholarly care and penetrating insight, *Metanoia* offers us a broad sweeping reset for how change happens in our lives and our organizations. Not for the faint of heart, nor for those who only want to think and not do, Hirsch and Kelly's book forces us to reconsider the depths of Christian metanoia for how we live and how we lead. For every church, pastor, and Christian leader longing for Christ's inbreaking future.

DAVID FITCH, BR Lindner Chair of Theology, Northern Seminary, Chicago; author, *Faithful Presence*

There are few writers I know who write with such prophetic insight as Alan Hirsch. We are still reaping fruits from *The Forgotten Ways* many years later. *Metanoia* is as catalytic, perhaps more so than anything Alan has written to date. I believe that *Metanoia* will rank among the books that changed things in the twenty-first century.

PEYTON JONES, author, *Church Plantology*; director, The mX Platform; founder, NewBreed Training

Metanoia is exactly what the church needs today. Hirsch and Kelly not only present an accurate diagnosis of what ails the church, but they also provide a compelling remedy for the cure. I instantly desired to make personal application to my own life and ministry. I absolutely love this book!

BRAD BRISCO, director, Bivocational Church Planting for the North American Mission Board; author, *Missional Essentials*, *Next Door as It Is in Heaven*, and *Covocational Church Planting*

Of all the people that I've known and worked with in ministry for these past forty years, Alan Hirsch has had as much profound impact on the Western church as anyone I've personally known. Together with my friend, Rob Kelly, in *Metanoia*, he's once again delivered "North Star" guidance by which to set a course. The strategically thoughtful, experientially informed, personally challenging, and collectively transformative content has been written for today with tomorrow in view. It is visionary in scope yet practical in nature for leaders no longer content with the status quo of docile acquiescence. If Alan's writing, I'm reading ... and you should, too!

DR. MARK DEYMAZ, directional leader, Mosaic Church (Little Rock); CEO, Mosaix Global Network; author, *The Coming Revolution in Church Economics*

Hirsch and Kelly present a profound and urgent message to the church today. The call to metanoia can no longer be a mere prologue. It must be the leitmotif of the life and mission of the Christian and the church. Read at your own risk, and prepare to have your mind blown.

FR. JAMES MALLON, pastor; author; founder, Divine Renovation Ministry

For two decades, Alan Hirsch has been a leading voice at the intersection of gospel, church, and culture. In *Metanoia*, along with Rob Kelly, Alan is once again prompting the church to find her best self through rethinking everything, reviewing all her plans and programs in light of Jesus and his gospel of the kingdom. This is a courageous book for passionate leaders.

TODD HUNTER, founder, The Center for Formation, Justice and Peace; former national director, Association of Vineyard Churches; author, *Christianity Beyond Belief*

Today's church in the Western world holds a dangerously anaemic vision for repentance. More than ever, the church must lean into the deeply robust vision for repentance (metanoia) with the hope of dismantling toxic systems and turning toward a more vibrant and bright future. Alan Hirsch and Rob Kelly have been sounding this alarm for more than a decade, and now they prophetically and pastorally call the church to repent, relearn, and re-embrace the mind of Christ. If more church leaders read this book and submit to the way of metanoia in the power of the Spirit, a radiant future could be ahead of us.

TARA BETH LEACH, pastor; author, *Radiant Church*

This is a mind-blowing book, literally. In *Metanoia*, my friends Alan Hirsch and Rob Kelly lay out both the promise and the pathways for the kind of personal and collective conversions we desperately need if we want to see God's shalom reigning in and through us. Redeeming the often misused and misunderstood word "repent," they show the beauty of the kind of transformation Jesus promised. An inside-out transformation that holds the promise of renewal. Our culture is struggling. It's ripe for renewal. Will we be ready?

KEVIN PALAU, president, Luis Palau Association; author, *Unlikely*

This book is so awesome that I don't know if I can find words to do it justice! In it, Alan and Rob give a much needed powerfully prophetic word to the Western church. This book should come with a warning label because you will not be the same after you read it. Your discipleship and engagement with the local church will be forever changed, and it will impact everything you do.

DANA ALLIN, synod executive, Evangelical Order of Presbyterians; author, *Simple Discipleship*

Decades of the "missional" conversation have not led to church-as-movement. Why? Perhaps because we cannot go from unlearning our inherited paradigm to learning anew without wholeheartedly embracing Jesus' call to metanoia. This book describes that indispensable, painful, and beautiful process of biblical transformation so that we can see and be the church Jesus promised to build: multiplying networks of disciples in communal relationships who exist in and beyond the gathered expression. Take the red pill, and brace yourself for a paradigm-shifting journey.

WES WATKINS, facilitator, Motus Dei Network; missiologist, One Collective

We long for change. *Metanoia* reminds us that the deep transformation we want for ourselves and our mission will not be possible until we are willing to be changed. It invites a rigorous assessment of where we are and casts a vision of where we could be. To go forward may look like turning around.

MANDY SMITH, pastor; author, *Unfettered* and *The Vulnerable Pastor*

This book is a refreshingly honest look at our need to embrace repentance. Alan and Rob dive deeply into the idea of metanoia and portray it as a gift of God for us and our churches if only we would heed and respond to its call. They weave theology, social change theory, and practical tools together in a way that not only convinced me afresh of my need for repentance but also filled me with hope for deep and lasting change in the Australian church. It's a must-read for Christian leaders!

BREE MILLS, director, Micro Churches Australia; Australia director, The Company

A significant shift needs to happen for the church to embrace a broader understanding of her kingdom calling—one that is truly Christlike, gospel-fluent, movement-minded, and city-renewing. This is especially true of my tribe, the Latino church. But we cannot just jump to change. We need to first be awakened to change to avoid the typical "plug and play" pragmatic approach that, in the case of the Latino church, has perpetuated colonized expressions of ministry. Being trained and coached by Alan and his team in the journey of metanoia helped me and the leaders I serve understand that before we step into the new, we need to deeply reflect on the old and enter the journey of painful deconstruction. Then, and only then, can we be awakened (metanoia) enough to journey into the new with different paradigms, platforms, and practices. This book is a must for servant leaders who are serious about ushering movemental changes in their churches, organizations, and cities.

ROBERT GUERRERO, vice president catalyst, Redeemer City to City; founder, Avance

The church is living in the midst of a tectonic shift in American religion. Needed more than ever is a theology for navigating this cultural paradigm shift. This book provides a theology for embracing change through a biblical analysis of metanoia. This is an essential read for aspiring church-based changemakers. It is both inspirational and practical, while maintaining missional faithfulness. This is a book about hope, not despair.

DR. DAVID JOHN SEEL, JR., author, *The New Copernicans* and *Network Power*

Every Christian leader who longs for personal, church, or organizational transformation needs to read this book! Alan and Rob aren't just talking about distant theories; they are speaking of what they know and have experienced for themselves. Get ready for true and radical change when you apply the wisdom from these trusted guides.

REV. DR. NICOLE MARTIN, chief impact officer, *Christianity Today*; author, *Made to Lead* and *Leaning In, Letting Go*

For those wanting to close and address the gap between the church and its missional engagement with the culture, this book outlines the hard and humbling journey we must undertake together.

MARK REYNOLDS, senior strategic advisor, Redeemer City to City

Metanoia is a prophetic masterpiece of the highest order. Hirsch—now with Rob Kelly—has led the way in helping us see the need to shift our ecclesial paradigm from Christendom to a postmodern apostolic framework. Together they have shown us how to do it. Overcoming the knowledge-practice gap is always the challenge. *Metanoia* unpacks the biblical process—step-by-step—for unlearning and relearning what we need to activate the church's apostolic DNA. A must-read for any disciple-leader that wants total transformation in the church now.

DR. MICHEL THERRIEN, founder and president, Preambula Group, Pittsburgh, PA; former academic dean, St. Vincent Seminary; author, *The Catholic Faith Explained*

New strategies don't fully work unless we let go of the old ways that no longer serve the needs of the hour. Taking a new route involves leaving the old route behind. Alan Hirsch and Rob Kelly show how this conversion to the new involves reversal, reorientation, and mindset shift. There is simply no change without it. This book reveals how metanoia is the root of ongoing fruitfulness. A great addition to the literature!

MICHAEL FROST, Morling College, Sydney

Jesus' most important words occur within the Lord's Prayer: "on earth as it is in heaven." The gospel movement from heaven toward earth is captured in doctrines of incarnation, revelation, and kairos. The gospel response from human beings is captured in the idea of metanoia. Discipleship is a journey of aligning ourselves with an ever-agile Jesus who leads us on a journey toward healing and repairing the broken creation. Hirsch and Kelly have done a great service in describing how this happens, not only within individual lives but also for organizations becoming discipled to align with the movement of Jesus.

JOHN CHANDLER, founder, Uptick; author, *Uptick: A Blueprint for Finding and Forming the Next Generation of Pioneering Kingdom Leaders*

Alan Hirsch and Rob Kelly have written the right book at the right time. At this moment of global upheaval and escalating cultural change, the church has struggled to meet the enormous challenge it presents. As the title of their book indicates, what is needed now is metanoia, a deep, thoroughgoing change, both individual and corporate. The strength of this book is in its clear definition of the nature of metanoia, its determination to lay hold of radical Christocentric change, and an insightful, accessible model that sheds light on a pathway to that change.

PETER HERBECK, executive vice president and director, Missions for Renewal Ministries

The word "reset" has become a byword. God's word for reset is "metanoia." It has personal, communal, and cosmic dimensions that "reset" can never reach. Hirsch and Kelly's exploration of metanoia in the Christian's spiritual life and its outworking in ministry is compelling and provocative. Their journey through the theoretical and practical elements will capture the reader's attention. If ever there was a key to the Christian life, metanoia is it. Getting your life and your ministry in sync with the flow of the Spirit will generate new fruitfulness. It will be risky and challenging, but it is God's default setting for renewal.

STUART DEVENISH, independent scholar, writer, practitioner, teacher, and researcher in Christian formation, spirituality, and ministry

When the world is changing so fast, what about us? Are we reacting to these volatile, uncertain, complex, and ambiguous times by digging in our heels or changing our hearts? Alan and Rob have reversed my thinking on metanoia in this timely read. Warning: the word "change" is found on 109 pages! Take it in, and let it do its work. The world is desperate for Jesus' church to look more like its Founder.

DR. TAMMY DUNAHOO, executive dean, Portland Seminary; author, *Cultivating a Disciple-Centric Growth Culture*

The Christian life has been described as a series of commitments, big and small, that we make in response to every new commitment God offers to us in Christ. If that is the transforming journey for us individually, it is also the paradigm shift for the community of Jesus, which Alan Hirsch and Rob Kelly so vividly call for in this book.

LEIGHTON FORD, founder, Leighton Ford Ministries; author, *Transforming Leadership*

In this book Hirsch and Kelly restore repentance (metanoia) to its true priority and significance, rescuing it from a once-for-all personal piety and restoring it to its foundational role in both personal discipleship and the ongoing transformation of churches and organizations. Metanoia is disclosed as a joy, not just a turning from, but a turning to a fuller engagement with Jesus and his kingdom. The processes described in part two make profound institutional change imaginable.

GRAHAM CRAY, honorary assistant bishop, Diocese of York; former archbishops' missioner; leader, UK Fresh Expressions Team; author

God's invitation has always been toward metanoia. A seed must fall to the ground. New wineskins are needed to rightly hold the new wine. And we too need to be converted and become like children, over and over again in order to change and grow. In *Metanoia*, Alan and Rob invite the church to join God's process for growth, change, and renewing impact.

DR. ERIC SWANSON, senior fellow, Leadership Network; coauthor, *To Transform a City*

It has been vogue for decades to speak about brokenness in the Christian life. What Hirsch and Kelly do in *Metanoia* is move us beyond a trite expression of a superficial spirituality to the deep and rich language of repentance. Their call to both personal and organizational metanoia is a first step to seeing a genuine movement of God in the West. Such repentance presents new possibilities, even ways of thinking, for us and the ministries we lead. The unlearning that needs to take place to get us in a posture that genuinely acknowledges Christ as the head of the church presents a learning curve that isn't insurmountable but will certainly require humility and contrition as well as the mind of Christ. These are not easy waters to navigate. Alan and Rob expertly steer us through what must be considered nothing less than the spiritual discipline of metanoia—a superpower for Hirsch and Kelly.

MICHAEL T. COOPER, professor, Missiological Theology; author, *When Evangelicals Sneeze* and award-winning *Ephesiology*

At Moore Theological College, one of my lecturers used to say, "All of life is repentance (metanoia)." It puzzled me at the time. Wasn't "repentance" the word for a one-off transformation: becoming a Christian? After decades of living, loving, and leading, I have slowly realized, in my own kind of "repentance," just how right my professor was. In *Metanoia*, Alan Hirsch and Rob Kelly have unpacked this important insight for both the individual and the community, both the Christian church and (dare I say) any organization that wants to be nimble, flexible, and just! Scriptural, psychological, and sociological—here is an exciting guide to becoming a perpetual learner, always guided by the higher things, never settling for the idiosyncrasies of our often-misguided selves.

DR. JOHN DICKSON, author; Jean Kvamme Distinguished Professor, Wheaton College, Illinois

Disruptive times call for a new kind of leadership. *Metanoia* is a guidebook for those ready to unlearn existing paradigms, small-minded thinking, and obsolete practices. It directs us back to the invitation of Jesus and Paul, to discover a wholehearted spirituality that emerges from repentance and openness and embraces new rhythms and habits. Alan Hirsch and Rob Kelly will guide you and your tribe to "Eureka!" experiences of deep transformative change that are essential for us as individual leaders and the churches and training systems we serve.

DARREN CRONSHAW, Baptist pastor; mission catalyst; research director and professor of Missional Leadership, Australian College of Ministries, Sydney College of Divinity; author, *Credible Witness* and *Dangerous Prayer*; coauthor, *Sentness*

In this liminal time in which we live, *Metanoia* is a gift to the church. My friends Alan Hirsch and Rob Kelly have given us a unique combination of a deeply theological, yet practical guide for any leader or organization seeking to reorient themselves to the mind and mission of Jesus.

DAVE RUNYON, coauthor, *The Art of Neighboring*

"Do not be conformed to the patterns of this world, but be transformed by the renewing of your mind. Then you will be able to test and approve what God's will is," wrote Paul in Romans 12:2. But how do we, the people of God, experience this kind of deep transformation together, and where will it take us? Hirsch and Kelly call it "metanoia," and in this book, they help us explore who the church can be if she attunes herself to this deep work of God in human life. So inspiring and helpful. A wonderful read.

LINDA BERGQUIST, church planting catalyst; adjunct seminary professor; coauthor

Alan and Rob have written a masterful missiology rooted in repentance, naming our collective need to unlearn, turn, and be transformed by Jesus in every dimension, so that we might build the movements that God imagines. This hopeful book is a wise guide to reimagining the future for the church.

TYLER PRIEB, founder, Missional Labs, New York City

Once again, Alan Hirsch (with Rob Kelly) has disturbed my status quo and forced me to acknowledge my false assumptions and blindness to different ways of seeing the world. *Metanoia* frames repentance in a much bigger, richer, more grace-filled perspective that sets us free from the epidemic levels of anxiety, discouragement, and frustration that many of us feel. Christendom is changing and, more than ever, we need a paradigm shift, a metanoia, to allow Christ to renew our minds and see the mission he has given us with new eyes. I welcome this disturbance!

RIC THORPE, bishop of Islington; acting bishop of Kensington; director, The Gregory Centre for Church Multiplication

I am convinced the global church has an opportunity to change and return to its movemental design. I call it "our John 15 moment." The old must be pruned so the new can grow. But to endure this John 15 moment will require us to repent of the old and see the new again. Change is hard. Yet, I think you will agree the church must change. The hard part is how to change and, more importantly, what must be changed. Change begins with repentance, which is challenging for all of us and is why this book will disrupt your paradigms.

PATRICK O'CONNELL, global director, NewThing

metanoia

Foreword by Dennae Pierre

meta noia

How God Radically Transforms People, Churches, and Organizations From the Inside Out

Alan Hirsch with Rob Kelly

100 MOVEMENTS
PUBLISHING

First published in 2023 by 100 Movements Publishing
www.100mpublishing.com
Copyright © 2023 by Alan Hirsch and Rob Kelly

Library of Congress Control Number: 2023903855

ISBN: 978-1-955142-37-3 (print)
ISBN: 978-1-955142-39-7 (ebook)

Cover design by Karen Sawrey
Interior design by Revo Creative
Copy-editing by Carolyn Smith
Proofreading by Sarah Giles

100 Movements Publishing
An imprint of Movement Leaders Collective
Cody, Wyoming
www.movementleaderscollective.com
www.catalysechange.org

Men learn so much about Jesus and his kingdom (love, service, humility, empathy, kindness, etc.) from the various women in our lives and in the world. And yet, universally, women go largely unrecognized and unrewarded and are all too often shamefully marginalized and violently oppressed. Despite this, women everywhere continue to bear witness to the form of Christ in the world, simply by being themselves. All I want to say is that I see you, my dear sisters, and I, for one, am beyond thankful. I can't imagine what this world would be like without you! All I know is that I would not want to be in it. This book is dedicated to you.
—Alan

For Ani, Addison, and RJ.
—Rob

Contents

FOREWORD
DENNAE PIERRE

My daughter Rosa, a vivacious fifteen-month-old, loves exploring the world around her. Other kids her age run *away* from danger, but open doors and busy intersections seem to exert a magnetic pull on her tiny legs. We've learned that closed doors keep Rosa safe because they separate her from potential danger. We make especially sure that every door leading out to the street stays *shut*!

Closing doors is only *part* of our plan in raising Rosa. Our grander purpose—and our ultimate desire—is that she would be able to enjoy the full freedom of exploration and discovery in the huge, wide world that is our backyard. Fenced in and cultivated specifically for her, the backyard is a world filled with all kinds of awe and wonder to satisfy her wide-eyed longing to explore. So, we intentionally *open* doors that let us take her out there.

The mental frames of Western Christianity have often focused on means of protection while neglecting the grander purpose for which those protections were put in place. We tend to think of obedience and sin-avoidance as closed doors—ways of staying away from the dangers of the street. In so doing, we fail to cultivate an imagination for obedience as an invitation to explore God's expansive kingdom.

And that's not the worst of it. Even more tragic is that our spiritual formation and communal practices are often anemic, making it difficult for us to discover God's reality in any depth. This results in a lack of attunement to the Spirit's adaptive and progressive work in our lives, churches, and organizations. Imagine what would happen if our family continued to keep the doors shut, to keep Rosa safe into her teenage years. Certainly when she becomes a young adult, Rosa will need a dose of healthy fear as she is handed car keys and backs out of our driveway. But we will need to gradually change our parenting methods between now and then to ensure she is ready to drive a vehicle and explore our city. Similarly, the one-size-fits-all, cookie-cutter solutions, and "magic pills" the church offers for discipleship, church planting, and theological formation expose an immaturity in our understanding of the journey we each must take to see true transformation. The consequences are evident in our own lives with God, each other, and our neighbors.

We need metanoia.

Rather than a simple solution, metanoia is an invitation to a process of making visible what is currently invisible. It invites us to see differently and to learn to behave differently, from a deep place of personal and corporate transformation. It requires us to have the courage to sit in discomfort, sorrow, anger, and shame as we inhabit the mind of Christ so that we may be transformed, healed, and renewed. Metanoia will form us not only to see the broken patterns of our lives and world simply as an objective fact, but also to see through the eyes and heart of God himself.

The practice of metanoia deepens our yearning for God in ways that increase our longing to experience his kingdom on earth as it is in heaven. It attunes us to God's wondrous reality. It increases our capacity to look at brokenness in the world *through* the mind of Christ, melting away the very shame and pride that keeps us from looking in the first place. I believe this is what God is doing in the church today. The Spirit is awakening us to new ways of seeing and being in order to have greater communion with himself and each other. He is asking us to look again at that plot of dirt and *see* the treasure he has hidden just below the surface. He is inviting us to leave everything behind to purchase that field!

Metanoia is a practice the church desperately needs today; and because we, as leaders, have so often failed to engage with it, we have gained a public reputation for misusing power, maintaining oppressive systems, and ignoring injustice. All the while, we are churning out church services and discipleship models that do little to challenge consumerism and individualism and are insufficient for cultivating Christians commissioned to live courageous lives of radical love in this world. If you are grieved by the state of the church or by the state of your own spirituality; if you are unsettled with Christian community that feels far from being a taste of heaven-on-earth; if you are discontent with the countless men and women far from Christ who struggle to discover him in our churches; if you ache for a visible witness of God's kingdom to break through in our everyday lives, then receive the gift of grace that is metanoia.

It is for this reason that I am incredibly grateful for Alan and Rob's work on this book. We are in deep need of this significant theological contribution and its invitation to inhabit the glorious mind of Christ! I have been deeply prayerful for Alan and Rob as they study and write, hoping that their work invites countless men and women into a practice of living that resists conformity to the powers and principalities of this present age and seeks conformity to the King and his kingdom.

Holy Spirit, please grant your people the courage to live in solidarity with Christ's sufferings as we follow in his steps and discover the healing and joy offered to us. Empower us to demonstrate the radical love of Jesus to a world deeply in need of him. Grant us the grace required to pursue metanoia!

A Briefing for the (Metanoic) Journey

The whole conception of the Kingdom is so novel that only those who are ready to make a new start can even see it, let alone enter into it.

WILLIAM TEMPLE

It is one of the sad ironies of aging, that after decades of struggle and learning, one finally discovers an idea that would have made all the difference had it been properly understood earlier on the journey. Metanoia has been such an idea for me (Alan). If I had understood this life-changing concept when I was younger, I believe my work with various organizations and denominations, as well as in local ministry, would have been far more effective. I have therefore written this book for Christian leaders, in the hope that they might see greater fruitfulness, as well as avoid significant frustration in their own discipleship and in their various organizations, whether churches, non-profits, or marketplace enterprises.

The Pre-History of This Book

This book has a rather unusual history. The idea of metanoia was explored as a key theme in the book I coauthored with Mark Nelson, *Reframation: Seeing God, People, and Mission Through Reenchanted Frames.*[1] As the title suggests, *Reframation* explores the importance of seeing things in a different frame in order to advance in our knowledge of God and his mission. Metanoia—paradigm shift and conversion that changes the heart—is the gateway for seeing through a different, Jesus-shaped lens and is therefore a topic explored throughout *Reframation*. The topic is also explored somewhat throughout all my writings—the missional paradigm shift in *The Forgotten Ways* and *On the Verge*, and the need to look again at the fivefold/APEST (apostle, prophet, evangelist, shepherd, teacher) ministry in 5Q, in particular.[2]

But the real stimulus for this book you are now reading started when Movement Leaders Collective, the organization I cofounded and colead, chose the theme of metanoia for our global gathering in May 2020—situated amid the ideological swirl of the Trump presidency and the early experience of the global pandemic. Given the apocalyptic nature of the global crisis, the theme resonated with all present and proved to be somewhat prophetic in nature. Because so little was known or understood by most Christians on the topic, and because it was so needed in these times, I decided it was important to write a book that focused solely on metanoia and how it can be implemented to bring transformative change in both self and society.

Early on, I approached Dennae Pierre to cowrite the book with me. As the highly capable leader of Redeemer City to City (North America) as well as Surge Network in Phoenix, Dennae is not only a remarkable young leader whom I deeply admire but also would have brought a much-needed female perspective to the book. I am convinced that many of the problems we currently face arise from the fact that almost all thought leaders and theologians (in the Protestant world at least) are male and therefore see things through a distinctly one-dimensional, male, outlook. This deficit in the female perspective means we are not getting the whole picture. And, with apologies to Einstein, we must recognize that we cannot solve our (decidedly male) problems with more of the same (male) kind of thinking that created them in the first place.[3] This necessitates an integration of the female mind and voice into the equation. By coauthoring, Dennae and I wanted to show we really do need each other to answer the problems we seek to resolve. However, Dennae had a season of growth in her work and family (including an unexpected fifth child joining her family!). She felt led to focus on developing the new leaders on her teams and decided the Spirit was calling her to forego the writing project with me. Thankfully, she did not pull out before she had offered some invaluable commentary and editorial feedback on the material I had written. And so I want to acknowledge her input into the shaping of this book. Watch out for Dr. Dennae Pierre! I believe she is a highly significant, thoroughly refreshing, emerging voice in missional movements.

Believing deeply in the synergistic value of coauthoring, I subsequently approached my dear friend and colleague, Rob Kelly—an energetic leader and advocate of city movements everywhere. Rob is a gem of a human, is super smart, and has a unique grasp of what it means to design movemental organizations that span whole cities. And like me, he loves theology, the social sciences, organizational leadership, and generally all things nerdy. We resonate deeply on just about everything. He was therefore a natural fit. Although I am the primary author of this book, Rob made a significant contribution to the material by taking the lead on three chapters in part two (chapters seven to nine) and by adding editorial comment throughout. Since I did secondary editing on his material, it is expressed using the common word "we." But every now and again, we will refer to the "I" when relaying autobiographical content, as I am doing now, and Rob will do later.

Issues of Style and Substance

If you have read any of my previous books, you will have something of a sense of my style and approach. This book is no different in that it seeks to provide substantive but distilled content applicable to discipleship and spirituality, as well as to leadership in the local church or organization.

True metanoia in the biblical sense is inseparable from the person of Jesus, and so Rob and I make no apology for using theology to guide best practitioners in a way that is consistent with the God we confess and love. To be a disciple means we can never rely solely on pure pragmatics and the can-do techniques so prevalent throughout church-growth thinking. Such pragmatism has brought about some of the many serious issues we are now facing—including celebrity leadership, one-dimensional churches, and expensive and complex structures that are almost impossible to change.[4] Besides, as God's beloved children, all believers are expected to become better at thinking thoughts after God and following his ways (Ephesians 5:1). Certainly, all Christian leaders are expected to operate from a theologically informed mind, arising from the discipline of seeing the world through the prism of God-logic.

Thinking and speaking theologically is also important because theology is the "authorized language" that reaches deep into our collective consciousness to retrieve reserves and resources that lie largely hidden and unused.[5] If we wish to properly motivate Jesus' church from the inside out, then we simply must speak the authority derived from deep within the Word.

As you read this book, keep in mind that, in the Scriptures, genuine knowledge of God cannot just be theoretical but involves the loving mutuality of knowing and being known (*yada* in Hebrew and *epignosis* in Greek). Knowledge of God can only come about through direct contact with God and not simply through abstract thinking about him. For example, there is a world of difference between *describing* the attributes of God's justice, generosity, and love, and *personally experiencing* all these things in our daily lives in such a way that they change us. In this latter form of knowledge, we are informed, impacted, touched, and transformed at the same time. To allow the content of this book to have this effect on you, we suggest you read it slowly, section by section, preferably on your knees. Prayerfully seek to attune yourself with what God is revealing to you along the way. This approach will lead you to a place of discovery and will allow you to look again ... to reframe.

Although we offer a distinctly biblical understanding of metanoia in the book, we want to also acknowledge that metanoia is by no means limited to the religious realm. Not only did the word (and the basic concept) originate in ancient Greek, but it is also experienced in all arenas of life. Ironically, some of the very best thinking on metanoia (yes, they actually use that term) is found in the secular marketplace, from authors such as Peter Senge, Otto Scharmer, Margaret Wheatley, and Fritjof Capra, among others. As such we will refer to them throughout. Adopting the language of leadership and organization, this book outlines a comprehensive "theory of change"—essentially how and why a desired change is expected to happen in a particular context. There is much to learn from the social sciences and organizational psychology in this regard.

Because of the way we use theological and sociological material, and because of the relative unfamiliarity with the depth of meanings inherent in the biblical theology of conversion and repentance, this work may feel dense and therefore may require careful attention. Contrary to our culture of quick reads and quick fixes, we encourage you to slow down, to look again, to break through the veil of familiarity you may have with these ideas. The teaching on repentance is a case in point. Although it's been in the Bible all along, it has all too rarely been understood in the way that Scripture itself intended. So we encourage you to be patient with the text.

Change in Two Dimensions (Personal and Collective)

In all genuinely biblical forms of spirituality, the personal encounter with God must inevitably lead to loving action in the world. When we wrestle with deep, transformational change at the personal level, we will become the kind of leaders who are able to deal with the exponentially more complex transformation required at the collective level—in the organizations we lead. This book will therefore seek to address metanoia in both the *personal* and the *collective* dimensions. It was psychologist Carl Rogers who famously noted that "what is most personal is most general." This is not only true for psychology but is also particularly true for spirituality, be it individual or communal. Henri Nouwen extrapolates,

> Anyone trying to live a spiritual life will soon discover that the most personal is the most universal, the most hidden is the most public, and the most solitary is the most communal. What we live in the most intimate places of our beings is not just for us but for all people. That is why our inner lives are lives for others … why our most secret thoughts affect our common life.[6]

Contemplation of God is the discipline that makes the heavenly dimension and truth of the Christian life present in the life of the disciple. What arises from these prayers is simply the working out of this truth in the transient conditions of this world.[7] In our deepest self-reflection, we discover that the roots of our personal problems are the same as those that permeate a sick society. In our personal struggle with brokenness, we cannot but become critics of the prevailing social order. On the other hand, as revolutionaries struggling to bring about a new world order, we will find that we are also fighting the same reactionary fears and false ambitions in ourselves that are laced throughout society. And so we soon discover that we cannot change the world without seeking to change ourselves. "Therefore, every true disciple is called to be a revolutionary at heart; the one who walks the way of Jesus is called to unmask the illusory quality of human society."[8]

Because these things are true, we will sometimes call for a personal experience of the joy of metanoia as we seek to follow Jesus in discipleship, and at other times we will highlight the need for collective (be it organization, broader community, or even national) recalibration and conversion. These are two sides of the same coin, which means that the process we suggest for one applies equally to the other. This is clearly the case throughout Scripture, where God addresses both the individual heart as well as the sins of the whole collective. This two-dimensional understanding of metanoia will become clearer as we proceed; we simply raise it now to guide you as you read.

Other Quirks of Style

Consistent with much of my previous writing, there are extensive endnotes throughout the book. This is meant to provide a deeper rationale to the concept being explored as well as stimulation for further study. We hope they will prove a fruitful resource to those wishing to pursue the topic at hand.

Throughout the book, we use the forward slash "/" to force double play on certain words—for example un/learn, re/define, re/calibrate. This is a deliberate technique so that the text is read more like poetry, enabling the sentence to be experienced in multiple dimensions.

The book refers to several appendices. If the topic is of interest, it can be found at www.themxplatform.com, where it can be read online or downloaded. (See page 191 for the QR code.)

Although part two of this book focuses on practical approaches, space does not allow us to include the numerous specific resources and tools that have been developed to help implement the insights learned along the way. We will therefore be publishing a follow-up practical field guide, which will help those leading organizations and churches to take others through the journey of metanoia.

Go to www.themxplatform.com/onlineshop for more details.

Overview of Contents

This book seeks to articulate a thoroughgoing understanding of metanoia, why it is critical, how it works, and suggests ways it can be implemented.

Part one focuses on the theological and sociological basis of metanoia and why it is critical for both an ongoing relationship with God and for our fruitfulness—whether as an individual disciple or as part of a collective. We will focus not only on the serious challenge that repentance is to our current ways of thinking and acting but also on the incredible blessings it brings—the mind-blowing, vision-enhancing, spiritually rich life God intended for us as his people.

Part two focuses on providing a model of metanoia that is entirely consistent with the content of part one, but that has been tried and tested in the white-hot context of key organizations seeking to become dynamic, innovative movements. The process suggested here has been developed for the various training and consulting services provided by Movement Leaders Collective (MLC, www.movementleaderscollective.com). And this is where Rob Kelly comes into the picture. Rob not only elaborates on the Metanoia Journey process developed by Rich Robinson (the global director of MLC) and myself, but he also brings his own unique insight and expertise to the equation. Rob has significant experience in this area, particularly with regard to platforms and the role of networking for movements that seek to scale across cities and regions. We trust that part two will provide a tangible, actionable way to bring transformational change for those organizations willing to undergo the corporate metanoia required.

This is not a book for the fainthearted. It is dense and somewhat heady at times, but it is also intended to strike at the heart of our prevailing understanding of things—our paradigms. You will not be able read this book and remain unmoved, uninformed, and unchanged. Obviously, we encourage you to read the whole book because there is a certain logic to each chapter. However, if your pragmatic self is straining with the more mind-bending, conceptual content of part one, and you are pining for some practical material that brings change to your system, we suggest you *must* at least read chapter two (on basic definitions—so that you know what we are referring to when we use the term "metanoia") and chapter three (which provides a compelling rationale for why *we* as a church need metanoia and why *you* as an individual leader need to repent) before moving to the practical content. Having conceded that, we seriously urge you to wrestle with part one … because tussling with the ideas there will make all the difference to your practice later.

In all this, we hope that you, like us, will find this material a challenging read in that it will not only call into question the many assumptions you might hold but will also be an exhilarating journey into the realm of ever-greater possibility.

Part One

Why Metanoia

In part one of this book, we propose a thorough framework for *why* metanoia is crucial for Christians in any era—but particularly in ours.

We lament deeply that a genuinely biblical understanding of metanoia has been all but forgotten by large swathes of the church in the West. Certainly, our (Protestant) traditions passed on a highly reduced understanding of metanoia. How it is that we have managed to bypass, or even actively suppress, the incredible revelation given to the church on this vital topic? Much frustration could have been avoided if we realized that God has indeed bequeathed to us a potent avenue of change built into the faith itself. Missing this has been disastrous in the life of the disciple, but perhaps even more so for the communities that are called to be the dynamic presence of Jesus in the world.

About a decade ago, I (Alan) cofounded a program that aimed to help a group of megachurches adopt a scalable and disciple-reproducing model. We took roughly 250 large churches through the program in about five years. It pains me to admit that, despite all the effort and cost, it made precious little difference on the ground. Although most of the participants were highly capable leaders who loved the *idea* of multiplication movements, they tended to lean toward a more pragmatic style and therefore did not have the patience or desire to grapple with the mental mapping needed to inform and sustain significant organizational change. But beyond that, even those who managed to make the required paradigm shifts often lacked the deeply spiritual, transformational *process* that would lead to long-term change. We didn't understand the importance of *unlearning* as a precondition for new learning, nor did we comprehend the process of conscious remapping in bringing about genuinely paradigmatic change. In other words, we failed largely because we did not understand the importance of collective metanoia in instigating change in both human lives and organizations.

For the benefit of all involved, I hope to never make that mistake again. All my work with organizations and leaders is now predicated on both the *idea* as well as the *process* of metanoia. Before moving to organizational re/design and leadership, I now encourage participants to take significant time to become consciously aware of their own roles as stakeholders in the legacy system, of the often unspoken assumptions built into their mental models, of the flaws inherent in the dominant thinking, and of the many hindrances to movement that are latent in the culture and deeply embedded, like muscle memory, in the practices of the organization. This is only the beginning of the process, but it is an essential part. We are beginning to see evidence of real change, as viable movements emerge from this challenging and disruptive season in which we find ourselves.[1]

In our work, we have found that individuals and leaders (and their organizations) who are willing to explore and appropriate the sheer grace of metanoia find themselves ushered into a place of new possibilities and increasing faithfulness. The reason for this, as we shall soon explore, is that metanoia involves having a radically open mind. From this perspective, change is not something to be avoided but rather is a form of sanctification—the process of being increasingly attuned to God and to his purposes in the world. To be a disciple—a person seeking increased conformity to the human archetype of Jesus (God's way of being human)—means to be committed to an ongoing journey of change, of letting go and letting be. It is not only entry to the kingdom of God that requires metanoia (Mark 1:15) but also being increasingly attuned to God (Romans 8:29; 2 Corinthians 3:18). Metanoia is, and ought to be, integrated into the process of becoming more and more like Jesus.

In our work with organizations seeking to embrace the mission of the church, we believe the stifling status quo is caused partly by our inability to bypass obsolete ideas and practices and to instead tap into better, more situationally appropriate ways of thinking and acting. All these issues, and more besides, require metanoia—paradigm shift and conversions that change the heart—if they are ever to be resolved.

At the collective level, metanoia ushers the organization into becoming what social scientists call a "learning organization"—an organization skilled at creating, acquiring, and transferring knowledge, and at modifying its behavior to reflect new knowledge and insights. Clearly, new ideas are essential if any learning is to take place, but these can only be accessed and appropriated through the collective un/learning that takes place in a genuinely metanoic process. The basis of this will be laid out in part one. We will start with an exploration of why metanoia is particularly appropriate in these apocalyptic times (chapter one); we will provide rich definition and nuance to the biblical teaching on topic in chapter two; chapter three will give a comprehensive rationale as to *why* metanoia is critical across the system and throughout life; chapter four will show how metanoia leads us into seeing the world through the mind of Christ; and chapter five will propose an "anthropology of the heart" and why it is critical to bring the mind, soul, and will into the equation of transformational change. By the end of part one, it should be clear that change is not only possible but necessary to the life of faith as well as to the effective missional impact of the church.

Chapter One

The Apocalypse of the (Ecclesial) Soul

Glimpses into the Problems and Potentials of the Church

After a time of decay comes the turning point. The powerful light that has been banished returns. There is movement, but it is not brought about by force. The movement is natural, arising spontaneously. The old is discarded and the new is introduced. Both measures accord with the time; therefore no harm results.

ANCIENT CHINESE SAYING

These are moments in life that can be ripe for change and conversion. Each of us has had their own "stoppage," or if we haven't yet, we will someday: illness, the failure of a marriage or a business, some great disappointment or betrayal. As in the Covid lockdown, those moments generate a tension, a crisis that reveals what is in our hearts.

POPE FRANCIS

See, I am doing a new thing. Now it springs up; do you not perceive it?

ISAIAH 43:19

Over the past decade, our world has experienced something epochal. Commentator Andy Crouch famously described it as a "cultural ice age"—an era that will usher in a lasting shift in our ways of thinking and acting throughout the domains of society.[1] It's hard to argue with this assertion; most of us instinctively know that something fundamental has changed, but we are not yet sure of its consequences. The dangerous ideological fractures in recent US politics, the seismic shifts in geopolitical power, the impact of the global pandemic—all exacerbated by the ever-encroaching realities of an inescapable environmental crisis and the advance of artificial intelligence—have all contributed to this particularly fraught moment in time. The cultural madness and ideological warfare that recent events have exposed are nothing short of alarming. How did so-called "civilization" arrive at the cusp of a new cold war that threatens to get so hot that it engulfs us all? Have we not learned anything from the precipitous events of the twentieth century, the deadliest century in recorded history?

For these, and many more reasons, the use of the biblical term "apocalyptic" is entirely fitting. The word *apocalypsis* in the Greek literally means to expose, to unveil, or to reveal something previously unknown, obscured, or hidden. The experience of an apocalyptic moment involves the exposure of previously hidden patterns in corporate human culture as well as in the individual human soul. These cultural patterns can be so deep that they hide in plain sight and replicate themselves indefinitely until the apocalyptic event reveals them for what they are.[2]

In the Scriptures, events such as these are also called "kairos moments"—saturated time, opportune moments when God calls people to account, and ultimately to repentance ... to *metanoia*.[3]

> "The time [*kairos*] has come," he said. "The kingdom of God has come near. Repent [*metanoiete*] and believe the good news!"
>
> MARK 1:15

Metanoia has always been fundamental to our life as Christ-followers. When Jesus began his earthly ministry and invited people to follow him and encounter the kingdom of God, there was simply one condition: *metanoia*, or, as we have narrowly and inadequately translated it, "repentance." We will more fully explore the meaning of the word in subsequent chapters, but for now, it is enough to say that the word *meta* simply means beyond, above, or overarching. And the word *noia* (a derivative of the noun *nous*) refers to a way of thinking. Metanoia therefore involves paradigm shift, the recognition and rejection of various false frameworks for understanding the world itself and waking up to a whole new world in which Christ is Lord and King.

Examples of the call to metanoia abound throughout the Scriptures. A disquieting example is found in the book of Revelation, where Jesus confronts the various churches directly and calls them to repent of their sins, disloyalties, small-mindedness, and cold-heartedness (Revelation 2, 3). He warns them that if they don't "metanoia," he himself will remove their lampstand as an act of sovereign judgment.[4]

But because this is part of *biblical* revelation, it's not just about "them"; it is about "us" as well. As an authentic expression of the prophetic function, the apocalyptic visions in the book of Revelation are not to be viewed simply as some historically encoded description of the future of world history but rather as a depiction of the ever-new intersection of the drama now taking place between heaven and earth.[5]

> Prophecy here, of course, does not mean foretelling the future but knowing what God's righteousness demands in any particular instant; knowing how, from the standpoint of God, to assign to things and to human beings, to events and their configurations, their place in the overall pattern. *The tangled threads of time are unravelled, and "the system" is laid bare.*[6]

For instance, the COVID-19 pandemic—without doubt the most disruptive event for the church since World War II—provided a revelatory experience whereby the hidden and unconscious ecclesial system was laid bare, forcing church leaders across the Western world to re-evaluate the long-held belief (and practice) that the church exists primarily in its once-a-week expression. Our reliance on fragile practices was "apocalypsed." This in turn has stimulated many to reflect apostolically on the church as a distributed, incarnational, network—the classic signature of transformative movements that change the world. Despite the painful disruption the crisis brought to many, it appears God has nonetheless used it to compel church leaders to reflect on the assumptions on which their prevailing expressions of church were built and to explore more adaptive, fluid, and non-fragile expressions of *ecclesia*. God has given us all an opportunity to investigate the system, to discern the numerous fault lines, to repent of our reductionisms (heresies), to recognize our fragilities, and to align ourselves more faithfully to him and to his purposes.

If we don't take this opportunity as it presents itself to us *now*, in our own kairos God-moment, we fear we will be doomed to a deepening frustration with defunct forms of church and an ongoing existential crisis in relationship to our faithfulness to Jesus and his kingdom way.[7]

Never Waste a *Krisis*

Although this revelatory *kairos* moment is disruptive and presents demanding adaptive challenges, as believers we must recognize that the sovereign Lord of history is somehow at work. Throughout the Bible, history cannot be viewed as a neutral process or as mere fate but, rather, can only be rightly understood as the theater of God's sovereign actions and judgments in the human realm. God is always deeply involved in world events, albeit in profoundly mysterious ways. If we are to believe the biblical testimony to God's sovereignty in world affairs, we must not dodge the implication that not only the world as a whole, but also *we* as his people, are being collectively weighed in the balance. We are being tried and tested. We are told that judgment begins with the household of God (1 Peter 4:17), and so we ought not to be surprised but rather seek to discern what God is saying. We must always respond by interrogating our systems and our roles within them: What is God saying to us in these portentous events? What is being revealed about us in this crisis? What must change? What specifically does God require of me/us?

Addressing and responding to questions such as these will help us faithfully engage with our kairos moment and God's call to metanoia—to change the way we think and act.

Truly, it seems that we have come to a point of "crisis"—a word which Webster's dictionary defines as "the point of time when it is to be decided whether any affair or course of action must go on or be modified or terminate; the decisive moment; the turning point."[8] This definition squares with the biblical term *krisis* as the refining judgment of God that determines events. In other words, we, as the church of Jesus, should acknowledge and receive these events as a time for correction, refinement, and growth—both individually and collectively.

This *krisis* for the church is multifaceted:

- It is a *spiritual crisis.* There is a pandemic of fear and anxiety, hatred and violence throughout society, as well as within Jesus' church. This alone is cause for much repentance.

- It is a *missiological crisis*. The church's credibility and witness before a watching world has been compromised. Our corporate inability to deliver our message in a meaningful way has been spotlighted.

- It is a *theological crisis*. We are forced to take a serious look at our understanding of God's nature and his kingdom purposes in the world. It is time for us to repent of our various idolatries and ideologies and enlarge our understanding of God.

- It is an *ecclesiological crisis*. A fragile, unfaithful, and ineffective understanding of the church has been exposed. We must unearth our core, misguided paradigm and redesign from there.

- It is a *christological crisis*. It has become apparent that the church lacks clarity on the nature of Jesus and the centrality of his character and purpose in *every dimension* of our affairs. We must correct any fundamental misalignments and acknowledge that Jesus is the only legitimate center and measure of the church. It's always reJesus time,[9] but particularly so at present. Failure here means we fail everywhere.

We must do something about these crises.

If we fail to respond faithfully to our particular kairos moment, then we effectively abdicate our responsibility before God to ensure our lives and our organizations are correctly aligned with Jesus and his mission in the world. If we fail to respond to our individual crises, we will experience ongoing frustration and despair—like Sisyphus, doomed to endlessly push the rock up the hill, only to have it roll down again.

Or perhaps it's like the storyline of the classic 1993 movie *Groundhog Day*, where Bill Murray plays a somewhat narcissistic and self-centered weatherman who is forced to live through the same day repeatedly until he finally learns how to love others and show human gratitude and perseverance. Only when he finally learns the lessons of his kairos moment, his crisis, is he freed from the maddeningly repetitive time loop in which he has been trapped.[10]

This is not only a powerful parable for individuals who can't seem to break free of addictive behaviors but also for churches and organizational leaders who find their organizations in various ruts that are seemingly impossible to escape. If we fail to make the necessary changes now—if we simply kick the can down the road—our actions aren't just cowardly and foolish, they are plain unfaithful.

This is clearly a problem with more liturgical ("high") churches that simply try to repeat past successes, but perhaps it also explains why other "low church" denominations are still wired for the kind of revivalism that occurred in the late nineteenth century or why many charismatic churches are trying to relive their heyday of the 1970s and '80s. It's like they are stuck in their own version of *Groundhog Day*. What is the lesson they must learn to escape the loop? Have they even bothered to ask?

Without metanoia we will continue in our various loops of despair and incompetence, either until we eventually learn, or until our organizations simply disappear in the rubble of history. Ever wonder how many of the seven churches in Revelation actually managed to repent, to break their own time loops?

Like Israel, many of us find ourselves wanting to go back to Egypt rather than experience the challenges of the desert. But it's no good continuing the way things are or doubling down on our current understandings. In this unique cultural moment, God is revealing things to us so that we might *do* something about them. The only way to resolve the issues arising from our broken paradigms is to repent, or—in the language of this book—to experience thoroughgoing metanoia. Part two of this book will explore how we as leaders can help people and organizations do precisely this, but first we must become aware of what God is calling us to repent of.

It's VUCA, You Schmooka!

Viewing our current times apocalyptically—as an exposure or unveiling of what was previously hidden—provides us with a uniquely *theological* form of knowledge. This is critical in helping God's people understand and respond to the various revelatory moments he puts before us and to which we are called to faithfully respond.

The social sciences also propose some compelling lenses which highlight the need for radical metanoic change. For instance, a well-developed sociological framework is expressed in the acronym VUCA, which describes the world as volatile, uncertain, complex, and ambiguous. These terms accurately portray the situation of constant, unpredictable change that is increasingly the norm throughout all societies, cultures, and economies in the world.

- *Volatility* refers to the speed of change in a cultural setting. The more volatile the world is, the more and faster things change.

- *Uncertainty* refers to the extent to which we can confidently predict the future. Uncertainty is associated with people's inability to understand what is going on. The more uncertain the world is, the harder it is to predict.

- *Complexity* refers to the number of factors we need to take into account, their variety, and the relationships between them. In situations of high complexity, it is impossible to fully analyze the environment and come to rational conclusions. The more complex the world is, the harder it is to analyze.

- *Ambiguity* refers to a lack of clarity about how to interpret something. A situation is ambiguous, for example, when information is incomplete, contradictory, or too inaccurate to draw clear conclusions. The more ambiguous the world is, the harder it is to interpret.[11]

When these factors combine, as they do in our day, they present a real threat to the societies that are experiencing them—as well as a compelling opportunity for revolutionary change. However, this VUCA world also has radical implications for a church that is alarmingly ill-equipped to negotiate such contexts. This rapidly changing situation demands a corresponding change in imagination and competencies in the church. The problem is that the reductionist formulations of church and organization we have inherited are derived from a significantly different, and less missionally challenging, context than that of the twenty-first century. The maps no longer fit the territories and, even more importantly, they do not fully square with the New Testament itself. As a result, we have a serious systemic, paradigmatic issue. We are wise to heed the words of Peter Drucker here—that the greatest danger in times of turbulence is not the turbulence itself; it is to act with yesterday's logic.[12]

This problem with trying to negotiate today's challenges with yesterday's logic is all too real. For instance, in my [Alan] work in helping people grapple with the nature of church-as-movement, I have found that the problem of change does not really lie in people misunderstanding the "new" ideas of missional movement. (Such ideas are actually ancient but have been forgotten.) Rather, the problem is in helping people escape the old ideas so deeply entrenched in the collective rationality and rooted in habits and practices. We seem to prefer to cling to the old wineskins even though we know they are inadequate to contain the new wine (Luke 5:39). Although we no longer live in Christendom (the form of church birthed out of the Constantinian marriage of church and state), it appears, when it comes to thinking about the church, that Constantine is still the emperor of our imaginations. A profoundly non-missional paradigm therefore continues to hold the Western church firmly in its grip. To escape the innumerable traps of yesterday's logic enshrined in the Christendom paradigm, and to faithfully negotiate the new territories we find ourselves in, *will* require metanoia—there can be no dodging it.

To be clear here, we are not criticizing those who work tirelessly on the frontlines of the church. The problem runs far deeper than the average disciple or leader—it is a collective problem in which we all participate. For instance, if we now regard the war in Vietnam with disdain, we can't necessarily fault the soldiers who fought there, but we can blame the ideologically loaded political rationale that caused the war in the first place. Similarly, if a child is facing psychological problems because of factors in society (for example, unhealthy competition, bullying, or the beauty myth), the problem is not *just* a problem inside the child; it's rooted in the culture, the system, in which that child is growing up. Lasting change only takes place when the ideas that created the problems themselves are changed. It's therefore essential to address the inherited concepts that infuse our thinking and our subsequent habits. We need to see things differently. And for this we are going to need the grace of both individual and collective metanoia.

Toward Promise and Prize

The good news is that apocalypse is not all doom and gloom. The apocalyptic moment not only presents a threat but, as Albert Einstein said, "In the midst of every crisis, lies great opportunity." Similarly, in Chinese script, the word "crisis" can mean either *danger* or *opportunity,* depending on context. This is more than a linguistic cue; it is true to life itself because crises nearly always lead to great change. Of course, there is always the possibility that the change will be for the worse. But there is also the opportunity to change for the better—to reform and improve. Likewise, the apocalyptic moment reveals our flaws, our sins, and our indirection, but it also comes with a promise for those who overcome. Metanoia not only enables ongoing faithfulness to God and our respective callings, but it also brings about a renewed sense of clarity about the situation and our role in it. And, because it inevitably involves some form of recalibration, it also ushers in promised new insight, a defining prize … missional impact.

We will explore this more fully in the next chapter, but at this point it is worth noting that there are many positive outcomes of metanoia. For one, it involves a transformational cleansing of perception—it allows us to see things in their truer, more infinite, light. In other words, it opens up a new mental map of the world, the very thing we need in times of *krisis*. Metanoia is therefore a critical key to ongoing transformation and the growth in all knowledge— especially knowledge of the eternal God. It allows us to think bigger and to grow in maturity.[13]

Therefore, for those willing to undergo the paradigm shift metanoia brings, the crisis unlocks possibilities and prizes previously unknown and unseen. For example, the crisis of the pandemic forced the church to take its "sentness" seriously because it found itself dispersed among the people (Acts 11:19–24). Ironic indeed because this is precisely what Jesus had specified for his people in the Great Commission (Matthew 28:16–20). The pandemic offered a perfect opportunity to live into our sentness and to reorganize accordingly (1 Peter 1:1–2; cf. the theme of a faithful diaspora in the book of Hebrews). I (Alan) heard a leader of a megachurch say that under the COVID-19 lockdown, the church was not closing down (as many of his peers were lamenting) but rather that the church was opening up in thousands of other places. He was able to see the situation not as a threat but as an opportunity, and because of this was able to discern the promise in the peril, the prize in the problem. Those who are open-minded enough to discern God's hand in contemporary events and respond appropriately are game changers because they are willing to adapt amid disruptive conditions.

No less than the great theologian Karl Barth fully recognized this idea of crisis as opportunity when he gave guidance to an anxious pastor in then-Marxist East Germany who was struggling to see how the Lutheran church—which was now radically decentered, delegitimized, and persecuted—could continue to be the church as he had always understood it. In other words, he was struggling with the issue of how a *state* church (with all its Christendom thinking, reliance on buildings, seminaries, and state funding) could possibly operate by going underground. Barth wisely maintained that, in light of the demise of Christendom across the West, *all* of God's people, not just those in the communist bloc, would be wise to ask certain questions of themselves and in every case render a clear answer of *yes* or *no*. He himself suggested that,

> *No*, the church's existence does not always have to possess the same form in the future that it possessed in the past as though this were the only possible pattern.
>
> *No*, the continuance and victory of the cause of God, which the Christian Church is to serve with her witness, is not unconditionally linked with the forms of existence which it has had until now.
>
> *Yes*, the hour may strike, and perhaps has already struck, when God, to our discomfit, but to his glory and for the salvation of mankind, will put an end to this mode of existence because it lacks integrity.
>
> *Yes*, it could be our duty to free ourselves inwardly from our dependency on that mode of existence even while it still lasts. Indeed, on the assumption that it may one day entirely disappear, we definitely should look about us for new ventures in new directions.
>
> *Yes*, as the Church of God we may depend on it that if only we are attentive, God will show us such new ways as we can hardly anticipate now. And as the people who are bound to God, we may even now claim unconquerable security for ourselves through him. For his name is above all names.[14]

When we lose our way in complex times, the God-given grace of metanoia helps us correct our direction and jettison obsolete practices, enabling us to be courageous enough to walk a different way and to innovate. Rather than feeling ashamed of losing our way from God, metanoia is an invitation to turn in a different direction, to draw closer to God and renew our commitment to the mission of the ever-greater God we love, serve, and follow.

There is simply no way of short-circuiting ongoing repentance in a life of faith. We are wise to understand it and to practice it as we negotiate life and God faithfully. This book will go on to explore this in depth and present ways in which we can access the deep joy and blessing metanoia brings.

Chapter Two

Metanoi-eh?

The Spiritual Art of Re/Turning and Re/Tuning

Leave off buying and selling, and start looking. Open your eyes. And you'll wake up in the New Jerusalem.

G. K. CHESTERTON

If the doors of perception were cleansed every thing would appear to man as it is, Infinite. For man has closed himself up, till he sees all things thro' narrow chinks of his cavern.

WILLIAM BLAKE

I was struck as if by lightning ... I needed only to "leave everything and follow."

HANS URS VON BALTHASAR

"You see," said Aslan. "They will not let us help them. They have chosen cunning instead of belief. Their prison is only in their own minds, yet they are in that prison; and so afraid of being taken in that they cannot be taken out."

C. S. LEWIS

Until the twentieth century, up to a quarter of all children died from disease—whether through smallpox, diphtheria, whooping cough, tetanus, measles, or mumps. Yet in the United States today, only 0.1 percent of under-five-year-olds die, and the figure is even lower in the UK and Australia.[1]

This dramatic reduction in infant mortality was brought about not primarily by vaccines but by an even earlier discovery: germ theory. Before the discovery of germs, most scientists believed diseases were caused by miasma (a bad air or mist) or an invasion of some alien spirit. It wasn't until the nineteenth century that scientists such as Louis Pasteur, Joseph Lister, and Robert Koch began to show credible evidence that supported the germ theory—the idea that microscopic organisms were the cause of most diseases. Once this theory was adopted, it led to more effective treatments, containment of disease, vaccines, and a subsequent drop in mortality. Today, we forget how rare it was for parents before the twentieth century to see all their children survive to adulthood.

But none of this would have been possible without a significant paradigm shift (metanoia). It was only when a group of scientists looked at the world with different eyes, recalibrated their thinking, and unlearned what they had previously held as truth, that they were able to discover a greater truth.

Our beliefs, our paradigms, and our perceptions not only shape our thinking but also our activity. If we don't understand the danger of germs, then there is no compelling reason to clean the scalpel, wear fresh scrubs, or sanitize wounds.

As twenty-first-century Western Christians, we have inherited beliefs and mindsets that not only significantly affect how we perceive God, the church, and the world, but also how we operate as disciples of Jesus and as leaders. To further extend the germ-theory metaphor, we are functioning somewhat like doctors walking into open heart surgery with unwashed hands, using the same scalpel from the last surgery, oblivious to the potential danger to those around us.

The issue of metanoia deals with the issue of paradigms, paradigm-blindness, and paradigm shifts; and this is why it is critical that we negotiate the rapidly changing VUCA context in which we find ourselves. Unless we address the problem of the underlying paradigm, no meaningful or lasting change will be possible. I (Alan) have seen this firsthand. After decades of teaching about mission and missional forms of church, I have come to the rather unnerving conclusion that it is our faulty paradigms that are causing us major problems. Take for instance our paradigms in the task of church planting. Because the primary paradigm of church in the West revolves around a peculiarly styled building, designed almost exclusively to host an audience for a Sunday gathering, most "church-planters" begin their challenging work with this stunted understanding of "church" in mind. And so, instead of planting churches as networks of disciples in communal relationships that exist in and beyond the gathered expression, they opt for a model aligned with their ecclesial mindset. If they are predominantly Reformed or Baptist in their thinking, they end up merely planting pulpits; if they harken from the more charismatic denominations, they plant praise and worship services; and if they are from a high church tradition, they plant eucharist dispensaries. Everything is designed around the somewhat narrowed understanding of what the Sunday-service experience ought to look and feel like. Because these significantly reduced understandings of the New Testament expression of *ecclesia* tend to dominate the thinking and practices of most church leaders, they seldom stop to consider that the early church itself did not even have distinctive church buildings, let alone pews, stages, vestries, or pulpits. And we wonder why we don't see the same kind of impact in our churches that was evident throughout the early church, even though it was always marginal and often persecuted. Our understanding of *ecclesia* is paradigmatically different from theirs.

Our lack of understanding can be caused by a number of factors. Some leaders feel too busy to stop and reflect on the problems with the inherited paradigm; others simply prefer to remain in denial about how dire things really are. Many of us are overly familiar with what we believe church to be—we think we have it all figured out. But we need to take another look. It was the French artist Henri Matisse who said that to look at something as though we had never seen it before requires great courage;[2] that to see an object in all its uniqueness, we must *let go* of the safety of a familiar view of reality. So, for example, for an artist to truly paint the rose right in front of them, they must forget all the roses that were ever painted. We suggest this is precisely true when it comes to our deeply entrenched over-familiarity with *what we think* the church really is. This ability to get another take on reality is a critical dimension of metanoia.

The paradigm problem is exacerbated when people are so deeply invested in the current system—receiving salary, status, and kudos—that they cannot, or will not, call it into question.[3] Certainly we know from history and sociology that resistance to innovation does not generally come from the ignorant masses but rather from the "professionals" who have a vested interest in maintaining the status quo. Church can indeed evolve beyond a lecture/worship/performance event, but not without significant self-awareness and repentance from the current leadership.

It is therefore critical that we gain a biblical understanding of what metanoia is and why it is essential in the life of the believer and the people of God. To help us further unpack the concept of metanoia, we will explore the idea of repentance—in the fullest sense of the term—in both the Old and New Testaments.

Time to Re/Turn—Old Testament Understandings

As strange as it might seem, there is no exact Hebrew equivalent for the English term "repentance." Rather, what we have come to know as repentance is best expressed by several different actions and metaphors that suggest a radical change in thinking and attitude toward God and his world.[4] The most prominent Hebrew terms/metaphors come in the words *shuv* and *teshuva,* which can best be translated into English as "turning" and "returning," respectively. To capture the Old Testament essence of the term, we will simply refer to *te/shuva* as re/turning or re/orienting.

As the word suggests, re/turning signifies a reorientation of perspective, like when you turn around and proceed in a different direction. It involves a reversal, conversion, and reorientation that is often felt before the mind can even grasp it; and it is critical to apprehending and joining in the work of God to restore all things—including the self.[5] Re/turning therefore involves not just a turning *from* but a turning *toward.*[6] *Te/shuva* clearly points to the re/direction of life, a re/turning *toward God,* a right re/ordering of life.[7] So important was *te/shuva* in Judaism that the rabbis taught that it was one of the seven pillars on which God established the world (Proverbs 9:1).[8] By this they meant that the possibility of conversion was built into the "operating system" of the universe itself.

Te/shuva, like all genuinely biblical ideas, is grounded in the reality of the covenant between God and his people. This covenant involved a relationship that required regular and all-encompassing orientation to the One God, along with a willingness to be increasingly attuned to his ways.[9] The people regularly lost their way and needed to constantly re/turn to maintain their relationship with YHWH. This meant a continuous renunciation of all forms of idolatry—of those things that hindered their connection with God, things that not only distracted them but also distorted their experience of God. Because the Israelites (like us today) were natural sinners and therefore inclined to covenantal unfaithfulness, the phenomenon of constant re/turning was factored into the covenant relationship that Israel had with God. It was the only way a relationship with the holy God could be maintained.

The concept of re/turning also assumes we are not always inclined to make the right choices; sometimes we deliberately take paths that lead us astray, and at other times we simply lose our way for lack of direction. We all make errors, whether deliberately or unintentionally, and we reap the consequences, good or bad. Therefore, we all need regular course corrections if we are to negotiate life's complexities. C. S. Lewis put it this way:

> We all want to progress. But progress means getting nearer to the place where you want to be. And if you have taken a wrong turning, then to go forward does not get you any nearer. If you are on the wrong road, progress means doing an about-turn and walking back to the right road; and in that case [the person] who turns back soonest is the most progressive [person] … There is nothing progressive about being pig-headed and refusing to admit a mistake. And I think if you look at the present state of the world it is pretty plain that humanity has been making some big mistakes. We are on the wrong road. And if that is so, we must go back. Going back is the quickest way on.[10]

More often than not, instead of re/turning, we find ways to minimize or ignore our "mistakes." Embarrassed about our faults and indirection, we tend to justify these "mistakes" with Christian platitudes that focus on the "good" that God brought about, despite evidence that suggests we have brought harm to ourselves, to others, or to the purposes God has called us to.

A Time to Tune In—New Testament Understandings

If the Old Testament notion of repentance encompasses the idea of re/turning, then the New Testament one points to the idea of tuning in. The New Testament fully incorporates the Old Testament's *te/shuva* but develops it by focusing on the role of conversion as not only changing our direction but also *transforming* us in the process—in other words it is *metamorphic*. The New Testament consistently teaches that repentance changes the way we perceive and make sense of our world—a change that goes to the very heart of consciousness. And here we arrive at the New Testament concept of metanoia, upon which this book is centered.

The word *metanoia* is typically translated in the Bible as "repentance." But this is not a particularly accurate or comprehensive translation. This diminished understanding of the biblical concept of repentance stems from the fourth century, when St. Jerome mistranslated the Greek word *metanoia* into the Latin word *poenitentia*, thus limiting its meaning to the idea of doing penance. This idea of penitence had strong moral and personal overtones, and so when we hear the word "repent," we tend to think about our own personal guilt, shame, or sorrow and about how we can engage in some form of restitution by actively trying to change and improve. There is nothing wrong with this in itself—clearly, we are called to feel some level of remorse in relation to our sins, as well as some form of restitution as evidence of radical change—but apart from being reductionistic, it does not actually convey what is meant by the word *metanoia*. Consider instead Alister McGrath's take:

> The Greek term metanoia—traditionally and inadequately translated as "repentance"—means something more like "a radical change of mind," or "a fundamental intellectual re-orientation," through which we turn away from older habits of thought and action and embrace a new way of thinking and living. Repentance means not primarily a sense of regret, but a renunciation of narrow and sectarian human views which are not large enough for God's mystery. It is about a transformed metaphysical vision of reality.[11]

A renunciation of small-minded thinking along with a transformed vision of reality! And if this sounds over the top, what McGrath is asserting is clear in the linguistic structure (etymology) of the word itself. Look at the word. The first part is *meta,* which is the same root we use in words like *meta*morphosis (change into something completely different); *meta*verse (the virtual above-reality world where users can interact, game, and experience things like they would in the real world); or *meta*physics (physics beyond ordinary physics). The root *meta* simply means "beyond," "above," or "overarching." Used as a prefix it means "more comprehensive" or "transcending." It implies a deepening or expansion of some sort—an opening up to something at a higher level of reality.

The second part of the word is *noia*, which is derived from the Greek word *nous*. In the New Testament, it refers to a person or society's outlook, mental filter, orientation, or mindset. The *nous* is made up of a complex system of narratives, assumptions, concepts, values, and practices that constitutes a way of viewing reality for the community that shares them. It is a "way of thinking" or a paradigm.[12] "[It] is the whole group of faculties which compose intelligence: It is sight and perception, thought and reflection, apprehension and comprehension—all that is popularly known as the intellect or understanding. But it also embraces more than this, namely, a large portion of the moral and affectional nature. It occupies the realm of the heart."[13]

Taken together, we believe the best translation of *meta-noia* is simply "paradigm shift"—or perhaps more colloquially, the experience of having your mind blown. Using the more disciplined language of the scholar, missiologist and philosopher Stuart Devenish says that the person undergoing metanoia experiences the inception of a new, ultimate, and alternate consciousness, which is contrary to anything they have previously known: "*Metanoia* can be defined as being either 'another mind' or a 'higher consciousness' or 'meta-knowledge.'"[14]

Clearly, metanoia is a much broader concept than the standard reduced mistranslation of repentance conveys. As theologian Richard Niebuhr observes, "The Christian responsibility 'to repent' demands more than simply expressing feelings of regret for moral wrong-doing and a vague desire for reform. [Rather,] it involves the recognition and rejection of various false frameworks for understanding the world itself."[15] Radical metanoia always brings with it a corresponding transformation. Metanoia renews our relationship with God, bringing with it an intense desire for him, deep gratitude, and a growth in self-awareness that increases our freedom to love. This clearly has huge implications for fruitful discipleship as well as for faithful living in the kingdom.[16] Crucially, as we will explore in chapter four, metanoia is the doorway to having the mind of Christ. All in all, metanoia is something like the red pill in the 1999 film *The Matrix*.[17] Take it and everything changes; you wake up in a new world.

And importantly, with regards to our various VUCA situations, we believe that when individuals and organizations embrace metanoia, it increases their ability to adapt, to mature, to persevere, and to be resilient in the difficulties of our cultural milieu. It also forms them into more hopeful and innovative people in the midst of trials. (Much more of this in part two.) And yet, we seem not to have grasped the sheer importance of this gift, nor have we meaningfully appropriated it in our individual and corporate discipleship. The net result is that our collective mind (*nous*) has been significantly closed; our spiritual instincts have been suppressed and dulled; and our ability to learn, adapt, and respond to the leading of the ever-greater God has been severely impaired.

Far from the stereotypical negative perception of repentance, which leaves us feeling diminished and ashamed, it is time for us to see metanoia as the beautiful grace of God that enables us to transcend the narrowed confines of our current condition and opens us up to an ever-greater, multi-dimensional understanding of God, our world, our organizations, and ourselves.

> Correctly understood, repentance is not negative, but positive. It means, not self-pity or even remorse, but conversion, the re-centering of our whole life on the Trinity. It is to look, not backward with regret, but forward with hope; not downwards at our own shortcomings, but upwards at God's love. It is to see, not merely what we have failed to be, but what by divine grace we can now become; and it is to act upon what we see. To repent is to open our eyes to the light.[18]

In the rest of this chapter, we want to highlight the many dimensions of metanoia and how it can bring about fruitful change in both our lives and our ministries.

Metanoia as a Mind-Blowing Transformation of Understanding

The first sentence in Jesus' active ministry could have included any number of topics. He would later give us the Great Commandments and the Great Commission, teach the Sermon on the Mount, engage in Upper Room Discourse, and pray a high priestly prayer for the unity of his church. But those weren't the focus of his first words. Instead, he announced, "The time has come ... the kingdom of God has come near. *Metanoiete* and believe the good news!" (Mark 1:15). The lesson? To even be able to hear and understand the most profound truths that Jesus teaches, we must first open our minds and hearts and undergo metanoia. It's the doorway to a real experience of God.

We encounter the Lord Jesus, and he immediately invites us to fundamental transformation—to metanoia! To know God *is* to change. Therefore, the true following of Jesus (discipleship) is marked by a significant reorientation that involves centering our whole being around the reality of God. Metanoia is the doorway to the spiritual revolution of Jesus. It allows us to discover that God is not "out there" but that we are in God and God is in us. And because we have been united to God in the person of our Lord Jesus Christ, the source of all reality, we no longer look out *at* reality; we now look out *from* reality. That's what it means to have the mind of Christ—the place where *everything* changes.

Stuart Devenish has conducted exhaustive study on the idea of conversion, and says that authentic metanoia—because it integrates the biblically related dimensions of a radical re/orienting of life, together with a re/framing of the very way we comprehend the world—provides disciples with a whole new way of processing their lives and negotiating their worlds:[19] "In an event which parallels the second phase of the Apostle Paul's conversion when scales fell from his eyes (Acts 9:18), the convert undergoes a venturing or opening of the mind toward hitherto unknown and unrecognized dimensions of reality."[20]

We can perhaps now better understand what Paul means when he admonishes all believers to be *constantly* "transformed by the renewing of [our] mind[s]" (Romans 12:2).[21] The person who undergoes this transformational experience will gain a renewed way of understanding themselves, their relationships, and the world around them; and their scale of moral values is also thoroughly reevaluated. Metanoia allows us to experience the boundless and unexpected; something beyond (*meta*) prevailing customs, attitudes, or ideas; something that sparks a deeper connection to God and to others; a phenomenon that brings a newfound clarity of our own role in the world; and offers a deepened perspective on things. Theologian Bernard Lonergan says that this new way of seeing the world involves what he calls a "horizon change" or a "paradigm shift."[22] In that *revelatory* moment, we are literally seized by a "way," a vision, and we begin to experience our lives as meaningful through serving the new construct. Everything, including our mental maps and core commitments, are reordered as a result. Metanoia therefore involves the capacity to imagine new possibilities—the idea of an open and invigorated imagination. It is much more than a confession of personal guilt or doing penance!

Likewise, theologians such as von Balthasar and Heschel see conversion as being awakened to wonder, even though this wonder is usually somewhat contained at first. The full implications of our conversion are not always immediately evident. It would be too much for us to grasp in one go, and we need time to assimilate what it is that we have experienced. Metanoia is therefore both an event that ushers in a single momentous and permanent change but also a process spread out over a lifetime.[23] This ought not to surprise us. For instance, the Bible teaches that sanctification is both instantaneous as well as ongoing, as is the filling of the Spirit (Ephesians 5:18). It is the same with salvation. We are both "saved" in a moment in time, but we are also called to "work out [our] salvation with fear and trembling" (Philippians 2:12). This twin nature of conversion is counter to much of Western evangelicalism, which places undue emphasis on conversion as a one-time, momentary decision. Our language reflects this viewpoint, with phrases such as "Get 'em saved," and "If you died tonight, do you know where you would go? Repent and believe in the Lord Jesus." But conversion, as Eugene Peterson puts it, is also a long obedience in the same direction.[24] We never stop learning; genuine learning involves a prolonged process that will occupy a whole lifetime. This is the essence of discipleship.

Metanoia is powerful because the smallest realization and new discovery can lead to new habits, patterns, and ways of relating to the world. Breakthrough thinker Olivia Fox Cabane notes that "break-through involves a shift in your understanding of the world, because the lens through which you view the world has been suddenly, gloriously changed … A breakthrough is a sudden advance in your knowledge or understanding that moves you past a barrier and makes you see things, understand things in a new way."[25]

Unfortunately, these moments can be all too rare. But this ought not to be so! Openness to ongoing metanoia ought to characterize the life of all people committed to loving, worshipping, and serving the ever-greater God.

Metanoia as an Ever-Expansive Reframing of Reality

As humans, we have the propensity to be bound by ideologies (reduced truth that claims to be the only defining truth) and by idolatries (reductions in our understanding of God, of making God small) that claim our allegiance. The only way to be released from such ideologies and idolatries is to reevaluate them in light of a greater truth.[26] Metanoia involves a transformational cleansing of perception, which enables a new, expansive, way of viewing the world.[27] It is therefore essential for ongoing transformation and the growth in all knowledge, especially when it comes to experiencing the God who is ever greater.

If we fail to engage with conversion as an ongoing reality, we will always remain somewhat misdirected and distracted, distanced from God, and therefore unable to experience the spiritually intimate relationship envisaged in our union with him through Christ.[28] By excluding metanoia in principle, we are no longer able to recognize the ever-widening greatness of the living God who has an eternity of revelation to show us. Maturity (*telos*), fullness (*pleroma*), and the ever-expansive mind of Christ will always evade people and organizations who/that do so.

Metanoia as a Crack in Your Cosmic Egg

Metanoia brings with it paradigmatic insight and learning that is characteristic of breakthrough moments—those "Eureka!" experiences that seem to radically reorient our lives and trajectories. Consider, for example, creative philosopher Joseph Chilton Pearce's description of the creative process itself as an experience of becoming aware of a crack in our seemingly self-contained worldview (what he likens to an "egg") that eventually leads to a paradigm change at a certain point in time. His own story is one that many of us can relate to.

I've been writing since I was old enough to read, and I have always thought it odd that I'd get a vague idea or notion, and then would walk around with it for a few days or weeks or months (and in one case several years) feeling sort of like I was pregnant with something, but that it wasn't ready to birth. I'd catch glimpses in daydreams, in synchronistic readings or discussions, in things I saw in the world. And then, suddenly, it would have to come out, and I'd pick up a pad and pen or sit at my typewriter (and now my computer) and the words would all pour out, be they a poem or a story or the first draft of a non-fiction book—with a clarity and precision and completeness that I never could have achieved if I'd tried to assemble them step-by-step, word-by-word, or if I'd tried to put them down on paper early in the process while I was still pregnant with the concept but not yet birthing. I discovered in this book that the way I write and the way others create is similar, that we become aware of the egg, and then a small crack in it, and then—by serendipity or magic or the grace of God—the crack suddenly opens enough that the light of understanding flows in and it's all just so clear and easy to express.[29]

My (Alan) own experiences are eerily similar. For instance, my book *The Forgotten Ways* started as a quest to understand the intrinsic nature of movements that was initiated by hearing a question that utterly gripped my imagination. I felt called to answer it in a way that was meaningful for the church in our time. For the next three years, *every day*, I sought to find possible answers and clues to an answer through reading, observation, conversations with others, and concentrated reflection. Throughout this time, I felt God was birthing something in and through me. However, the "answer" to my quest—the "cracking of my cosmic egg," so to speak— came all at once while I was sitting at a coffee shop, sipping a latte. The "answer" came in what I experienced as an "Aha!" moment, a revelation, a download; and for the next three hours, I sought to capture the deluge in a teacup.[30]

One of the characteristic features of metanoic experience is that, by and large, it is experienced with the force of a conversion. Although the ideas might have been bubbling below the surface, there seems to be a catalytic moment of realization as their significance dawns upon a person and can be described as a revelatory event ... a moment of sudden, triumphant discovery, inspiration, or insight in which we are turned, reoriented ... *converted*. These insights are not gained abstractly, without deep personal involvement in the subject matter. Rather, they are experienced as something directly *given*—a universal insight into some objective dimension of reality. These experiences are at the summit of human learning, where such works as the last string quartets of Beethoven came into being, or where Einstein first grasped the theory of relativity.[31]

Theologian David Schindler calls these breakthroughs "originary experiences"—those fertile moments that lie at the roots of a paradigm shift. The history of Christianity (as well as breakthroughs in science and arts) has been formed and indelibly shaped by countless such experiences.[32]

We tend to retreat from metanoia, imagining it to be a miserable process of highlighting our failures and shameful acts, but the process of metanoia allows us to see with fresh eyes the beauty awaiting us if we turn toward God's reality. And when many leaders within Christ's church are experiencing epidemic levels of anxiety, discouragement, and frustration, perhaps there could be no better time for leaders and their organizations to re/turn, re/orient, and re/tune to experience the full and abundant life that Jesus established in his incarnation.

Chapter Three

Why We Need to Repent

A Compelling Rationale for Metanoia

Our sole avenue to reality is through prayer, repentance,
and adoration, through the deep heart's way of knowing.

C. S. LEWIS

Wanderers in the land of Osten Ard are cautioned not to put
blind trust in old rules and forms, and to observe all rituals
with a careful eye, for they often mask being with seeming …
Visitors to this land should take heed: Avoid assumptions.

TAD WILLIAMS, *THE DRAGONBONE CHAIR*

Each wrong idea we follow is a crime
committed against future generations.

ARTHUR KOESTLER

A change of worldview can change the world viewed.

JOSEPH CHILTON PEARCE

In his book *A Guide for the Perplexed*, philosopher E. F. Schumacher talks about visiting Stalingrad in the communist era of the USSR. He was taken on a tour of what is now called St. Petersburg, and at a certain point consulted a map to try to locate his whereabouts. In the square where he was standing, he could see several enormous cathedrals and churches, and yet there was no trace of them on the map. Curious, he asked his guide why this was the case, and he was informed that in the USSR, churches, especially ones with active congregations, had been systematically eliminated from public consciousness; they were deliberately excluded not just topographically but also from the cultural terrain.[1]

Schumacher uses this incident as a metaphor to represent the modern atheistic/materialist worldview. He asks his readers what has been deliberately excluded from their mental maps, their inherited paradigms, and why this might be the case. He then invites the reader to look around with fresh eyes—to see what they are *not* now seeing—and challenges them to integrate their renewed sight into their prevailing cultural and mental maps. In other words, he invites his readers to experience metanoia by including significant, previously excluded, information into the frame. This is the hard work we too must engage in if we are to allow God to reshape and realign our personal and collective expressions of faith.

Speaking of mental maps, perhaps the greatest obstacle to charting a viable way forward is the illusion that our current understandings are the right place to start a journey to a more faithful future. Or, as Charlie Brown wisely notes, "How can you do 'new math' problems with an 'old math' mind?" Epictetus, the Greek philosopher, once noted that it is impossible for a person to learn what they think they already know. This is the closed-minded, non-metanoic mind that refuses new insights and relies on inherited understandings. Sadly, this form of closed-mindedness means that better ways of doing things will forever remain unexplored.

I (Alan) have long held that if paradigm change does not occur, it is impossible for a fundamental shift to take place in either the individual or organization.[2] What we need are re/newed mental maps as well as a re/newed sense of orientation and direction. Re/newed here does not imply fabricating new ways of thinking out of nowhere but involves a retrieval of the church's most primal way of conceiving and negotiating our world—through becoming individuals and a people with the mind of Christ.

As we have noted in the preceding chapters, we simply must come to grips with the various dimensions of conversion if we are to recalibrate the church, restore spiritual integrity, and repair the broken fabric of a fragmented faith and a fragmenting church. We need metanoia if we are to experience the radical, system-wide, Spirit-generated paradigm shift that ought to be a feature of Christian existence and which we so evidently need at this particular apocalyptic moment. In this chapter we seek to answer the question, Why is metanoia needed within the church, perhaps now more than ever?

Because We Generally Suck at It

I (Alan) once had a vigorous conversation with an old friend who also happened to be one of Europe's leading missiologists. We were talking about the seeming inability of the European church to shift its thinking and practice, especially in light of radical changes in the cultural context. Because the majority of European churches were designed and calibrated toward previous historic eras and situations, they were not able to respond to the challenges of contemporary mission. As a result, many now exist largely as monuments to a totally different time. This inability to adapt and respond faithfully to today's issues has resulted in the significant decline (and often closure) of European churches. This is not an overstatement. Current statistics indicate we are likely seeing the last generation of biblical forms of Christianity in many European countries.[3]

As part of the same conversation, I lamented the long, shameful history of violent and oppressive antisemitism that is associated with European Christendom. As a Jew of European descent, this is of particular concern to me. I commented that the church's demise seemed to be bound up with an inability to confess, repent, and so be released from their collective sins, whatever they might be. My friend could simply not fathom the idea of whole churches and/or denominations repenting. He viewed repentance as only for individuals. A similar resistance to collective repentance can be witnessed in the US, as the nation—as well as its churches—try to jump over their own dark shadows when it comes to systemic racism and nationalistic ideologies. This inability to recognize ancestral sins and collective responsibility before God might well account for the loss of spiritual authority, as well as much of the decline of the church, in these contexts.

If the church is itself unwilling to repent, how can it possibly call broader society to the kind of change that a living relationship with God demands? Is not the gospel itself predicated on the call to metanoia?

H. R. Niebuhr suggests that the church ought to be the very first to repent for the sins of a society, and that it is to repent on behalf of all. In this way, we become something of a prefigurative community that embodies a prophetic call to repentance in society at large.

> When it becomes apparent that slavery is transgression of the divine commandment, then the Church repents of it, turns its back upon it, abolishes it within itself. It does this not as the holy community separate from the world but as the pioneer and representative. It repents for the sin of the whole society and leads in the social act of repentance. When the institutions of society are subject to question because innocent suffering illuminates their antagonism to the will of God, then the Church undertakes to change its own use of these institutions and to lead society in their reformation. So also the Church becomes a pioneer and representative of society in the practice of equality before God, in the reformation of institutions of rulership, in the acceptance of mutual responsibility of individuals for one another.[4]

It might surprise us to learn that, throughout Scripture, the call to repentance (*te/shuva* and *metanoia*) is addressed mainly to corporate entities ... to whole nations, such as Israel, Nineveh, and Egypt; and to Jesus' church.[5] Consider these texts from the old and new covenants, for example:

> This is what the LORD says to the people of Judah and Jerusalem: "Plow up the hard ground of your hearts! Do not waste your good seed among thorns. O people of Judah and Jerusalem, surrender your pride and power. Change your hearts before the LORD, or my anger will burn like an unquenchable fire because of all your sins."

JEREMIAH 4:3–4 NLT

> "Yet I hold this against you: You have forsaken the love you had at first. Consider how far you have fallen! Repent [*metanoia*—change your frames, push reset] and do the things you did at first. If you do not repent, I will come to you and remove your lampstand from its place ... Whoever has ears, let them hear what the Spirit says to the churches. To those who are victorious, I will give the right to eat from the tree of life, which is in the paradise of God."

REVELATION 2:4–5, 7

So, if God would call Israel as well as these original—and in a real sense *archetypal*—churches to account, what makes us think we get a free pass when we corporately sin against God or collectively lose our way? Should God not have held the German church complicit in the rise of Nazism and for actively participating in, or turning a blind eye to, what became known as the Holocaust?[6] If God holds individuals responsible for murder, why would he not hold collectives accountable for the egregious horrors of mass murder?[7] Is the church in South Africa not accountable for the sin of theologically legitimized, systemic racism in the era of apartheid?[8] Claiming to be believers, or a church, or a "Christian nation," does not give people a free pass to sin against the holy God.

It might well be that our collective sins are greater and more serious than our individual sins—a negative synergy at work on the collective level. People will do in groups what they would never do on their own. Gang rape and mass murder are extreme examples, but think also of the countless ways we each contribute to the destruction of the earth, to global poverty, and to the shameful oppression of women.[9] Abuses and injustices we'd be mortified to commit on our own are normalized within our cultural milieu, allowing us to "benefit" from a society that lives in resistance to God's ways and perpetuates evil against his image bearers. Because it happens at such a grand scale, we, as individuals, are convinced we are not responsible, even though we are part of the collective. It seems we still have much to learn about what it means to keep covenant with the holy God.[10] We must repent!

Because any Advance in Our Knowledge of God Requires Repentance

If we truly believe God is transcendent, eternal, and infinite—and we as humans are not—then any move toward him will require a radical opening of the mind and heart.

God's revelation always shatters our preconceptions and exposes God's infinite nature. The divine name YHWH ("I will be as I will be" or "I will appear as I will appear") indicates that God is always surprising and uncategorizable. He can never be pinned down, which is why von Balthasar, echoing Augustine and Anselm, rightly says that "if you have 'grasped' something, whatever it is you think you have grasped, it is not God."[11] God will not be put into any box, doctrinal or otherwise.

> The early church fathers and mothers, who were theological virtuosos when it came to exploring the boundaries of what can, and cannot, be known about God, were right to remind us that when dealing with the Lord of the Universe there is *always more*. Even in our best attempts, we never arrive at a totally comprehensive understanding of God … if anyone claims to have done so, then it is not God that they have understood.[12]

At the heart of human sin and idolatry is the desire to make God smaller, more controllable, and more containable. And, as C. S. Lewis rightly observes, God being God simply *has to* confront and bring down our idols. God is the great iconoclast, and it is an act of sheer grace that he shatters our small, idolatrous conceptions of him and liberates us to know him more truly.[13] We must always remember that God transcends any human notion of him and therefore any move toward him will by definition *always* require metanoia … the willingness to have our minds thoroughly blown, time and time again![14] The metanoic mind is therefore a humble mind that is willing to learn, to change, to respond to new truths and information. Only in this way will we adapt to God's self-revelation and move beyond our own limited frames.

Faith must never be limited to intellectual assent or to abstract propositions about God. At a more fundamental level, metanoia enables us to see, hear, and experience God. The revelation of God is an inherently transformative event, but to grasp it in a way that is transformative requires a conversion of the recipient's mind, passions, and will.

The alternative to the metanoic mind is a fearful mind which resists change, especially when new information threatens the inherited maps of meaning. This is precisely the problem with all forms of religious fundamentalism. The fundamentalist Christian is the natural reductionist who loves three-point gospel formulas, five-step personal miracle recipes, pre-digested sermons (which they almost immediately forget), self-sealing arguments, dualistic black or white, us-vs-them categories, and so forth. Fundamentalism is therefore a non-metanoic mental trap because it lacks the means required to grow in knowledge of God, the self, and the world. It can never mature! This should alarm us. Surely, the purpose of the work and teachings of Jesus was *not* to generate dangerously reductionist, grumpy, and moralistic religion. Something has gone seriously wrong. We need to repent!

Because if We Fall in Love With Our System, We Lose the Capacity to Change It

It was Upton Sinclair who once noted that it is difficult to get someone to understand something when their salary depends on them not understanding it.[15] This startling idea highlights how certain people become captive to the demand for loyalty that many organizations require over their adherents/employees. Change becomes difficult precisely because stakeholders and power brokers in the system are often still able to benefit, even if all else in the system is visibly suffering.[16]

Over the years, we have trained leaders embedded in different Christian institutions and churches who wanted to see change. Regularly these leaders awaken to new ideas and ways of engaging in mission but lack the skill to bring about change within the institution itself. Leading organizations through metanoia requires a willingness to oppose significant forces that are resistant to change. (We will address the issue of deep organizational change in part two.) Over time, attempts to change often fall short, and leaders are either expelled from the organization or remove themselves. Hierarchical structures, cultural norms, budget designs, and decision-making processes are all created to subconsciously (or overtly) support the status quo. Even when there is no one in the system who wants to maintain the status quo, people tend to subconsciously reinforce the accepted cultural norms! The invisibility of these restraining forces in the system hints at their possible spiritual nature as manifestations of the powers and the principalities. We struggle not against flesh and blood (Ephesians 6:12).

Loyalty to the institution itself can be dangerously misguided, partly because no impersonal institution ought to require this level of allegiance from us, but also because it creates a blindness to the faults and sins of the organization itself. Organizations tend to exert a "towering effect" on us (appropriating undue and overwhelming significance). They must be seen for what they truly are: mere products of human activity that cannot ultimately affect our intrinsic worth. The rejection of Jesus by the religious and political establishment of his day bears witness to the tendency of institutions to develop their own metrics and categories for what should, and should not, be valued or deemed essential. It is in Jesus alone that we can find the higher authority—one that transcends the intimidating effect of institutions—with which to speak the corrective word into our context. Even a traditional Catholic like von Balthasar can say, "To honor the tradition does not excuse one from the obligation of beginning everything from the beginning each time, not with Augustine or Thomas or Newman, but with Christ."[17]

This is particularly significant in relation to our understandings of the church—our ecclesiology. When we "hallow" the institution itself, we put it beyond reach of any criticism, thus contributing to the mesmerizing effect mentioned above. This "hallowed institution" stuns us into silence because it gives the impression that, in critiquing it, we are somehow critiquing God. But the institutional structure of the church is not God. When we unduly exalt it, the forms of the church will never change, adapt, or learn. We do well to remember with Bishop Newbigin that the church is simply the sign, symbol, instrument, and foretaste of the kingdom of God and not the kingdom itself.[18] To be faithful to this description of the church will require constant adaptation and response to the ongoing challenges of living in Jesus' kingdom.

It was the hard-eyed religious folk—people just like us—who missed what God was doing in Jesus more than anyone else because they were convinced their prevailing views of God were right. They were in love with their own system and tradition of interpretation and could not critique or change them. This is why Jesus continually said to them, "You have heard that it was said ... but I tell you" (Matthew 5:21–22) and why he also said, "They may be ever seeing but never perceiving, and ever hearing but never understanding" (Mark 4:12). We are all locked into ideas and notions that might well be wrong, but we believe them to be true. This is a particular danger for all religious people. G. K. Chesterton once said that, "Madness does not come by breaking out, but by giving in; by settling down in some dirty, little, self-repeating circle of ideas; by being tamed."[19] To avoid such a spiritual predicament, something religious folk particularly fall prey to time and again, we need to factor deep and ongoing change into our very definitions of the church itself; metanoia ought to be incorporated in the system from the get-go.

If change and growth are not programmed into your spirituality, if there are not serious warnings about the blinding nature of fear and fanaticism, your religion will always end up worshiping the status quo and protecting your present ego position and personal advantage—*as if it were God!* Although Jesus' first preached message is clearly "change!"

(as in Mark 1:15 and Matthew 4:17), where he told his listeners to "repent," which literally means to "change your mind," it did not strongly influence Christian history. This resistance to change is so common, in fact, that it is almost what we expect from religious people, who tend to love the past more than the future or the present … Yet even the intelligence of animals is determined by their ability to change and adjust their behavior in response to new circumstances. Those who do not, become extinct.[20]

We must be careful not to fall in love with and become mesmerized by our own organizations, tools, and methods. This is especially true when they mask themselves with denominational and institutional authority.[21] Leadership guru Peter Drucker says, "The most probable assumption is no currently working business theory will be valid ten years hence … And yet few executives accept that turning around a business requires fundamental changes in the assumptions on which the business is run. It requires a different business."[22] Similarly, the biggest blockage to the *next* experience of God is often the *last* experience of God, because we get locked into it. Much angst, burn-out, missional ineffectiveness, and spiritual apathy comes from expecting God to fit into preconstructed boxes and mental frames. To avoid being trapped in these various prisons, we must engage in regular paradigm shift … regular metanoia. Become a drifter every now and again, hit the road, take a trip to yet *another* way of experiencing God's reality and presence. Repent!

Because We Can't Lug It All Along With Us

It might seem obvious at first, but no matter how much you want to honor your organizational tradition, you simply can't do *everything* your predecessors or ancestors did. It's impossible. And yet most churches (and individuals) feel somehow obligated to repeat past formulas and successes in order to be faithful to Jesus today. Now don't hear what we are *not* saying; we fully recognize that in a faith community, tradition can represent the collective memory of our best thinking and practice and is therefore an important source of insight and instruction. But we must remember that tradition is not in itself authoritative. Only Scripture—as the canonical source of God's Word, illuminated by the Holy Spirit, and prayerfully interpreted in and by the community of faith—holds this kind of authoritative value.[23]

Whereas tradition is usually positive, tradition*ism* is almost always not. Tradition is important because it connects us to a historically rooted "way" and confers upon us the wisdom of the past. Traditionalism, on the other hand, is inherently lazy; instead of doing the thinking we ourselves must do, it outsources it to other historical agents and binds us to that past. Just ask Jesus what *he* thinks of traditionalism, and you'll no doubt get the point (e.g., Matthew 5:17–48). Being the Prophet that he is, Jesus seems to issue an unrelenting challenge to all religious convention.

The confused blurring of tradition with canonical Scripture lay at the core of the problems the Jewish religious leaders (scribes, Pharisees, Sadducees, priests, and so forth) had with Jesus. For these leaders, their tradition had become another -*ism;* a mental prison that closed them off from perceiving what God was doing in Jesus.[24] There is no doubt that Jesus saw their traditionalism as sinful and perverse. It placed an intolerable burden on people's shoulders without raising a finger to help them carry it. And so we need to become aware when we are casually allowing our predecessors to do our thinking and to predetermine our ways of acting. Metanoia frees us from enslavement to past ideas and behaviors that have now become dogmatic expressions of ideology.

For those who are anxious about the need to preserve tradition, we have a suggestion: Don't simply wear Grandad's old hat (and require others to do the same) but instead *have children.* Our offspring not only carry our genetics carried into the future but also—if we have been good parents—our narrative. Although the narrative will evolve and vary (only domineering parents impose *their* will and story upon their children), it will be lived out in the lives of our children and their children and so forth.

I [Alan] recently watched a PBS documentary on seminaries and the dilemma they now face. It compared seminary pedagogy to teaching people to repair phone booths. Remember those things we used to have on every main street? Here's the subversive question buried in the metaphor: Are we doing the equivalent of teaching phone-booth repair to a generation that has replaced them with smart phones? Sadly, we think the answer might well be yes.

Those who still seek to build and repair phone booths might justify their actions by referring to the adage about the reliability of "the tried and the true." But listen to Seth Godin:

The tried and true is beyond reproach. It's been tried, and of course, it's true. True because it worked. In times of change, though, most of the tried is in fact, false. False because what used to work, doesn't, at least not any longer. Sure, it might be what you've always done. But that doesn't make it true, or right, or best. It just means that you already tried it … The nature of revolutions is that they destroy the perfect and enable the impossible.[25]

Godin ends by noting that seeking out the "tried and true" is actually the wrong direction to take in chaotic times. The tried, if applied willy-nilly in these circumstances, turns out not to be true but its very opposite … the false way. The classic theological formulation *semper reformanda* (always reforming according to the Word/will of God) was meant to keep us in an adaptive learning posture; it implies an unrelenting willingness to reform the church and not to just proceed on the assumption that the tried *is* the true. Reforming—creating new culturally adaptive "forms"—by its very nature requires a metanoic mind and constant willingness to grow, develop, change, and learn.

Eliminating old ways of thinking is crucial to our existence. Just as every living organism must discover ways of getting nutrition to survive, they must *also* have ways to expel the waste products from their system.[26] Insofar as it enables us to discern obsolescence and rid ourselves of it, consider metanoia as vital to the health of all individuals and organizations—without which the system will eventually die a rather unfortunate death. Talk about a literal "Oh, crap" moment![27]

The more entrepreneurial-type leaders may be thinking *Amen!* as they read this critique on traditionalism, but it's worth noting that the antidote to stifling traditionalism is not entrepreneurship *per se*—rather, it is metanoia. The pragmatic marketplace syncretism—which simply looks for "what works" and then uncritically replicates it in another context—has dominated much of evangelical thinking over the last forty or so years. Besides, in many ways, every church-growth guru has created their own "tradition," even if they do not call it by that name. Doubt this? Then ask yourself why so many contemporary forms of church look and sound so similar. Through conferences and church-growth books, "traditions" are passed on, as people seek to rapidly grow a congregation and find tools that "work." Metanoia, however, gets at the very definition of what we consider "success" in relation to our worship and Christian formation, helping us to ask questions like, What does Jesus think of our uncritical traditionalism/s—ancient and contemporary? What does "church growth" mean in the movements that Jesus started?

Friends, the only yoke we are to take upon ourselves is not the yoke of tradition but the yoke of Jesus, which by contrast is easy and light (Matthew 11:30). That's more than enough. And remember; you cannot do *everything* your predecessors did ... nor should you. Unburden yourselves. Be free. Repent!

Because We Need to Redraw the Maps to Fit the New Territories

The metaphor of maps is useful in grappling with the concept of metanoia. Charles Taylor calls the inherited mapping embedded in culture "social imaginary." These inherited cultural maps determine the way in which we seek to maintain the society in which we live.[28] We are all born into and shaped by a cultural world that has deeply ingrained mental maps about how the world works and how we are to function within it.[29]

As author Len Hjalmarson notes, humans develop mental maps as aids in orienting a complex world. They act as a kind of shorthand, so that we can pay attention to other things. They become the implicit lenses through which we see the world, and they vary in breadth and detail. Peter Senge notes that,

> "Mental models" are deeply ingrained assumptions, generalizations, or even pictures or images that influence how we understand the world and how we take action. Very often, we are not consciously aware of our mental models or the effects they have on our behavior ... Many insights into new markets or outmoded organizational practices fail to get put into practice because they conflict with powerful, tacit mental models ...
>
> The discipline of working with mental models starts with turning the mirror inward; learning to unearth our internal pictures of the world, to bring them to the surface and hold them rigorously to scrutiny. It also includes the ability to carry on "learningful" conversations that balance inquiry and advocacy, where people expose their own thinking effectively and make that thinking open to the influence of others.[30]

Most of our maps are updated in small increments, but sometimes our maps are redrawn wholesale; and when this happens, we experience something like a conversion. The entire map is rewritten, and any landmarks that remain are reoriented.[31]

This map metaphor is powerful because it has become clear that the church's current mental maps—the prevailing social imaginary we use to maintain life and culture—no longer fit the territories in which we live. Most of our thinking about ourselves and our collective role in the world has been formulated in different times and places. For many Christians and Christian denominations/organizations, this means in effect that they are trying to negotiate twenty-first-century New York with a map of sixteenth-century London, Rome, or Geneva—depending on the denominational bent.[32]

The world evolves, conditions change, and new norms emerge. But instead of adapting, people find themselves stuck in their patterns of thinking and behaving. Most don't realize the new situational reality until it bites, and often religious groups are fearful of the changing conditions and cultural shifts. As Adam Grant reminds us, part of the problem is cognitive laziness:

> Some psychologists point out that we're mental misers: we often prefer the ease of hanging on to old views over the difficulty of grappling with new ones. Yet there are also deeper forces behind our resistance to rethinking. Questioning ourselves makes the world more unpredictable. It requires us to admit that the facts may have changed, that what was once right may now be wrong. Reconsidering something we believe deeply can threaten our identities, making it feel as if we're losing a part of ourselves.[33]

We need to be able to meta-think, to experience paradigm shift. To insist on adhering to obsolete paradigms is not only very foolish, but it is also ungodly—because it effectively excludes an openness to the Spirit, who leads his people into ever new frontiers of the gospel. The anxious attempt to "preserve" the status quo often comes from a fear that if we don't stick to the well-worn paths, the "faith" will be lost. Instead of carrying the gospel boldly into every context and every question, we fight battles to perpetuate the current state of affairs. We work hard to make sure the next generation knows to stick to the established paths of the generation before. This is akin to burying God's truth in the sand in a feeble attempt to safeguard our cultural norms for the next generation.

Instead, we must faithfully carry God's truth into new cultures, to address new questions and new problems. There is no lingering question or cultural context "out there" that is a threat to the gospel, but bringing the gospel to bear on new questions and new cultural norms will mean we need to see differently. Recharting our way in the world is going to require what I (Alan) call "soft eyes": the courage to look and think again; the cultivation of an explorer's heart; and the activation of a thoroughly metanoic mind. Repent!

Because When the System Gets Jammed Up, We Need to Push Reset

Addressing symptoms here and there is not enough to resolve the challenges facing the church today. The organizations and institutions we are leading need a thorough recalibration, a fresh start. When something is "calibrated," it is set or adjusted to a desired measure or standard. Therefore, to *recalibrate* something means returning it to the original (or desired) settings that have somehow been bypassed or reset. This is as good a metaphor for repentance as any. Repentance—involving conversion/redirection and meta-thinking—is just like rebooting the system. Repentance resets the ecclesial system to the basic theological algorithms and enables us to refresh and realign everything, bringing tangible hope for a more faithful future.

Most machines—whether computers, smart phones, or cars—will need recalibrating (a tune-up) from time to time. The same applies to humans and institutions, both of which experience various forms of mission drift involving loss of direction and purpose. This is as true for the church as with any institution. Although most people and organizations set out with a clear idea of who they are and why they exist, as the "what" and "how" are repeated, entities begin to focus on processes and lose sight of their purpose. Naturally, the longer we do something a certain way without thinking, the harder it becomes to stand back, get our bearings, and make sure we are still going in the right direction. Sometimes it takes a crisis to shock us into this; the benefit of the unique crisis we are currently in is that it has also given us the time and space to actively engage in this reset.

Put simply, recalibration is about ensuring there is alignment between a person or organization and their fundamental, defining values. It is about making sure that what you are doing and how you are doing it lines up with who you are and why you exist in the first place. It may not be particularly appealing or spectacular work, but it is critically important because being "off," even by a few degrees, can make all the difference when compounded over time.

The first key for an organization is to recalibrate itself with what the French call a *raison d'etre*—the fundamental reason or purpose for existence. What are the founder's purposes, and are we rightly aligned to them? We believe that now, more than ever, the most fundamental reset we need is to recalibrate the church back to Jesus. We need to reJesus.[34] We need to repent!

Because in Order to Learn, We Must First Unlearn

At the opening of the book 5Q, which focuses on the fivefold typology of the ministry of the biblical church, I (Alan) felt it important to encourage the reader to engage with metanoia. This is because the predominant inherited "mind" of the church in relation to the Ephesians 4 typology of ministry has been significantly reduced from that of the New Testament understanding of ministry. Without a metanoic openness to looking again at what has become too familiar ("soft eyes"), there is no way of escaping the old baked-in patterns that we have found ourselves locked into. Metanoia—involving as it does unlearning, reframing, and recalibrating—is the price we must pay to experience transformation. It changes how we see and experience God, people, the world, mission, and of course, the ministry of the church.

> But the desire, as well as the ability, to see things in their original wholeness exacts a price on those who find themselves captive to reductionisms of various sorts and varieties. The price of admission to the symphony [of fullness] is first and foremost repentance. Actually, repentance is the price required for any new learning in any domain— it's just that outside the church it's called unlearning, whereas inside the church it's called repentance. No one can learn who is not first prepared to unlearn. Likewise, no one can grow in God unless they are willing to repent regularly.[35]

When individuals and collective entities fail to evolve and mature, they find themselves in a rut of outdated practices that don't fully display God's character to their cultural context. That's why most denominations are still calibrated to some past experiences of success and try to perpetuate this through outworn formulas and approaches to worship, mission, evangelism, or whatever. Like the sad words of a U2 song, they are stuck in a moment, and they just can't seem to break out of it.

The idea of metanoia itself implies a willingness to be adaptive, agile, open-minded, and to learn again. It is beyond the scope of this book to fully explore the dynamics of learning itself, but it is important to simply note that educational philosophers now almost universally recognize that learning—consistent with an implicit *metanoic* process—is inevitably relational, emergent, and recursive, involving multiple logical levels, or leaps, in order to evolve.[36] In other words, learning involves *meta*-thinking … a thinking beyond/above our current thinking. We not only learn in the process but simultaneously we learn how to learn. Seminal cybernetics philosopher and anthropologist William Bateson sees learning as an "awakening to ecstasy" in that it enables the learner to stand outside of (*ek-stasis*), to transcend, him- or herself.[37] That's what you are doing right now in reading these very lines—you're becoming more aware; you're thinking about thinking; you're getting perspective, a new take on reality that invites you into the possibility of transcending your current, limited, understanding.

The metanoic mind is childlike, playful, adventurous, and experimental. Jesus says we must change and become like children if we are to enter the kingdom of God (Matthew 18:3–4). To do this we need to unlearn some of our "adultish" ways which have become inflexible and one-dimensional. Children have unprejudiced, humble, and curious eyes of wonder, and this keeps them open to un/learning. And this childlike reverence and awe is a prerequisite for grasping mysterious truth.[38]

We all know a variation of the folktale of the two con men who arrive at the capital city of an emperor who loves to spend lavishly on clothing. Posing as weavers, they offer to make him magnificent clothes that are visible only to those who are wise. The emperor hires them, and they begin their work. Various officials, and then the emperor himself, visit them to check their progress. Although each of them can see that the looms are empty, they pretend otherwise, lest they be considered fools. When the weavers report that the emperor's suit is finished, they mime dressing him, and he sets off in a procession before the whole city. The townsfolk go along with the pretense, not wanting to appear stupid or to offend the king. Eventually, when a child blurts out that the emperor has no clothes, the collective spell is broken, and everyone sees things as they truly are. It took a child to name the problem and expose the flawed thinking that surrounded it. How might childlike eyes help us better see the damage and ineffectiveness created by our collective idolatries?[39] For instance, what if, instead of hearing our own voice in its circular reasoning, we, as the church, listened to what our neighbors think about us? Perhaps if we really want people who are apparently far from Jesus to hear and learn the manifold wisdom of God, we ought to become aware of how our collective failures repel a watching world.

In order to be childlike, we must engage with metanoia as an inherent part of discipleship and the learning process itself:

> In the NT the disciples of the Nazarene are called "learners" (*matheiteis*). One never leaves learning behind, and consequently also never leaves unlearning behind. No one can learn, who is not prepared to unlearn. Entrance into the open air is gained only by those who break out of boundaries that have been set, who venture out of fixed paths into the unknown, and who do not let their heart and head be stunted by routine. Perhaps it may be claimed that only by what we can unlearn do we show whether and to what extent we are capable of learning.[40]

It has been said that every mile in the wrong direction is really a two-mile error. Unlearning is therefore twice as hard as learning. Social psychologist Barry O'Reilly has observed that the significant inhibitor in helping high-capacity individuals improve at what they do is not so much the inability to learn new things but rather the inability to *un*learn mindsets, behaviors, and methods that are no longer effective.

> Highly effective leaders are constantly searching for inspiration and for new ideas. But before any real breakthroughs can happen, we need to step away from the old models, mindsets, and behaviors that are limiting our potential and current performance. We must unlearn what brought us success in the past to find continued success in the future.[41]

O'Reilly goes on to note that when people reflect on what it takes to be mentally fit, the first idea that comes to mind is usually intelligence: the smarter you are, the more complex the problems you can solve—and the faster you can solve them. In this view, "intelligence is viewed as the ability to think and learn. Yet in a turbulent world, there's another set of cognitive skills that might matter more: the ability to rethink and unlearn."[42] This squares with futurist Alvin Toffler's famous quote on a new kind of literacy: "The illiterate of the 21st century will not be those who cannot read and write, but those who cannot learn, unlearn, and relearn."[43]

And un/learning is never a once-and-done event—it's a continuous loop of unlearning and relearning: a system of letting go and adapting to the situational reality of the present as we look to the future. Seminal philosopher Susanne Langer notes that in all true learning,

> the philosophical horizon is widened in all directions at once, as horizons do with every upward step ... Most new discoveries are suddenly-seen things that were always there. A new idea is a light that illuminates presences which simply had no form for us before the light fell on them. We turn the light on here, there, and everywhere, and the limits of thought recede before it. A new science, a new art, or a young and vigorous system of philosophy, is generated by such a basic innovation.[44]

Learning is inherently iterative in nature, involving a process of gaining an ever-greater comprehension.[45] Metanoia provides the gateway to transcend previous understandings. This is why real, *paradigmatic*, learning is almost always experienced as something like a religious experience ... a conversion if you will.

Metanoia helps us recognize that the things we have previously done may no longer be useful at this moment. The mission is to develop the capability to know when to move away from outdated practices, to absorb new information that can inform your thinking and adapt your behaviors as a result.[46]

> In an entrepreneurial society individuals face a tremendous challenge, a challenge they need to exploit as an opportunity: the need for continuous learning and relearning ... The correct assumption in an entrepreneurial society is that individuals will have to learn new things well after they have become adults—and maybe more than once. The correct assumption is that what individuals have learned by age twenty-one will begin to become obsolete five to ten years later and will have to be replaced—or at least refurbished—by new learning, new skills, new knowledge.[47]

Unlearning is not about forgetting. It's about the ability to choose an alternative mental model or way of doing things. It's about listening to people who were previously off our radar. What might our churches and organizations look like if we were constantly challenging how we equip church members for mission? Evangelize unchurched people? Form wholehearted disciples? Deepen the practice of community? When we learn, we add new skills or knowledge to what we already know. When we unlearn, we step outside the mental model in order to choose a different one. As Mark Nelson and I (Alan) said in *Reframation*:

> To be able to learn something new, whether it is related to God or to other forms of learning, we need to be willing to let go of obsolete ideas and open our eyes and our hearts to being willing to grow, mature, and get back on the road of discipleship and learn again. The learner needs to venture out of fixed paths into the unknown, and not allow their heart and head to be stunted by mere routine—this is especially true of religious routine. In fact, we suggest that new breakthroughs are only gained by those who break out of the arbitrary boundaries that have been set by mere convention—that's why they are called breakthroughs.[48]

Or, as poet Jack Gilbert says, "We must unlearn the constellations to see the stars."

We must repent![49]

Chapter Four

Christo-Logic

Seeing the World from Inside the Mind That Created It

*The Holy Spirit implants the mind of the Son of God into
our hearts so that we may fashion our lives accordingly.*

HANS URS VON BALTHASAR

*Christ is God, who has conformed himself to us so that we
may become conformed to him, so that we may be empowered
to understand, to love, and to experience the things of God.
He renews our understanding so that we may comprehend
what we otherwise cannot comprehend, and he renews our
hearts so that we may love what we do not love naturally.*

JEAN DANIÉLOU

*In every dimension of the life of Christ, God was at work in his
Son to shape minds, hearts, and imaginations, so that human
beings can draw forever after on these inexhaustible sources.*

AIDAN NICHOLS

*You were taught, with regard to your former way of life, to put
off your old self, which is being corrupted by its deceitful desires;
to be made new in the attitude of your minds; and to put on the
new self, created to be like God in true righteousness and holiness.*

EPHESIANS 4:17–24

In the remarkable book *Black Like Me*, author John Howard Griffin shares how he had his skin medically darkened in an attempt to comprehend the lives of Black people in 1950s America. Appearing to be Black, Griffin then journeyed through the Jim Crow South, from New Orleans to Atlanta, so that he could personally experience discrimination based on skin color.[1] Stepping into the shoes of a Black person allowed Griffin to experience some of the horrific violence and dehumanization that was the common lot of the person of color in that particular era in American history, and in many ways in today's era, too. Griffin describes one particular occurrence:

> Once again a "hate stare" drew my attention like a magnet. It came from a middle-aged, heavyset, well-dressed white man. He sat a few yards away, fixing his eyes on me. Nothing can describe the withering horror of this. You feel lost, sick at heart before such unmasked hatred, not so much because it threatens you as because it shows humans in such an inhuman light. You see a kind of insanity, something so obscene the very obscenity of it (rather than its threat) terrifies you. It was so new I could not take my eyes from the man's face.[2]

Griffin's example highlights how seeing the world through the eyes of others can change how we see ourselves and our world. As Griffin put on the skin of a Black person, he temporarily experienced first-hand the hatred and contempt that many Black people face.

Ponder now what it might look like to put on Jesus' skin and to see and experience the world the way Jesus does. Surely that would be nothing short of a mental revolution, a change in how we view absolutely everything. In this chapter we want to explore the implications of what it means to integrate the biblical teaching on the mentality (mind) of Christ—or thinking sacra*mentally*. Sacramentality is the ability to experience the whole world as the arena of divine theophany—of being able to perceive and discern God's presence and activity in the world.[3] Jesus saw the world through his Father's eyes and could readily discern the Father's will and handiwork in the world. In so doing, he was able to express the very thoughts of God. Sacramentality gets us into something of the same zone—it involves negotiating our world with the mind of Christ.

It becomes quickly apparent in reading the New Testament that this ability so characteristic of Jesus is given to those who love Jesus and adhere to him and his ways (see, for example 1 Corinthians 2:16;

Philippians 2:1–3). But, far from being something ethereal and elusive, this "mind of Christ" given to disciples enables them to behold this world as it really is because they can see the world through the *Logos*, the creative and redemptive person of Christ.[4] As the ancient liturgy proclaims: "Because through the mystery of the incarnate Word, the new light of your brightness has shone onto the eyes of our mind; that knowing God visibly, we might be snatched up by this into the love of invisible things."[5]

Metanoia as the Gateway to the "Mind of Christ"

So how do we access this mind of Christ, and what role does metanoia play in relation to it? Well, according to Alister McGrath, the purpose of metanoia is to provide the "process of spiritual and intellectual re-orientation and re-alignment, in which the believer comes to share in the mind (*nous*) of Christ."[6] In other words, it is through regular iterations of metanoia that the human mind is increasingly configured to the mind of God in Jesus and "our senses acquire something of the spiritual quality of the Lord's glorified senses ... so that, in him and together with him, we can grasp the Father and the Spirit and the entire world beyond."[7] In Christ, we are enabled to comprehend things differently from the world's standard forms of wisdom, whether they be science, philosophy, the arts, economics, or religion.[8] We "have access to these and all the mysteries which 'no eye has seen, nor ear heard'; no one who has not received the Spirit 'is able to understand them because they are spiritually discerned.'"[9] As we have already noted in a previous chapter, metanoia operates like something of a portal into an alternative universe, a gateway to the mind of God (the *Logos*), leading to a greater attunement to God and his purposes in the world.

Although access to the mind of Christ remains an inconceivable grace of God, given to his people, there are *some* conditions associated with experiencing its fullness. Paul says only those disciples who are committed to increasing conformity to Christ—Paul calls them "the mature"— are enabled to more fully understand, and operate with, divine logic.

> Yet among the mature we do speak wisdom, though it is not a wisdom of this age or of the rulers of this age, who are doomed to perish. But we speak God's wisdom, secret and hidden, which God decreed before the

ages for our glory. None of the rulers of this age understood this; for if they had, they would not have crucified the Lord of glory. But, as it is written,

> "What no eye has seen, nor ear heard,
> nor the human heart conceived,
> what God has prepared for those who love him"—

these things God has revealed to us through the Spirit; for the Spirit searches everything, even the depths of God. For what human being knows what is truly human except the human spirit that is within? So also no one comprehends what is truly God's except the Spirit of God. Now we have received not the spirit of the world, but the Spirit that is from God, so that we may understand the gifts bestowed on us by God. And we speak of these things in words not taught by human wisdom but taught by the Spirit, interpreting spiritual things to those who are spiritual.

Those who are unspiritual do not receive the gifts of God's Spirit, for they are foolishness to them, and they are unable to understand them because they are discerned spiritually. Those who are spiritual discern all things, and they are themselves subject to no one else's scrutiny.

> "For who has known the mind of the Lord
> so as to instruct him?"

But we have the mind of Christ.

1 CORINTHIANS 2:6–16 NRSV

In the broader context of these verses (1 Corinthians 1:18–31), Paul makes a clear distinction between the religious beliefs held by Jews, Greeks, and Christians, noting that those who had become believers had only done so by leaving behind their previous religious practices and beliefs in order to follow Christ—in other words through metanoia. In these verses, Paul is saying that what had previously supplied their answers and enlightened their minds no longer does—they have in effect *de-converted* from previous outlooks on life. As a result, Jesus has given them a new consciousness, a new mind and heart, and this has changed absolutely everything.[10] Receiving a new heart, as we shall explore in a later chapter, is like being given a new operating system, a new identity, a new way of seeing, and a new mental map of the world (Ephesians 4:23; Colossians 3:10–11; 1 Corinthians 2:16). And because of this, we have a much greater affinity and a deeper soul resonance with the things of God.

The Spirit of Christ and the Mind of Christ

As we have already noted, there is nothing automatic about receiving the mind of Christ. It is an action of God's pure and unimaginable grace, and it is only entrusted to true disciples, those believers committed to the process of sanctification, to an ever-greater attunement to the holy, and to becoming increasingly Christlike. Furthermore, having the mind of Christ is only achieved through the indwelling of God the Holy Spirit.

> [We] walk not according to the flesh but according to the Spirit. For those who live according to the flesh set their minds on the things of the flesh, but those who live according to the Spirit set their minds on the things of the Spirit. To set the mind on the flesh is death, but to set the mind on the Spirit is life and peace. For this reason the mind that is set on the flesh is hostile to God; it does not submit to God's law—indeed it cannot, and those who are in the flesh cannot please God. But you are not in the flesh; you are in the Spirit, since the Spirit of God dwells in you. Anyone who does not have the Spirit of Christ does not belong to him. But if Christ is in you, though the body is dead because of sin, the Spirit is life because of righteousness. If the Spirit of him who raised Jesus from the dead dwells in you, he who raised Christ from the dead will give life to your mortal bodies also through his Spirit that dwells in you.
>
> ROMANS 8:4B-11 NRSV

Receiving the mind of Christ is therefore a profoundly *spiritual* process. Von Balthasar notes that in this process "the Holy Spirit implants the mind of the Son of God into our hearts so that we may fashion our lives accordingly."[11] He goes on to say that "the Holy Spirit can be recognized at work in a person by establishing in them the mind of Jesus."[12] Jesus tells his disciples that the Spirit "will take what is mine and declare it to you" (John 16:15 ESV), and Paul tells the Corinthian church that "we all, with unveiled face, beholding the glory of the Lord, are being transformed into the same image ... For *this comes from the Lord who is the Spirit*" (2 Corinthians 3:18 ESV, italics ours).[13]

And so we discover that the Spirit's role in Christian community is not to replace an absent Jesus, but on the contrary to render him present in new, and intensely *personal*, ways. And it is the fundamental mission of the Holy Spirit to lead the Christian community into an ever-increasing concordance with Christ. The Spirit is the agent by which the mind of Christ is given.

[A] new intellect is created by the Spirit, who alone fathoms the depths of God and enables the intellect to grasp these realities [the facts of revelation] in an obscure but real manner. This new intellect is at first rudimentary, but, as it comes into play, it gradually grows more luminous; it shares in the knowledge that God has of himself … Developing through the gifts of the Holy Spirit, through the gift of knowledge and the gift of understanding, the new intellect makes the mind familiar with divine realities, and enables it to grasp them in all their fullness and to assess the evidence that they present.[14]

We are given access to depths and breadths, insights, ideas, and initiatives that we could never have received of our own accord and yet are now truly our own.[15] This new mind is able to understand, accept, and see correctly, widely, and wisely. This brings an instinctive sensitivity to God and a readiness to respond to his will and direction. And it is from within this distinctly spiritual wisdom that we can understand ourselves in a whole new light; to recognize the inherent design of things; to comprehend something of the eternal purposes of God in the world; to see and resolve all our problems by accessing and engaging the very mind that created and sustains the world.

Christo-Logic: Dimensions in the Mind of Christ

The experience of thinking with the mind of Christ can also be referred to as "Christo-logic." We will spend the rest of this chapter, as well as several of the appendices, in an attempt to understand what the mind of Christ really is, how to access it, and how to live according to its light.

Christo-Logic is Formatted According to the Pattern of Christ

Because metanoia calibrates the believer to Christ, who is also the Word of God, Christo-logic is therefore the kind of logic that is derived from the pattern of Jesus Christ. The only way we can be certain we know the Divine Mind and are operating accordingly is through the prism of Jesus' life and teachings—he is the "way and the truth and the life" (John 14:6). This is because Jesus is the fulfillment of the messianic logic laced throughout the Old Testament and, as the eternal Word (*Logos*), is *always* God's way of communicating his mind to us (Hebrews 1:1–3; Colossians 1:17). "Christ is the infinite form of truth revealed in the world … [Therefore] a faithful account of truth, of the God-World relation, can only be found in Christ."[16]

The Bible issues us with a summons to metanoia, to leave everything and to follow Jesus Christ, to take him as the measure of all things, as the singular point of reference for understanding ourselves and our world.[17] Therefore, the only way of knowing the truth of God is to root oneself fully in the thoughts, events, and actions of Jesus' life, and think outwards from there. Whoever wants to be Jesus' disciple is called first to repentance, then to take up their cross and follow Jesus by conforming their lives to him in discipleship (Matthew 16:24). It is by having Jesus at the center of our lives and consciousness, by being decentered from the false narratives and identities that have previously defined us, that we experience transformation: "And we all, who with unveiled faces contemplate the Lord's glory, are being transformed into his image with ever-increasing glory, which comes from the Lord, who is the Spirit" (2 Corinthians 3:18).

This ability to both recognize the Christ-pattern underlying the world and attune ourselves to it is critical. (See appendix four on conforming to the image of God in Jesus.) Absolutely everything is to be understood in relation to the pattern of life that Christ presents to the world—namely our particular calling and purpose; human life as God intended; how the church is meant to correspond to its God-intended form; how we make our daily decisions; discerning the hand of God in the world; and serving him appropriately with our lives.[18] Listen to Paul's ecstatic speech on the topic:

We look at this Son and see the God who cannot be seen. We look at this Son and see God's original purpose in everything created. For everything, absolutely everything, above and below, visible and invisible, rank after rank after rank of angels—*everything* got started in him and finds its purpose in him. He was there before any of it came into existence and holds it all together right up to this moment. And when it comes to the church, he organizes and holds it together, like a head does a body. He was supreme in the beginning and—leading the resurrection parade—he is supreme in the end. From beginning to end he's there, towering far above everything, everyone. So spacious is he, so expansive, that everything of God finds its proper place in him without crowding. Not only that, but all the broken and dislocated pieces of the universe—people and things, animals and atoms—get properly fixed and fit together in vibrant harmonies, all because of his death, his blood that poured down from the cross.

COLOSSIANS 1:15–20 MSG

According to Paul, the whole world is created by the Father in the pattern of the Son; and "in him all things hold together" (Colossians 1:17). Therefore, we must focus on Jesus to discern God's original purpose in everything created. Just as the individual pieces of a puzzle only make sense by being set within the completed puzzle, so "everything" finds its proper place in him, and all the fragmented and dislocated pieces of our world are put back together in him. The more we let the life and events of Christ's life inform and imprint us, the more we will be able to connect our own daily stories with the greater story of God's presence in our lives. Listen to Paul again:

> I ask—ask the God of our Master, Jesus Christ, the God of glory—*to make you intelligent and discerning in knowing him personally, your eyes focused and clear, so that you can see exactly what it is he is calling you to do, grasp the immensity of this glorious way of life he has for his followers*, oh, the utter extravagance of his work in us who trust him—endless energy, boundless strength! All this energy issues from Christ: God raised him from death and set him on a throne in deep heaven, in charge of running the universe, everything from galaxies to governments, no name and no power exempt from his rule. And not just for the time being, but *forever*. He is in charge of it all, has the final word on everything. At the center of all this, Christ rules the church. The church, you see, is not peripheral to the world; the world is peripheral to the church. The church is Christ's body, through which he speaks and acts, by which he fills everything with his presence.
>
> EPHESIANS 1:17-23 MSG, ITALICS OURS

If we miss what God is doing in Jesus, we are utterly lost, for we will never be able to comprehend God. But not only do we solely know God through Jesus (John 14:6), but Jesus is also the archetypal expression of humanity as God intended it. Or as N. T. Wright says,

> If you want to know who God is, look at Jesus. If you want to know what it means to be human, look at Jesus. If you want to know what love is, look at Jesus. If you want to know what grief is, look at Jesus. And go on looking until you're not just a spectator, but you're actually part of the drama which has him as the central character.[19]

In other words, Jesus is God's way of being human, and he sets the archetypal pattern for us to follow. "Christ's whole life in all its aspects must supply the norm for the life of the following Christian and thus for the life of the whole church."[20] The seventeenth-century French mathematician Blaise Pascal agrees: "Jesus is the center of all, the object of all; whoever does not know him, knows nothing aright, either of the world or of himself."[21] Bonhoeffer maintains that "[t]he way in which the form of Jesus Christ takes form in our world is the concrete, obedient, con-formation of human beings to the form of the biblical Christ, the man whose existence for others is the world's true reality."[22] Humans are therefore to be "ordered to" Jesus. Only in him is humanity comprehensible.

The church, as the communal human expression of the person and ministry of Christ, is by no means peripheral to what God is doing; it is right at the center. As the body of Christ, the church is meant to be the embodiment of Christ and therefore should be a visible demonstration— a living "proof of concept"—of what God intends for the entire human race. It was this insight into the church's true purpose and calling that enabled Bonhoeffer to recognize the profoundly *de*-formed "Christ-less Christianity" that presented itself in the form of the Nazi co-option of the church of his day. The so-called Christians of the time had become dangerous ideologues because they had lost a sense of the absolutely exclusive and archetypal significance that the Jesus of the Gospels has for his people. They had apparently forgotten that their primal responsibility, individually and communally, was to conform themselves to him in the lifelong call to discipleship. If there was no discipleship in the church, there would be no conformation to Jesus. Bonhoeffer saw that there was a direct correlation between non-discipleship and an ideologically captive church:

> Discipleship means adherence to Christ, and, because Christ is the object of that adherence, it must take the form of discipleship. An abstract Christology, a doctrinal system, a general religious knowledge on the subject of grace or on the forgiveness of sins, render discipleship superfluous, and in fact they positively exclude any idea of discipleship whatever, and are essentially inimical to the whole conception of following Christ … *Christianity without the living Christ is inevitably Christianity without discipleship, and Christianity without discipleship is always Christianity without Christ.*[23]

After losing their first (defining) love, much of the German church of Bonhoeffer's time had literally become a Christ-less abomination—a so-called church that no longer looked, acted, sounded, and thought like Jesus, their eternal Archetype, Founder, and Lord.[24]

And so the form of Christ is critically important because it helps us recognize and evaluate the authenticity of a group of people claiming to be a church. This is not as abstract as it might initially sound, but it does require a spiritual sensibility to understand and appropriate this logic. For instance, we need only look at our society and culture that is *not* formed in Christ to recognize a world that is deeply out of sync with God's intended design and purpose for it. The lack of Christoformity in the world should jar us. As people who have been "born from above," we should *feel it* deeply. But we should also be able to sense how things might be corrected and brought into more recognizable alignment with Jesus. But we can only do this by assessing what we see against the archetypal pattern of life perfectly represented in Jesus Christ (Ephesians 4:13). (See appendix one on attunement to Jesus as an elaboration of Christoformity.)

Thankfully, we are not left to our own devices regarding our deepening attunement to God in Jesus. It is the role of the indwelling Spirit—in the individual disciple as well as in the believing community— to make Jesus known to us so that we might thereby conform ourselves to him.

> It is the work of the Holy Spirit to accomplish the continuing enfleshment of the Word in a universal fashion. It is the Spirit who transposes Christ's historical existence into a form that becomes the immediate and inward norm of every life. In this way the Holy Spirit creates the missions of the Church and individuals as applications of the life of Christ to every Christian life and the whole life of the Church.[25]

Only by undergoing metanoia can we, as people who are committed to being indexed to Jesus through prayer and discipleship, relinquish prior definitions of what is real and find our true measure in Jesus alone.

Christo-Logic is Seeing Everything from God's Perspective

We have already noted that metanoia is the door by which we gain access to the mind of Christ. This is because metanoia creates the appropriate posture for the soul to be receptive to revelation, a soul willing to encounter God and to be changed and transformed. As inconceivable as it sounds at first, metanoia enables us to share in Jesus' own consciousness; and because of this, disciples gain a Christlike perspective on the world rather than a human perspective (which the Bible calls "the mind governed by the flesh" [Romans 8:6]).[26] Paul exhorts the church in Colossae to "look up, and be alert to what is going on around Christ— that's where the action is. See things from *his* perspective" (Colossians 3:2 MSG).[27] It is through the mind of Christ that we can see the world with panoramic and unambiguous vision. In his book *Seeing and Believing*, Devenish says that, through metanoia,

> [Believers] have been given access to a new dimension of reality that has inducted them into new vistas of knowing, being, and seeing. They have been made privy to a special kind of knowledge that does not originate with themselves but out of the mind of God. In order to sustain this transformative vision, this luminescent wisdom in the midst of the multiplicity of visions and distracting images, they must hold their gaze … When we do [on occasion] turn our eyes away to look at other things, we are prompted to remember our calling and to return our gaze once again to the face of Christ. To look inwardly is to see the face of Christ; to look outwardly is to see from Jesus' point of view.[28]

Many of the problems we face come from having our own finite perspective rather than seeing things from God's infinite perspective. It was a limited, earthly perspective that lay at the core of Peter's reproach of Jesus in Matthew 16. Although Peter's earlier declaration of Jesus as the Messiah was revealed to him by the Father (16:17), moments later he rebuked Jesus for setting his mind on the forthcoming ordeal of the cross. At which point, "Jesus turned to Peter and said, 'Get away from me, Satan! You are a dangerous trap to me. You are seeing things merely from a human point of view, not from God's'" (16:23 NLT). It seems that Peter—and we with him—had been going about things in the wrong way. Instead of trying to see God, he should have tried to see as God sees.[29] Without the benefit of the mind of Christ, we will remain trapped within a culturally defined, reductive, and "worldly" logic. This limited logic is futile because it is what created the problems we face in the first place. Echoing this idea, missiologist and missionary Ralph Winter used to constantly remind us that "every major decision you make will be faulty until you see the whole world as God sees it."[30]

Here is a little exercise to test this issue of perspective in your own life. Prayerfully ask Jesus what he thinks about the issues of wealth and money and about the assumptions that are built into the capitalist understanding of how the world ought to work (for example, meritocracy, plutocracy, property rights). Got some in mind? Write them down as bullet points on one side of a piece of paper. Then, on the other half of the paper, jot down what the world outside of Christ thinks about the same issues. Now compare the lists. How do these differ? No doubt you will quickly observe how contrary Jesus' way is to the world's "normal." Now, try tackling the complex issues of power and its abuse, using the same approach. As part of this exercise, ask yourself how you are structuring the organization you lead in this respect. Ask yourself how we justify our attachments to hierarchy and top-down forms of leadership when Jesus expressly forbids this to his followers (Matthew 20:25–28; cf. Philippians 2:1–11). What about issues of race, of gender, forgiveness, service, or how to treat enemies? What about how we view suffering or the trials we face? Things are very different when you compare the human-only view ("the mind of the flesh") with Jesus' perspective.

It is because the ways of Jesus are so confronting to our standard ways of seeing that we can acknowledge why repentance is essential for us to gain his perspective on our world and our role within it.

Christo-Logic is a Form of Thinking That Can Always Transcend Itself

In an earlier chapter, we discovered that learning—growing in awareness and tending towards maturity and fullness—requires you to have an open, metanoic, self-transcending mind.

> A mind delighting in discovery,
> As love of learning turned to learning love
> And explanation deepened mystery[31]

This "delighting in discovery" is a key part of our formation in the way of Christ. Any genuine encounter with the God who created the universe confirms this—we are mere graced recipients of the God who has reached down to us and now reveals himself to us. God is always greater than we can ever conceive or imagine. We can confirm with Gregory of Nyssa that "when the eye of the soul turns towards God, it is thrown back by the lightning flash of the Infinite."[32] Because God is by nature infinite and eternal, any advance in our understanding of him must therefore blow the self-enclosed categories of the human mind. Christians have long confessed that while God is indeed fully immanent and can be found in *all* things, he is also transcendent and cannot be fully contained in any created thing. Just when we think we have God all worked out, we quickly realize we haven't even really started.[33] In other words, God's truth has ascendancy over our own truth, and we ought to live our lives accordingly.

If this is the case when it comes to the knowledge of God, then it must also mean that metanoia—the process of constantly having our minds blown—plays an essential role. There can be no dodging it. Gregory of Nyssa taught that to "find God" means that we must always thereafter be also committed to seeking him unceasingly. "The reward of the search is to go on searching," he notes. "The soul's desire is fulfilled by the very fact of its remaining unsatisfied, for really to see God is never to have had one's fill of desiring Him."[34]

Authentic belief in God assumes we are somehow related to a Being that is infinitely greater. This eternal God is revealed and known in Jesus, but this God can never be pinned down by human thought or rationality. As any number multiplied by infinity is infinite, so we must recognize that the eternal, because it is eternal, qualifies everything.

Theologians have long used the phrase *sub specie aeternitatis* to describe the idea of seeing the world through the lens of eternity, in which we acknowledge our own limited thinking. We believe such infinity-thinking comes from having the mind of Christ.[35] Infinity-thinking is not just necessary for the mystical knowledge of God; it gives the believer a distinctive perspective in any arena of life.

This approach to thinking is not only important in the realm of theology, but it is also a useful category in the world of leadership and organization. Infinity-thinking means being able to always think beyond the current categories. For instance, leadership guru Simon Sinek uses the metaphor of what he calls "the infinite game" to suggest that infinity-thinking is critical to remaining adaptive and responsive to ever-changing conditions. He notes that games such as basketball and chess are finite, with firm rules and clear endpoints; but business or politics (or church for that matter) is an infinite game. There's ultimately no such thing as "winning" in these types of "games" because there's always a new set of challenges to deal with. Therefore, those who thrive in the long run are those who play by infinite rules. This enables them to maneuver, innovate, and thrive in VUCA conditions.[36]

However, this way of thinking is not easy. Most people operate with a thoroughly non-metanoic way of seeing the world. A closed mind locks them into their prevailing thinking on any matter. Sinek again:

> For all its benefits, acting with an infinite, long-term view is not easy. It takes real effort. As human beings we are naturally inclined to seek out immediate solutions to uncomfortable problems and prioritize quick wins to advance our ambitions. We tend to see the world in terms of successes and failures, winners and losers. This default win-lose mode can sometimes work for the short term; however, as a strategy for how companies and organizations operate, it can have grave consequences over the longer term.[37]

The non-metanoic mind is unable to transcend itself because it is established by self-sealing arguments and reaffirmed by confirmation bias.[38] This closed-loop thinking pays more attention to things that confirm existing beliefs, while at the same time discounting any evidence that challenges these beliefs. This pathological echo-chamber, conspiracy-theory thinking is evident for all to see on social media feeds. It is the type of dangerous thinking that infuses the close-minded, ideologically motivated, fundamentalist religion/s of our day, be they Christian, Muslim, Hindu, or any other faith.

Very few people evolve much beyond the thinking of their last experience of formal education, such as high school or university.[39] As Sinek notes, it takes significant courage to vacate outmoded ideas, and because of this distinctly spiritual form of laziness, many of us remain bound to the obsolete—things that once worked but no longer do. This is the key issue for many Christian leaders, who often have an outworn view of church and ministry.

Metanoia broadens our horizons and offers us a wider perspective on things. We recognize opportunities and paths that were unexpected or even unimagined. We find ourselves in a "bigger world," compelled to work toward a vision we have been granted of a "better world." With such enlargement of vision comes an invitation to bring more of ourselves than we may have even known existed, with full commitment to a task or role we could not have imagined.

This is a time for un/learning if ever there was one. And the advantages of un/learning are significant—the ability to change your mind, to learn, to adapt, is a superpower. The rate at which you learn and progress in the world largely depends on your willingness to weigh the merit of new ideas, even if you don't at first agree with them; perhaps *especially* if you feel threatened by them. As we have already noted, one of the great gifts of Christo-logic is that it allows us to solve the problems of our world from outside of the closed-loop thinking that created those problems in the first place.[40]

Christo-Logic is Holistic Thinking

Many of our problems derive from an innate tendency to fall prey to the all-too-human proclivity to demystify, to eliminate paradox, and make big things small and more controllable. This tendency is a problem that occurs in all forms of human knowledge and arises when we try to analyze and describe a complex phenomenon by its simple or funda-mental constituents. These reduced ways of seeing reality become the primary and exclusive way of understanding the phenomenon, mistaking these minimal and fragmented formulas for reality itself. Now to be clear, *analysis* is necessary to understand the world, but analysis is just one dimension of the process of knowledge. The other, counterbalancing, dimension of true knowledge is *synthesis,* in which things are understood in light of a greater whole.

Science and philosophy call the results of this over-analysis "reduc-tionism." The Bible also has a term for it: "heresy." No kidding! Heresy is simply theological reductionism—making big ideas small. At its core, it is a form of idolatry. As N. T. Wright notes, "Heresies do not come about by straightforward denial ... They happen when an element which may even be important, but isn't central, looms so large that people can't help talking about it, fixating on it, debating different views of it as though this were the only thing that mattered."[41] Or, as C. S. Lewis says, "We have all departed from that total plan [of Christianity] in different ways, and each of us wants to make out that his own modification of the original plan is the plan itself ... [E]very one is attracted by bits of it and wants to pick out those bits and leave the rest."[42] Heresy is like the parable of the various blind men who each grab a piece of the elephant and mistake it for a whole object. For example, the man who grabs the trunk believes he is holding a snake; the man who grabs a leg believes he is holding a tree, and so forth.

In other words, heresy produces a fragmented consciousness incapable of experiencing the fullness that is offered to us through Jesus. We suggest that most of the problems we now face as Christian leaders arise from reductionism, or in theological language, from heretical thinking.[43]

The only way to heal our reduced thinking therefore involves the reversal that comes through metanoia—the ability to think beyond the current limitations by reintegrating the fragmented part back into the universal whole—by reframing it. This "universal whole" is what is meant when theologians say that truth is "catholic" or "universal." The term catholic (not to be confused with *Roman* Catholic here) is derived from the Greek words *kata+holon* and literally means that we are to measure all things "according to the whole." This is similar to the Hebrew idea of *shalom*, which not only means peace as the absence of conflict but also as the presence of a cohesive wholeness, integrity, and harmony. To see things *catholically* is to understand all things as parts of a greater whole.

This is where the mind of Christ comes into play. We have already seen that, for Christians, the whole of reality can only be understood through the person of Jesus Christ who integrates and restores the world through his life, ministry, death, and resurrection. "He is before all things, and in him all things hold together … For God was pleased to have all his fullness dwell in him, and through him to reconcile to himself all things, whether things on earth or things in heaven" (Colossians 1:17–20; see also Ephesians 1:3–15). And so—like the puzzle we referred to earlier, or a mosaic that can only make sense when all the pieces are put together to create a meaningful picture—thinking through the mind of Christ helps us to see beyond the fragmentary understandings of things and enables us to sense the synthetic whole: the purposes of God in and through all things.

Synthesis—the healing of our heresies—tends to explain reality by understanding that the whole is greater than the sum of its parts. Theologian Hans Urs von Balthasar (as well as social psychologist Daniel Pink) calls this reach for wholeness *symphonic* thinking. Think about an orchestra tuning up; the notes are discordant until the sounds of various instruments combine and blend to create an emergent new sound. Symphonic theology, like all forms of true art, requires imagination, holism, and play, along with diversity in unity. By renewing and enlarging imagination and vision, it leads directly to innovation and other various forms of creative learning. Theologically, we can say that because God's truth is living and dynamic and continues to unfold itself in new and fresh ways, it is essentially "symphonic."[44]

Renewal—spiritual, social, or organizational—in some sense means always returning the fragments to the originating whole and in so doing rediscovering new meanings.[45] It means understanding things through the mind of Christ. As Mark Nelson and I (Alan) say in *Reframation*, we resolve our current problems not by more (reductive) analysis but by more synthesis. It is this symphonic way of thinking that connects the dots, opens doors, and cleanses perceptions to enable us to really see again.[46] This "thinking through the mind of the Creator" will always involve counter-reductionist thinking—thinking bigger, never smaller.

Christo-Logic is Spiritual Instinct

The New Testament clearly teaches that when an individual comes to exist in Christ, Christ in turn exists in them. This is precisely what is conveyed in the mutual-abiding teaching in John's Gospel (e.g., John 15:1–17) as well as the "in Christ" teaching found throughout Paul's writings (e.g., Romans 6). Known as the doctrine of "union with Christ," it has *huge* implications for the life of a believer.

As disciples, this union with Christ is usually experienced as an inbuilt *bias* to all-things-Jesus. This instinct for Jesus involves a sense of attunement to God's will, which is always consistent with his love (John 15:1–17). This spiritual inclination will include a sense of the whole in the parts; an awareness of truth; a gut instinct born out of increasing attunement to Christ. Although this instinct is experienced at the level of precognitive intuition, it is not mere guesswork; it follows a definite, Christoform pattern. It is the wisdom inherent in the mind of Christ.[47]

Spiritual instinct therefore is that aspect of Christo-logic that enables us to *intuit* ways to solve our problems and to negotiate the complexities of life by following the pattern of Christ our Inner Teacher, as seen in Scripture (e.g., 1 John 2:27), and under the active leadership and guidance of the Spirit.[48]

An analogy of this implicit, instinctive knowledge can be seen in animals. For instance, sharks are clearly adept swimmers, and yet they do so without ever cognitively "knowing" anything at all about a theory of "swimming." This innate knowledge of complex hydrodynamics is somehow built into the very nature and purpose, latent in the DNA, of the shark itself. The same can be said about the uncanny ability of migratory birds to navigate from one single point in the globe to another without cognitively knowing *anything* about global positioning and navigation: pure instinct. All of God's creatures live according to such instinct.

Because of our penchant for both rationalizing and controlling life, it sometimes takes liminal situations to force us to rediscover these more instinctive dimensions in life. For example, this capacity to access intuitive knowledge is well demonstrated in what is called the "startle reflex/response"; those situations where people exposed to mortal danger can activate powers not readily available to them in their ordinary mode of existence. For instance, a person in pitch darkness who becomes aware of the threat of a dangerous animal growling close by is somehow able to scale a rock face that would normally be almost impossible for them in the daylight. In startle responses, a primal, instinctive "tacit-knowledge" seems to take over.[49]

In these situations, the standard logic does not readily apply, and we find ourselves operating on gut instinct—what Daniel Kahneman refers to as "thinking fast" and Malcolm Gladwell calls "blink" insight. Gladwell reminds us that some of the most momentous choices in life are made when we "think without thinking"—in the blink of an eye—and so, in order to develop and evolve, we should learn to trust the power of "blink" to help chart our way through the complexities of life. He notes that sometimes having too much information can impede our judgment—a state of mind commonly referred to as the "paralysis of analysis." Gladwell maintains that spontaneous decisions are often as good as, or even better than, carefully planned and considered ones.[50] Godin agrees: "Intuition: That's what people call successful decision making that happens without a narrative. Intuition isn't guessing. It's sophisticated pattern matching, honed over time. Don't dismiss intuition merely because it's difficult to understand. You can get better at it by practicing."[51]

It therefore should not surprise us that a corresponding *superna-tural* instinct ought to pervade the Christian life as well. We need to learn to trust our deepest inclinations, recognizing that whatever God teaches us through spiritual instinct will not contradict what is known through Scripture, nor will it violate the truth vouchsafed to the whole community of the church. In other words, "the discernment of spirits" (1 Corinthians 12:10) is necessary if we are to avoid wrong thinking and behavior. Discernment means to think through our decisions and actions, not just by rational calculation but by listening for the Holy Spirit; in prayer, recognizing God's motives, invitations, and will; ensuring that it conforms to the law of love and does not violate the pattern of Jesus' life and teaching.[52]

The examples of intuition found in the natural world help us understand the presence of a similar intuitive form of knowledge built into the being of the body of Christ. The mind of Christ is therefore a form of tacit knowledge, latent throughout the church, as well as in individual disciples. This latency, or blink-instinct, is a dimension of Christo-logic that is available to all of God's people through the Holy Spirit—who connects us to Jesus and the latent intelligences built into his body.

Perhaps the most explicit example of latent spiritual instincts is found in Paul's teaching on the five intelligences and instincts (what I refer to as *fivefold intelligence* or *5Q*) bequeathed to the body of Christ (Ephesians 4:1–16).[53] The self-same instincts that shaped and directed Jesus' own calling and ministry (Jesus as the archetypal apostle, prophet, evangelist, shepherd, and teacher ... APEST) are "given" to the church in its very foundation ... in the commissioning at the ascension, no less. Barth goes as far as to call APEST "the modes of Christ's royal presence in the church"![54] Ponder what is being said here: *APEST is the means by which Jesus is present and active among his people.* Talk about primal instinct and latent capacity! As distinctive expressions of the mind of Christ, these intelligences are readily accessible (latent) for those willing to act on them, and according to Paul, we can always get better ("mature" Ephesians 4:13, 15) at them.[55]

Because we have been given access to the mind of Christ through metanoia, an instinct for all things Jesus and his mission should direct and pervade all aspects of Christian life and ministry. Certainly this instinct informed the apostolic ministry of the church as it ventured outward in its Holy Spirit inspired Jesus-mission to change the world. That same mind of Christ is operating in us and ought therefore to infuse our current efforts as we seek to walk in his way and extend his mission.

Christo-Logic is Discerning What God is Doing and Joining with Him

As we saw in chapter two, because conversion involves a radical reorientation and recentering on Jesus (*te/shuva*), as well as a reception of a whole new mind (meta-noia), we find ourselves more aligned to God and therefore more able to discern his purposes in our world so that we might join with him. Once again, the archetype of this is found in Jesus himself.

Everything Jesus did, and everything about him as the Son of God, was received from, and calibrated to, God the Father. Jesus said, "The truth is that the Son does nothing on His own; *all these actions are led by the Father. The Son watches the Father closely and then mimics the work of the Father*" (John 5:19 The Voice). Whether in a church gathering or at the pub, Jesus is always looking for what the Father is already doing, and he subsequently partners with the Father in that work. Listen again to Jesus:

> "I have not ever acted, and will not in the future act, on My own. I listen *to the directions of the One who sent Me* and *act on these divine instructions. For this reason*, My judgment is always fair and never self-serving. I'm committed to pursuing God's agenda and not My own."
>
> JOHN 5:30-31 THE VOICE

Jesus' perspective did not originate from egoistic self-centeredness but came from seeing the world with a God's-eye point of view.

And when Jesus taught the disciples, he intended that they would increasingly adopt his point of view as their own (Philippians 2:5). And that is precisely what happened. After his death, resurrection, and ascension, the apostles began to participate in Jesus' mission to the world. This was not a project of their own imaginings. They were operating Christo-logically, following the traces of the redeeming God in the world. Their actions were consistent with everything Jesus commanded them to do. They applied the same point of view they saw Jesus apply. They literally looked through Jesus' eyes rather than their own eyes and saw the supernatural kingdom of God at work in them and through them.[56] Through their conversion, they had become "insiders" of Jesus' own understandings and experience of God.

> "I'm no longer calling you servants because servants don't understand what their master is thinking and planning. No, I've named you friends because I've let you in on everything I've heard from the Father."
>
> JOHN 15:15 MSG

We believe this ability to find God everywhere and join in whatever he is doing lies at the core of Jesus' consciousness and must therefore be an aspect of the mind of Christ bequeathed to his people. This means we must pay attention. We must learn to become aware of *what* God is doing, as well as *how* and *where* he is doing it. Therefore, instead of ministry being all about human ingenuity and what we can do for God, it is more about discovering what God is already doing, and—considering our gifts and resources—discerning how he wants us to join him.[57]

> Be assured that from the first day we heard of you, we haven't stopped praying for you, asking God to give you wise minds and spirits attuned to his will, and so acquire a thorough understanding of the ways in which God works.
>
> COLOSSIANS 1:9 MSG

And so we have discovered that metanoia allows us to perceive and understand the pattern and form of Christ, respond to it, and to align ourselves with it. As such it provides us the portal through which we gain access to the infinite mind of God in Christ.

> In a living faith, human inadequacy and ignorance are outbalanced by divine omnipotence and omniscience; it is part of the contemplative's act of faith to cling to this: "for we do not know how to pray as we ought, but the Spirit himself intercedes for us with sighs too deep for words", by calling Abba, Father, not somewhere outside or above us, but actually in us and from within us.[58]

Metanoia starts with repentance, re/turning, re/orienting, and re/framing; and leads to re/newal, re/storation, re/aligning, and re/calibrating of the church and individual disciple.

Chapter Five

Wholehearted Metanoia

Activating Mind, Soul, and Will

To experience metanoia is to quicken the conscience by the holiness of God, to feed the mind with the truth of God, to purge the imagination by the beauty of God, to open the heart to the love of God, and to devote the will to the purpose of God.

WILLIAM TEMPLE

Faith is a way of experiencing which is undertaken with one's whole being, all out, "with all one's heart, with all one's soul, and with all one's might." Faith is our way of leaning into life.

MICHAEL EIGEN

And when you return, you will remove every trace of idol worship. I will give you a whole heart and a new spirit; I will take from you your hearts of stone and give you tender hearts of love for God, so that you can obey my laws and be my people, and I will be your God.

EZEKIEL 11:18–20, AUTHORS' TRANSLATION

Jesus wants faith from the heart. He wants the very center of our being and not just a couple of nerve-twitches from the threshold of our ego.

HELMUT THIELICKE

We speak of "having a change of heart" so often that the phrase seems pretty ordinary—even banal, perhaps. But understood biblically, to have a "change of heart"—or similarly "to change your mind"—is not merely to think differently: *it is to become someone else*. "Thus to change your heart is to experience a transformation of being—a renovation of one's personal ethos."[1]

Having explored the dynamics and definitions of metanoia, as well as how it is the gateway to the mind of Christ, we now want to explore *how* this transformation—this change of heart—might take place. We are thus exploring how human beings might live in dynamic, open responsiveness to God; how we might grow as disciples; how we can mature as human beings; and how we can increasingly align ourselves to Jesus and his purposes in our lives.

We must first tackle the biblical issue of the heart and why it matters in determining our identity and our actions. Failure to understand the dynamics of the heart and to live accordingly will inevitably end in a mess of bungled attempts at repentance. This can create a sense of despair as we question whether change is even possible. Or we might experience some form of change but without any lasting, transformative, impact.

This despair can equally apply to organizations as to individuals; perhaps even more so because every organization comprises a complex fusion of people, each with their individual complexities. Collective metanoia is often resisted because many institutions seek to preserve the past and to prevent change by enshrining recognizability, repeatability, and predictability. Metanoia—the openness to ongoing reframing and remapping at the level of paradigm and beyond—threatens the intrinsically *conservative* nature of the institution. This is perhaps why metanoia is never taught as a foundational principle of the institution itself. And this also explains why institutions struggle to innovate and adapt to changing conditions.

Any leader reading this book will know all too well how difficult it is to get any lasting, system-wide changes in organizations, even relatively small ones. (Just think of a small denominational church, for instance.) But this is perhaps especially true of religious organizations because of the misguided theological significance we assign to them due to a distinctly non-movemental understanding of the church of Scripture and history.[2] As we noted in an earlier chapter, by appropriating such theological significance, religious institutions readily gain what is called a "towering effect," where members feel somewhat "stood over" and overwhelmed by the sheer embeddedness of traditional thinking and behaviors laced throughout the organization.

This resistance to change is as old as human organization itself. We need only consider Judaism in Jesus' times to see the reality of religious entrenchment. Jesus absolutely requires metanoia as a precondition to understanding and participating in what God is doing in and through him (Mark 1:15). As we have seen, without repentance, Israel was effectively locked into previous patterns of thinking that had been shaped by unfaithfulness as much as by faithfulness. But unfaithfulness is hardly unique to ancient Israel. We observe similar patterns throughout church history, providing plenty of examples of degenerate institutions that need regular and ongoing reform and renewal. Alas, very few such institutions in history experience change. We suggest that this lack of change is in part due to the failure to understand metanoia and how to focus the psychosocial resources to bring it about. Those in history who have managed to experience radical renewal have done so by integrating their collective mind, soul, and will and focusing these toward un/learning and transformation.

Once again, we encourage the reader to constantly apply the ideas in this book, both individually (as a disciple) and collectively (as a leader). Resist the temptation to read the Bible individualistically. Remember, it is primarily directed at communities (for example, Israel and church) and only at individuals in and through them. It is only when we read the Bible in this way that we can feel the profound significance of the biblical teaching for personal life as well as whole societies. In the end, all the desires, longings, and plans associated with all that is human are issues of the heart—individual and/or collective—and so, if we are to experience some level of transformation at all, we will need to get a handle on the heart and how it works.

God Wants (to Change) Your Heart

Woven into the revelatory fabric of the Bible is an unavoidable and consistent appeal for a wholehearted change. The primary words for "heart" in the Scriptures (*leb* in Hebrew and *kardia* in Greek) occur over 750 times. Teaching about the heart is therefore not incidental and cannot be overlooked if we are to understand both the nature of revelation and our human response. Very rarely is the word "heart" used to refer to the actual physical organ that pumps our blood. In other words, it is primarily used as a metaphor. This gives the concept profound significance, delivering invaluable insights for biblical anthropology, psychology, and spirituality.[3]

Our understanding of the heart is particularly significant in relation to the knowledge of God ... *theology*. Thinking about God is so closely wedded to the heart that an understanding of one is quite impossible without an understanding of the other. Consider the prophetic proclamation about God giving his people (note the collective dimension) a new heart (Ezekiel 36:26; Jeremiah 31:33; Hebrews 8:10) or God altering/circumcising the heart (Deuteronomy 10:16, 30:6; Romans 2:25–29). Both examples demonstrate the critical role of the heart in authentic human response and responsibility, in the ongoing covenantal relationship between God and his people, in regeneration, and in ongoing worship.

The heart is also the seat of understanding, the source of thought and reflection, as well as the root of the will and therefore the origin of all resolve.[4] In other words, the heart is the real source of all significant human actions. And because the heart is the source of all loyalties, its separation from God is what lies at the roots of rebellion and idolatry.[5] The heart is not a neutral place; it cannot avoid choosing one lord over others. Each desire represents a lord; many lords are therefore at work in the same heart, each soliciting obedience.[6]

Seen in this light, the heart is a complex battlefield. Because it is the hidden source of all thought, desire, volition, loyalty, and hope, it can readily become the scene of deadly conflicts, as one desire competes with others and where one treasure must be chosen over many alternatives. It is the source of both good and evil; therefore, failure to understand or master it can be catastrophic. Dedicating your heart to some cause can create not only great mathematicians and saints but also Nazis and suicide bombers.[7]

And so when God effectively says, "Give me your heart" (e.g., Joel 2:12–13), he is saying, "Give me your internal reality; give me the source of your imagination—the root of your capacity for image making and false worship. Give me your will to obey, your will to love me. Give me your passions and your evil urges." It appears that if God can get our heart, he gets the whole of us. He gets direct access to the very center of our life, consciousness, and experience. It is as if God says to humanity, "When your heart is Mine, then I know that you are Mine!"[8] The possibility of authentic change and deeply spiritual connection with God is therefore clearly a matter of the heart.[9]

Before we explore the multi-dimensional nature of the heart, it's important for us as Westerners to appreciate how we tend to limit the heart to the realm of emotions (notice how we express this reduction in emoticons, such as, "I 'heart' you") or in romantic love songs. Although the emotional/affective dimension is a key function of the heart, the biblical writers used the metaphor to highlight a much broader understanding. The Bible locates the affections in the "soul" (the spiritual life force). Though emotions are involved, the idea of the soul extends far beyond this understanding. So when the Bible talks about the heart, it means much more than our desires and emotions. We need to open our minds (metanoia) to take in the biblical sense of the heart and why it is important.

One Heart in Three Dimensions

In the Scriptures, the heart is made up of at least three discernible, but profoundly interrelated, dimensions: mind, soul, and will.

Although these components have some areas of functional overlap, each comprise discrete elements that together form the whole heart. For the biblical writers, human transformation takes place through the *uniting* of the disparate elements of *mind/intellect, soul/pathos,* and *will/ free choice,* in such a way that engages the whole human being at the very core of his or her consciousness. Likewise, throughout Christian history, faith has been represented as *notitia* (the intellectual element), *assensus* (the emotional element), and *fiducia* (the volitional element). These together comprise a holistic, three-dimensional understanding of faith and correspond *directly* to the three-dimensional model of the heart presented here.[10]

Consider the following diagram, which locates wholeheartedness in the intersection of all three separate dimensions. The more these interpenetrate and coalesce around the center, the more wholehearted is the metanoic experience. In a completely whole heart, all three will be totally integrated—so that all that can be seen is "the heart."

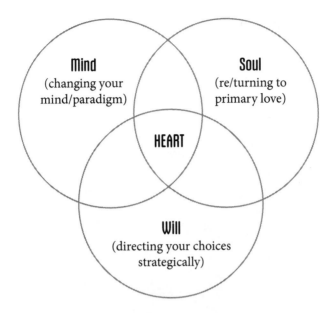

The Whole Heart

Once again, we must recognize both individual and corporate dimensions of the model above. The local church—or any organization because of their collective nature as extensions of human life—can exhibit a divided heart at least as much, if not more so, than individuals. And if the leaders of the organization are unable to integrate the collective mind, soul, and will, transformational change will remain something of an illusion, and decline will be inevitable.

It is important to keep in mind the primary and holistic nature of the heart if we are to understand and experience radical metanoia. The three dimensions form one reality of the heart. (See appendix two on the relationship of wholeheartedness to the transcendentals of being.) In the last section of this chapter, as well as in part two, we will propose a way toward greater individual and collective wholeheartedness.

The Mind and Mindfulness

We noted in chapter two that in the Scriptures the words "*nous-noia*"—commonly translated as "mind"—do not primarily refer to the physical organ of thought (i.e., the brain) but are best understood as a certain way of thinking, a rationality, or a mindset. The mind is that part of us that receives, assimilates, and makes sense of our experience of the world, whether spiritual or material.[11]

Because the mind is an inseparable dimension of the heart, any change of mind involves a change of heart, and every change of heart is soon a change of mind.[12] The heart is not governed by mindless emotion or thoughtless action. Rather, the mind is an inextricable part of a holistic intellect, especially when it is integrated with the mind of Christ.[13]

If transformation and paradigm shift are to take place, it is critical to address the prevailing rationality of the individual or group and do the serious work of reframing ideas. *Meaning*ful change cannot take place without this. As we have already noted, authentic metanoia involves radically evaluating previous belief systems and appropriating a new way of seeing the world—adopting a new mental map.[14]

Being conscious of, and actively rescripting, this mental map is a critical part of the wholehearted change process. A constant reassessment of the individual or collective mind lies at the core of un/learning and is therefore essential for transformational change. To leave the mind out of the equation is not only to end up mind-less (aka "stupid" or "dopey") but also undermines that aspect of the individual or organization that requires a sense of direction, meaning, and purpose to function. Meaninglessness only leads to debilitating despair and hopelessness, which also inevitably leads to a sense of directionlessness. We need to ask (and to some degree answer) questions like, Why are we doing this? What is the meaning of this for my life? How do I wisely and strategically negotiate the complexities involved? Is what I am doing built on truth, or is it a deception?

Being mindless works against the intelligence needed to adapt to the challenges of life and leadership.

The Soul and Soulfulness

Because the concept of the soul is particularly elusive, it warrants more clarification than the mind or the will. In Scripture, the terms for "soul" (*nephesh, ruach, psyche*) have a broad range of metaphorical meanings and can be variously translated—depending on the context—as "soul," "life," "consciousness," "person," "appetite," "desire," "emotion," "passion," and so forth. But importantly, the soul represents the animating principle of life—its "spirit"—and so it is sometimes used synonymously with the idea of spirit.[15]

The soul is also strongly associated with *pathos*; those aspects of human life that enthrall, that involve eros, empathy, compassion, and sympathy. The soul is the seat of the restless yearnings that inform the human heart: passion, desire, and the search for truth, integrity, meaning, and salvation. These yearnings drive and motivate our greatest endeavors. Furthermore (as Augustine well understood) the *psyche* is that part of us that is mysteriously drawn to the infinite; and thus it is the soul that senses, and responds to, the sacred in all things. It is therefore from the soul that all great art is generated.

The soul is also linked with the *senses* and therefore forms the basis of our primary experience of the world; that part of us that hears, tastes, feels, and sees.[16] When the senses are properly rooted in the heart, life will resonate more fully as all sensual activities are transformed into deeply *personal* acts of the whole human.[17] Humans have peak experiences when all the senses are engaged and activated—as in genuine lovemaking, or encountering beautiful art, music, or nature.

James Hillman, a psychologist who has sought to understand the nature and dynamics of the soul, says that the soul generally lies hidden behind our routines, dogmas, and fixed beliefs until it is awoken in moments of crisis that break the routine. For Hillman, the soul is the "imaginative possibility of our nature"—a possibility that is realized in reflective speculation, dream, image, and fantasy.[18] Clearly, our dreams and our imagination are functions of our psyche or soul.

In relation to motivational dimensions of the soul, eighteenth-century preacher and theologian Jonathan Edwards sought to articulate what he called "the religious affections" as part of his theology of the soul. Edwards's famous treatise on the religious affections (that which we love and attach ourselves to) was written to explain the nature of Christian conversion, no less. He maintained that if the soul is left unmoved, no spiritually significant action, let alone conversion, can or will take place.

> I am bold in saying this, but I believe that no one is ever changed, either by doctrine, by hearing the word, or by the preaching or teaching of another, unless the religious affections are moved by these things … In a word, there is never any great achievement by the things of religion without a heart deeply affected by those things … True religion is placed in the affections.[19]

Soulfulness, it appears, can be developed when individuals and communities live out their values and beliefs, and in so doing demonstrate sensitivity to God and his purposes for the world. To "have soul" therefore means to live from the inside out—where the outside is consistent with the inside. It is to wear your heart on your sleeve—being genuinely unpretentious. It means to have integrity, presence, *gravitas*. It is even said that in true love, the soul of a person envelops their body, which is why saints are often depicted with auras or halos.[20] Our great saints, our heroes in the faith, are inevitably those people who lived their messages with soul. I (Alan) recently met with the leaders of a remarkable Catholic lay movement called the Focalare Movement. These people did not need to say much about their organization. In one of the most compelling encounters I have had with Jesus in and with his people, I could feel what I can only describe as "Jesus-energy" in their very presence. Their soulful gravitas worked its magic on me, as I am now fascinated with this remarkable movement.

Organizations that have soul have a certain personality—a vibe, a feel, a mood. They too wear their beliefs on the outside for all to see. A soulful church, therefore, is one that reverberates with the presence of Jesus. It can be tangibly felt and directly experienced.

Activating the soul is therefore essential for the idea of wholehearted, lasting, metanoic transformation. Without bringing the soul into the equation, we will not only be soul-less, but we will also be half-hearted at best, heart-less at worst. Without activating the soul, we will lack the necessary passion and commitment required for transformation—our hearts, will not "be in it."

> It is not revolutions and upheavals
> That clear the road to new and better days,
> But revelations, lavishness and torments
> Of someone's soul, inspired and ablaze.[21]

The *passionate* pursuit of a goal alters the structure of reality.

The Will and Decisiveness

Perhaps getting a biblical handle on what is meant by the will is the easiest task in describing this anthropology of the heart. The soul and the mind tend to hide in plain sight, more on the level of un/consciousness and indescribable yearning. However, the will is much more evident. Every day, we feel the impact of our own choices, as well as those made by others. Acts of kindness are a case in point. We benefit from other people's positive choices to serve and love. But we also experience negative examples of the will. Ideologically driven politics are an obvious, and all too contemporary, example. You don't have to look too far to see this. Just think of the power politics at play in countries across the globe over recent years, as well as throughout history. What is patently clear is that we all have a will, and that it plays a large part in all our lives, for good or ill.

Dallas Willard says that will, or choice, involves the capacity of the person to originate things and events that would not otherwise be or occur.[22] This ability to "originate" things and events arises from human freedom and possibility and lies at the center of all creativity. To be human before God requires responsibility, direction, and choice. To choose God is to align your will with his will.

Our ability to choose is part of what it means to be created in the image and likeness of God. As humans, we can and must choose. In this way we can alter the course of our lives and determine something of our destiny in the world. No wonder Augustine was said to have called it "the dreaded gift of free will." It is a gift because it opens us to all kinds of possibilities; dreaded because it can also wreak utter havoc. The will therefore involves the uniquely human capacity to be proactive, to initiate, to create, to bring about what did not exist before.

It's not just our active choices that can create problems for us and others around us; passivity and indecision (the unwillingness to make a choice) can also cause all sorts of issues. Sins of omission can be just as serious as sins of commission. Some theologians even consider laziness (*acedia*) and decisionlessness to be the root of sin.[23] Martin Buber says that indecision, when combined with directionlessness, lies at the root of our problems with evil.[24] Passivity clearly plays a role in various psychological problems and can even be understood as the basis of demonic oppression and bondage, where humans relinquish their freedom to, and become subject to, darker spiritual forces. Those who understand the nature of spiritual deliverance often say that demonic oppression derives largely from an abuse of will, from repeated bad choices.

In this sense, full-on repentance—transformative change, conversion—requires definite actions of the will, along with the ability to be strategic and proactive, to reset the direction of our lives, and to make an impact in society and the world. It is by exercising our wills, by choosing and by responding, that we can create new futures. God's kingdom comes when and where his will is done.

The Symphony of a Whole Heart

The three-dimensional model of the heart is clearly evident in Israel's *Shema* of Deuteronomy 6:4–9, which is confirmed and supplemented in Jesus summation of the Torah and the greatest commandments—the call to "Love the Lord your God with all your heart and with all your soul and with all your mind and with all your strength [will]" (Mark 12:30).[25] When we integrate and unify the dimensions of the heart—soul, mind, and strength (will)—in what we have named as wholeheartedness, we can truly love and worship the One God.[26] By leaving any of these out of the equation, we can neither experience a true love of God nor fully undergo the deep metanoic change that comes with such an experience.[27]

Throughout history, various Christian traditions have sought to incorporate the three-dimensional understanding of the heart into their prayer, worship, and practice. Orthodox theologians, for example, speak of "the prayer of the heart" where prayer is understood as requiring the offering of the whole person—intellect, reason, will, and affections—as well as the physical body.[28]

The human heart—comprising mind, soul, and will—is the executive center of an individual's life.[29] In other words, it is the place of action where ideas and intentions, plans and passions are implemented. "The heart is where decisions and choices are made for the whole person. That is its function."[30] Furthermore, because the heart integrates the intellect, will, emotions, and senses, it unites the body and the mind, which is fundamental to human perception itself.

Our feelings are the way in which the heart integrates and unifies all that we engage with in life. As the activity of the heart, feelings are not to be regarded as a separate faculty alongside the intellect and the will, nor as in any way inferior to them. Feelings are the integration of all human faculties and are therefore eminently human.[31]

All three dimensions of the heart presuppose and ground one another. They are interrelated and cannot give their true contribution without being informed and impacted by the others. The mind needs the soul, which needs the will, which needs the mind, which needs the … and so forth. The more we can integrate these three dimensions, the more we can experience a transformed, changed, metanoic heart—a heart aligned with God's purposes and focus for our lives. Conversely, the more fragmented the heart, the more dysfunctional our lives will be.

The Pain of a Broken Heart

The problem of the "broken" heart—our incapacity to bring our whole heart to what we are doing—lies at the core of our broken lives and systems. This is because at least one of the three dimensions that bring metanoic transformation of the heart is missing from the equation. The broken (divided) heart is a heart confused by too many alternatives and is therefore unable to employ its integrative power.

Like a body whose core functions are at odds with one another, the half-hearted, double-minded, indecisive person/organization is out of sync, working against themselves/itself and tearing themselves/itself apart. For instance, every member of Alcoholics Anonymous must deeply *want* to break their addiction—with their *whole* heart—if they are to be successful in overcoming it. Without a wholly integrated mind, soul, and will, they can never be free. This is true for all radical personal and social change. It is especially true for human institutions because their collective extension of individual existence means change is more complex. We know that our institutions are so riddled with innumerable ruts, that they often try to operate with outworn thinking, and that they sometimes act just plain inhumanely. These are corporate patterns that need to change. But the point is that they must really *want* things to be different if they are to experience change at all. They need to activate all three dimensions of their corporate heart if they are to experience genuine metanoia.[32]

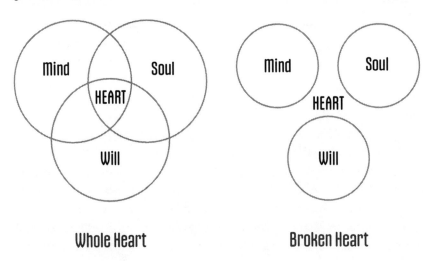

Whole Heart   Broken Heart

Think about the people or organizations you know that exhibit a whole heart. I (Alan) immediately think of Christine Caine, one of my dear friends and heroes, who founded Equip & Empower Ministries, Propel Women, Zoe Churches, and A21. Those who know her experience Christine as a wholehearted person. She is brimful of "soul" and passion and feels things deeply because she is radically open to God's transformation. She is exceptionally smart, carefully considers things, and informs herself deeply. She is strategic and proactive, making choices she sticks with. Because she is so radically open, critically aware, and predisposed to responsible action, she significantly impacts the world for God.

An important aside here regarding women and wholeheartedness: In my (Alan) experience, women are usually much better at integrating mind, soul, and will, partly because they don't tend to compartmentalize their lives in the way men tend to. For instance, contrast the woman who anointed Jesus with perfume with the religious elite who watched her. They sat at a safe distance, arms likely crossed, and assessed the incident rationally. She, on the other hand, engaged with heart, mind, body—as a whole person. She's the one who Jesus praised and whose story has been told through the ages (Mark 14:3–9; John 12:1–8).[33] There is much to learn from women in this regard. For instance, I was recently talking to a female colleague about how difficult it is for me to experience wholeheartedness, that I tend to engage primarily in one dimension. She said that the best way to integrate all three at once is to shed a tear because when we cry, all the pieces of the heart (as well as the two sides of the brain) come together. This tallied with my experience; most of my major metanoic/conversion/repentance moments have involved weeping.

Conversely, we can all recall people who operate from a fragmented center. For instance, we likely know individuals who are passionate for God and are even willing to make costly choices for him based on that passion, but their lack of wisdom causes all kinds of problems. Despite good intentions, they tend to create chaos wherever they go.

The same, of course, can be true of organizations. Some are overly theoretical, others are driven by emotionalism, and others by sheer willpower. For instance, in expressions of church, there are "mind-churches," which do not touch the heart; "soul-churches," which do not bother with the head; and "will-churches," which do not engage mind or soul but try to minister through sheer gritted teeth. Further, the head churches are usually not prayerful or contemplative; the soul churches have little discrimination or training in those aspects of ministry that allow members to be discerning in a world of deceptions; and the will-oriented people have either left the church or, even worse, stay in the pew but do not take it seriously as anything real, urgent, or wonderful.[34] Consider the following examples:

- Isolated from the guiding wisdom of the mind and the spiritual resonance of the soul, the will can be dangerous, forceful, and at times cruel (as in political authoritarianism, or in sexual assault, for instance). We need only recall a time when someone "forced their will" on us, usually resulting in some form of victimization and suffering.

- Without some form of intellectual grasp of why and what it is that you are doing, and without a resolve to ignite action, a passionate soul can render a person (or group) unhinged or overly emotional. Think of the fanaticism of the suicide bomber or, to a much lesser degree, the mindless irrationality of some charismatic sects.

- Without some real measure of love and soulfulness, along with the willingness to be a force for positive change in the world, the intellect becomes an unloving, oppressive, and technocratic dictator. Think of Dostoevsky's Grand Inquisitor—a brilliant technocrat who in pursuit of a grand humanistic vision of moral order, winds up creating a merciless institution that dehumanizes its members into functional units.

We need to bring all these dimensions together. And here we arrive at the idea of wholeheartedness.

A Model of Wholehearted Change

As part of the training systems of MLC, my dear friend and colleague Rich Robinson and I (Alan) developed a comprehensive model for understanding the wholehearted, transformative change process. It is incorporated in the model of personal and organizational change that we will elaborate on in chapters six to nine. Here, we simply address the matter of the heart as it relates to metanoic, transformational change, using the framework of mind-power, soul-power and will-power.

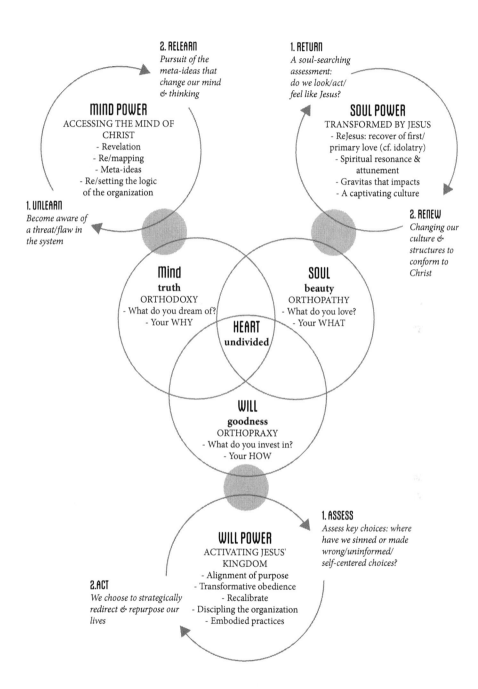

Activating Mind-Power

Leaders seeking to activate *mind-power* need to be proactive in helping their organizations consciously identify the ideas that drive them, evaluate whether these ideas are still valid, and, where necessary, discover and implement new ones. Once there is awareness of the relative strengths and weaknesses in the group, leaders will also need to facilitate the necessary unlearning so that members can readily adopt new ideas and pathways. Failure to do this will leave entrenched thought and behavioral patterns in place.

We need to be aware of our foundational ideas and principles—what MLC refers to as *meta-ideas*.[35] This is particularly important for ecclesial organizations, where core theology is critical in motivating action and shaping thinking.[36] If leaders are operating with the Christo-logic gifted to them in Jesus; and if they have an open and hungry mind, characteristic of the metanoic experience, they should be able to discern the foundational ideas and how they shape identity and practice. However, to identify and formulate these meta-ideas accurately, they will need to engage in intelligent reading and dedicated research for alternative ways of thinking on topic—to break from overfamiliarity with previous ideas. They will also need to consider how to re-map and reorder the way the organization thinks and digests information. (See appendix six on upstream-downstream processing.)

The processes above apply equally to the individual, except that the application is more personal. Essentially, we need to become increasingly self-aware, develop our critical-thinking abilities, and commit to growing in discernment and to becoming generally more informed. This can be achieved, for example, by dialoguing in book clubs; by committing to reading the thought-leaders in any field, even if it means learning whole new vocabularies; by learning to ask poignant questions and following through in a quest to answer them; and by limiting consumption of TV and other media that dumb us down and generate passivity. Always remember that the word "disciple" in the Greek (*matheiteis*) means *learner* or *student,* and so whatever else it means, it involves growing in wisdom and understanding. There can be no dodging or outsourcing our thinking if we are to mature as lifelong disciples of King Jesus.

Activating Soul-Power

As we have seen, the soul of an organization embodies the vibe or atmosphere of the organization—in effect, its resonant culture. Culture, as a dimension of the soul or spirit of the organization, acts like an invisible force field that influences everything we do. Leadership expert Peter Drucker reputedly remarked that culture eats strategy for breakfast. If this is the case, we are wise not to leave it unattended. Activating soul-power will require a significant focus on the issues of culture and its impact on the organization.

Organizational behaviorists have long taught that organizations are laced with invisible cultural elements—actions, values, language, symbols, purpose, and ethos. We are often blind to these forces of culture around us, but they directly affect our thoughts, actions, and communication. Newcomers approaching the ambit of an organization readily perceive its vibe and can feel constrained to behave in certain ways, even though no one explicitly tells them how to do so.[37]

The outward expression of an individual soul can be detected by looking at what is loved and desired because the soul arouses passions and focuses motivation. Soul is also evident in the core values of the community; and it is the felt presence of these values that attracts passionate commitment and allegiance, guides behavior, shapes thinking, and informs decision-making.

Without a resonant soul-power, the organization will over rely on power and rules to try to maintain itself. However, using this approach, it is unlikely to sustain itself over the long term and will inevitably languish and eventually fade into oblivion. Reactivating soul-power is therefore critical in revitalizing organizations.

Leaders should understand what gets people in the organization interested, what activates them, what makes them sad or happy. What do people feel passionate about? What language do they resonate with? We suggest that organization, as well as the artifacts within it (for example, buildings, music, art pieces) seek to be more artful, beautiful, and culturally resonant. The core values should not appeal just to the head but should also move the soul, making people feel things deeply.

Activating Will-Power

Passivity and indecision can be a significant problem for individuals as well as organizations. Churches or denominations that are full of complacent individuals have trouble getting anything done. There are many reasons for this complacency, but inevitably it involves some disorder of the will that leads to an inability to make meaningful choices and stick with them.[38] In Christian organizations, this results in a culture of resistance to the demands of the kingdom of God—a serious spiritual malady that will frustrate God's purposes in and through his people. Repentance will therefore inevitably involve obedience and a willful resolve to act in accordance with God's will.

Another disorder of the will manifests itself when individuals or collectives make many decisions, but they are haphazard and seem to have little lasting impact. What is lacking is a discernible, strategic plan of action that will change their circumstances. Instead, there is frustration and hopelessness, which leads to further passivity and inactivity.

In order to focus the organization's sense of will, we suggest that leaders consider issues strategically. What decisions made here and now will have maximum effect later? What are the goals and objectives of the organization, and how can you allocate resources to achieve these? Have a metric and stick to it. Be accountable for the choices you make … or those you fail to make.

All Together Now

Again, this comprehensive model of wholeheartedness will be built into the processes of metanoia that are explored in part two.

For now, try doing a quick test on 1) yourself and 2) your church or organization, to get a sense of the strengths and weaknesses of each. Use the results to develop a pathway to strengthen the areas that prevent you from being wholehearted and therefore unable to experience the transformative power of metanoia. We must not simply focus on our strengths and ignore our weaknesses. So, for instance, if the dimension of the mind is the strongest, there is no value in doubling down on thinking. Instead, pay attention to the dimension that undermines the functioning of the whole. We must attend to the weakest part of the system if we are to experience wholeheartedness.

On a scale of 1 to 5 (with 5 as strong), assess your own personal capacities and then those of the organization you lead.

What does your assessment tell you about yourself and/or your community? Are your relative strengths or weaknesses mirrored in the organization? What's missing, and what can you do about it? What are some of the distinct ways you can improve in your area of weakness? How can you hire/recruit to your weaknesses?

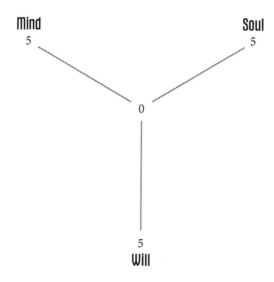

Unification of the heart and its direction toward God is how we are to *love* God, and it lies at the very heart of the biblical worldview. When Jesus said, "Blessed are the pure of heart for they shall see God" (Matthew 5:8), he was not only referring to the importance of personal holiness but also alluding to the biblical idea of being single-hearted. To be pure of heart means to have an undivided heart. As we have already noted, according to the monotheistic logic of the *Shema*, all the forces of human life (soul, mind, strength) are to be focused on the One God and not dispersed among many idols and ideologies that appeal to our hearts. We can only know and love God by integrating the disparate forces of the heart and directing these toward the One.[39] According to Jesus, it is only those who have undivided and simple hearts who are able to understand, to look upon, experience, perceive, and discern God.[40]

Wholeheartedness—corporate and individual—is essential to metanoia, and metanoia in turn is essential to our knowledge of God. A dynamic and integrated heart is the starting point for a genuinely transformative experience of metanoia. As Eugene Peterson translates the words of Jesus: "You're blessed when you get your inside world—your mind and heart—put right. Then you can see God in the outside world" (Matthew 5:8 MSG).

Part Two

How Metanoia

We now come to the second, more practical, section of the book. This content is derived from a process designed by Rich Robinson and myself (Alan) as a vital part of our work in MLC. In the chapters that follow, Rob brings his unique insights on platforms and networked organizations to bear, adding credibility and experience to the process. To be clear, MLC exists to help churches and Christian organizations become more movemental, and in doing so to have greater transformational impact. This process—what we here call the "Metanoia Journey"—has now been built into all our leadership development training, including our Movement Labs, the Starfish and the Spirit Accelerator, the mDNA Accelerator, The City Movement platforms, and the 5Q Church Planting Cohort.[1] It has, in turn, been embedded into many of the processes of the various movements we work with, including NewThing, City Leaders Collective, The Underground Network, Redeemer City to City, For Charlotte Network, The Salvation Army, and others.

We say this to demonstrate that metanoia is not simply a theoretical exercise. What follows incorporates all the core ideas in this book— metanoia as paradigm shift and re/learning, as participation in the mind of Christ, and as wholehearted change—and brings them together in an active process that will deliver real, enduring, and deeply spiritual change. Chapter six describes the necessary journey of un/raveling and un/learning that will make space for the process that follows; chapter seven explores the dynamics of paradigm shift that lead to a place of conscious clarity about the organization's mental model/map as well as the determining DNA; chapter eight proposes a way in which to create the platform of change through which the culture and structures predetermine the actions that follow; and chapter nine explores the habits, practices, and algorithms that shape the whole life of the organism/ organization.

Before we dig into the content of the Metanoia Journey, it's important to state that, in line with the purpose of this book to provide a thorough conceptual framework for metanoia as a whole, what we offer in this section is not so much the details of the process but an overall description of it. The nuts and bolts will be provided in the associated workbook and through the various learning cohorts and coaching offered by MLC. Therefore, please read these chapters as something of an overview of the process with some hints at tools and practices that enable change.

As we have already explored, metanoia is essential to any ongoing growth as disciples of Jesus, and the exact same metanoic process involved in individual discipleship applies on the collective level. The process needed for individuals to grow, adapt, and change mirrors the process that communities need to grow, adapt, and change. In other words, metanoia is a skill that leaders need if they are to not only disciple individuals but also to *disciple the organization* itself and bring it into greater conformity and attunement with God and his purposes in the world. If change and growth are not programmed into the equation of our churches and our discipleship, our religion will always end up protecting the status quo as if it were God.[2]

We have already noted that transforming a whole organization is far more complicated than changing an individual—and that is difficult enough. Even revamping a small traditional church is extremely challenging. This is because, over time, organizations that started as a movement tend to institutionalize in order to sustain themselves. Institutions are almost always conservative agencies, designed to preserve the status quo and to resist regular adaptation and change.[3] Of course, movements must be embodied in some form of organization, but once we begin to think of the church primarily in terms of organizational structure, it becomes one of the very principalities and powers that the gospel is supposed to withstand.[4] However, as we have already stated, in these VUCA times, the ability to innovate and adapt is absolutely critical to organizational survival. Under such conditions, leaders who lack an understanding of the complexities of change, and have no workable process of metanoia, will either be finally expelled from the organization or will be unable to fundamentally alter its trajectory of decline.

The Way of Un/learning

Humans almost always resist change. Part of the reason for this is that organizational insiders, and especially leaders, are the key beneficiaries of the current system and tend to work to maintain it. The existing paradigm therefore becomes something of a mental (and spiritual) prison of self-induced repetitiveness and bias. These are the deep, often unconscious, reasons for resistance to change, and so embarking on a process of trans-formation requires a fair bit of courage and a whole lot of self-insight. We need to unlearn a lot, it seems, to get back to that foundational life which is "hidden in God" (Colossians 3:3). Yes, transformation is often more about unlearning than learning, which is why we call it "conversion" or "repentance."

It's also important to understand and acknowledge the reality of spiritual warfare behind intransigence in the form of powers and principalities that seek to bind human behaviors through ideology, religious traditionalism, and oppressive patterns of behavior. *Stoicheia*,[5] (the "elemental spirits/principles") are the foundation of the religious, social, economic, and political certainties that give order and stability to life. They assume spiritual power when people give their allegiance to them as if they were themselves the source of meaning and significance. They enslave people, and religious institutions tend to be laden with them (Galatians 4:8–11). Paul warns us to not submit to the *stoichea*, expressed in human rules and religious ritual such as "Do not handle! Do not taste! Do not touch!" (Colossians 2:21). Institutions can have a "life" of their own and are often opposed to God's purposes. Leaders trying to help the church get back on a missional footing will need great spiritual discernment and a commitment to prayer because the struggle to advance the kingdom of God is not just a human battle but a spiritual one (Ephesians 6:12).

A glance at the Metanoia Journey diagram on page 92 shows the shape of the journey we need to take if we are to experience genuine

DECONSTRUCT (VIA NEGATIVA)

UNRAVEL
becoming aware of paradigmatic issues, identifying systemic dysfunction, wicked problem, embracing the adaptive challenge

UNCOVER
roaming of the mind, soft eyes, sensing the system, exposing flaws & movement blockers, unlearning, lamenting unfaithfulness

UNLOCK
exploring frontiers, broad mapping of contours, prayerful/playful prefiguring of possibilities, culture of experiential learning, spiritual receptivity

UNDERSTAND
reforming/reformulating paradigm, searching for patterns & prevailing meta-ideas, seeking the balance between order & chaos

Mind
from narrow/reduced thinking to an open mind

Will
from fear & competition to a submitted will

Soul
from cynicism, pragmatism & despair to a hopeful soul

HEART

DEFINING MOMENT
Clarity & Conviction
Metanoia/Eureka!/Aha! Moment
the turning point, the epiphany, reception of key insight/s, an intuition of the answer, the elegant solution

PARADIGM
engaging the mind of the organization, including forming/formulating a mental map, solidifying meta-ideas, formulating DNA that can be fractalized throughout the organization

PLATFORM
engaging the soul of the organization, setting the culture & vibrant spirituality, architecting movemental structures, ensuring scalability

PRACTICES
engaging the will of the organization, developing organizational rhythms & algorithms that refine core practices to embed meta-ideas, develop tools & training pathways for scale

PERFORM
movement scaling, learning & growth, cultural health, organizational sweet spot, reiterating & refining

SHARED PERCEPTION
Awareness
Hear

The Metanoia Journey
Metanoia

COLLECTIVE ACTION
Application
Obey

RECONSTRUCT (VIA POSITIVA)

transformation. The U-shape of the curve suggests we can only learn if we are first willing to go through something of an un/learning process. By doing so, we can emerge on the other side with a renewed ability to achieve our mission. This metanoic process releases individuals and the organization from cycles of brokenness and rehabituates them to patterns more consistent with Jesus and his cause.

This notion of un/learning is consistent with the ancient understanding of how we can know God. Theologians have long talked about the way of negation and unknowing (the *via negativa* or the apophatic way), and the way of knowing and understanding (the *via positiva* or the kataphatic way). At different times, and for different reasons, both forms are necessary to grow in our relationship with God.

The Hero's Journey

A willingness to trek through the valley follows the same archetypal pattern in the now universally recognized "hero's journey," which informs most of the defining narratives in human culture and religion. On this expedition, the hero is commissioned to undertake an arduous journey, during which they will undergo significant testing and existential struggle to eventually, and against all odds, emerge victorious and solve the threat to broader society. This pattern is not only found in myth and popular storytelling but can also be seen in the lives of many of the biblical heroes, including Abraham, Moses, Jeremiah, Mary, and Paul—but supremely in the life and ministry of the Arch Hero of the story, Jesus himself. The sending of the Son of God, his incarnation, his ministry, rejection by his people, the existential struggle in his passion, death, his victory in the resurrection, and the return to a new reality in the ascension—all follow this U-shaped journey, which results in Jesus bringing salvation to the world.[6] As we saw in chapter four, metanoia follows the pattern of Christ's life (incarnation, life, cross, and resurrection) and in so doing brings us in sync with the mind of Christ. There must be no avoiding metanoia—and the hero's journey we must take—if we are to be consistent to Jesus' "way." The hero's journey as a Metanoic Journey can be readily seen in the following diagram, which is based on Joseph Campbell's classic monomyth.[7]

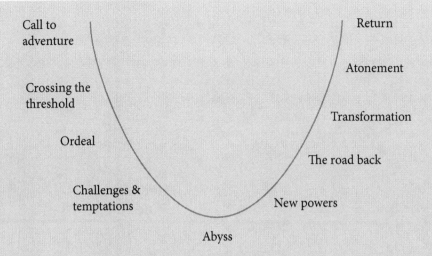

The Hero's Journey
(based on Campbell's Monomyth)

Developmental psychology also asserts that learning is achieved through an undulating U-shaped pattern that involves consecutive un/learning and re/learning processes. The U-curve (also known as the sigmoid curve) charts the process proposed by seminal educational philosophical thinkers such as Jean Piaget, James Fowler, Clare Graves, Kurt Fischer, Lawrence Kohlberg, and Carol Gilligan, among others, as well as the organizational-change models proposed by individuals such as Katrin Kaufer, Otto Sharmer, and Peter Senge. Is it any wonder that the greatest minds in psychology and organizational change affirm the biblical process God designed for us as his image bearers, and by extension our organizations, to most effectively be conformed into the image he intends for us?[8]

Journey Like Your Life Depends on It

As you begin the Metanoia Journey, it is imperative that you approach it as a quest in which everything important to you and your organization is at stake. In ways we are not always aware of, this really *is* already the truth of the situation. There can be no return to some form of an idealized past. There must be no more doubling down on attractional strategies if we want to achieve missional outcomes. It is a time of significant liminality.[9] If we don't change our systems and paradigms now, in this wet-cement cultural/apocalyptic moment, it is likely our standard organizations will eventually break down.

We must now search for a better way to be faithful witnesses of the kingdom. The journey into the future of the church can be understood as something of a pilgrimage—a liminal journey that takes us deeper into God than we have ever been before.[10] And, as is the case in certain similar conditions, if it doesn't kill you, it will make you stronger. Liminality, negotiated *faith*fully, really can be good for the mind, soul, and will. Therefore, engage with the liminality by being willing to live like a vagabond, as an itinerant on the road. Be desperate! Don't even bother to take a change of clothes, let alone food for the journey. Learn to depend on God's provision and guidance as you go (Luke 10:1–20). You should feel the all-too-real risk of failure—this will motivate you in ways you cannot even now imagine. Abandon the concept of "failure is not an option," recognizing that failure is only failure if you don't learn from it. Engage with the risk; let the liminality teach you what only liminality can. "Fill the gaps! Stay liquid! Survive!"[11]

Any attempt to change the trajectory of any organization—and perhaps especially the church—remains a tough challenge. But there are significant signs of hope among the ashes. If we are willing to unlearn, explore new possibilities, recalibrate, reframe the current ways of thinking, and rebuild a viable organization from there, we will not only discover resources within ourselves that we never thought possible, but we will also know God in a deeper and more profound way.

Chapter Six
The Metanoia Journey

Learning to Unlearn to Relearn

You never change things by fighting the existing reality. To change something, build a new model that makes the existing model obsolete.

BUCKMINSTER FULLER

If you want truly to understand something, try and change it.

KURT LEWIN

In a time of drastic change, it is the learners who inherit the future. The "learned" usually find themselves equipped to live in a world that no longer exists.

ERIC HOFFER

For this reason, since the day we heard about you, we have not stopped praying for you. We continually ask God to fill you with the knowledge of his will through all the wisdom and understanding that the Spirit gives.

COLOSSIANS 1:9

"It's the economy, stupid" was Bill Clinton's slogan when he successfully ran for the White House in 1992. The US was experiencing an economic recession, and the incumbent president, George H. W. Bush, was perceived as out of touch with the needs of ordinary Americans. Clinton's campaign staffers were therefore instructed to hammer home the importance of the economy every chance they got—the slogan was even framed and hung all over the campaign headquarters.

We want to co-opt that saying and claim (with all due respect), "It's the system, stupid." By this, we mean it is impossible to correct the almost universal decline of the church in the Western world without grappling with the system that has produced the decline in the first place. To miss the systemic nature of the problem will mean that all attempts to resolve it will be mere patchwork—quick-fix solutions—which will have no lasting effect. As Robert Pirsig famously stated,

> But to tear down a factory or to revolt against a government is to attack effects rather than causes; and as long as the attack is upon effects only, no change is possible. The true system, the real system, is our present construction of thought itself, rationality itself. If a factory is torn down but the rationality which produced it is left standing, then that rationality will simply produce another factory. If a revolution destroys a systematic government, but the systematic patterns of thought that produced that government are left intact, then those patterns will repeat themselves in the succeeding government.[1]

Witness, for instance, the failure of the democratic Arab Spring movement to overthrow systems of autocracy throughout the Middle East. Similarly, this inability to dethrone deeply entrenched systems of Christendom has been the story of the church for far too long. In the last few decades, leaders have sought to weaken the stranglehold with church-growth methodology, which has only further entrenched attractional paradigms and intensified the problem. For all the techniques and plug-and-play solutions adapted from various "successful" megachurch models, the fundamental Christendom paradigm has been left untouched.[2] This is evident in the panic-driven attempt to return to what was considered the "normal" church expression in the aftermath of the highly disruptive COVID-19 pandemic. But those who did this simply kicked the can down the road and will eventually have to deal with the problems of the system. The reality remains: If leaders fail to change the operating system of the organization itself, then anything we do is just a Band-Aid and, in the end, nothing will change. We must therefore dig down to the very roots of the problem; we need to get to the core of the system itself, and from there we must take responsibility for reconfiguring it.

The Downcurve (To Un/learn)

Leaders need to both understand the transformative power of metanoia *and* have a process by which they can guide the organization through meaningful, deep, spiritual change. The Metanoia Journey is precisely the kind of tool needed. As noted, many attempts at generating movements focus on a re/learning design process on the upcurve. However, what is critically lacking is the un/learning process of the downcurve. Without this, no real change can take place. The primary template of the organization remains deeply entrenched and largely invisible to the organizational insiders. Many pragmatic leaders, impatient with concepts, are like Evel Knievel—wanting to "jump the chasm" to avoid the hard learning journey. And, because they are also ardent pragmatists, they are always looking for the quick fix, the plug-and-play app, the seven-step miracle solution. But in so doing, they dodge the painful unraveling necessary to "convert" the organization from a more institutional form to being a more decidedly movemental one. We have seen this played out over many years, and painfully few organizations have attained the prize of being a Jesus movement. It's impossible to jump over your own shadow, and it's equally impossible to see transformative change without first doing the deep work of unlearning.

In the biblical way of metanoia, the shortest way to the next mountain peak is down through the valley. *The only way up is to go down.* We must be willing to descend into the dangerous valley if we are to get to the destination. We need to unravel and reach rock-bottom (as, for example, the Alcoholics Anonymous 12-step process affirms) before we are willing to pay the price of change. Only by journeying through the valley do we come to recognize that what really hinders new ways of thinking and doing is the prevailing way of seeing and doing. Franciscan friar Richard Rohr calls this process "falling upward." Leaders or organizations that fail to realize the necessity of this route will inevitably remain immature, fearful, and finally obsolete.[3]

This chapter will focus in some detail on each of the four stages of the downcurve: Unravel, Uncover, Unlock, and Understand. Because the downcurve content corresponds with the material already explored in part one of this book, we will cover these four stages briefly in this chapter and then will look in more depth at the three stages of the upcurve—Paradigm, Platform, and Practices—in the following three chapters. Perform, the fourth stage of the upcurve—addressed in the conclusion—enables organizations to bake ongoing metanoia into the system so that we can continue to un/learn and be effective and faithful to our calling.

Unravel

The journey to change begins with facing head-on what design thinkers call a "wicked problem." Wicked problems are those organizational dilemmas that are extremely difficult to solve because of their complex and interconnected nature. They are often not immediately obvious, but even when they are, the potential solutions are not risk-free. The COVID-19 pandemic presented something of a wicked problem to many established organizations (for example, hospitality, airlines, supermarkets, healthcare, and churches). Other examples of complex wicked problems are climate change, global poverty, and homelessness.

But there is a somewhat paradoxical dimension of a wicked problem in that although it can threaten to undo the organization if it is not properly addressed and resolved, if a solution can be found, it promises to take the organization (or individual) to a higher level of performance than ever before. In other words, solving a wicked problems brings with it a significant reward ... a prize.

Wicked problems present an adaptive challenge, which usually comes in one of two forms: 1) as an adapt-or-die scenario, where either a new way of operating must be found or the individual or organization will cease to exist, or 2) as an opportunity which offers a compelling reason to change.[4] In adaptive challenges, the problem is often unknown or hard to identify; it requires unraveling and may be tied to deeper patterns or dynamics. The solution likewise is also unknown and therefore requires learning. Facing the crisis head-on precipitates a search for new and innovative ways of achieving the organization's purposes—which is why leadership gurus suggest (as we said in chapter one) we should never waste a good crisis. Grappling with a wicked problem ought to trigger the un/learning process that, if followed well, leads to metanoia/paradigm shift, which

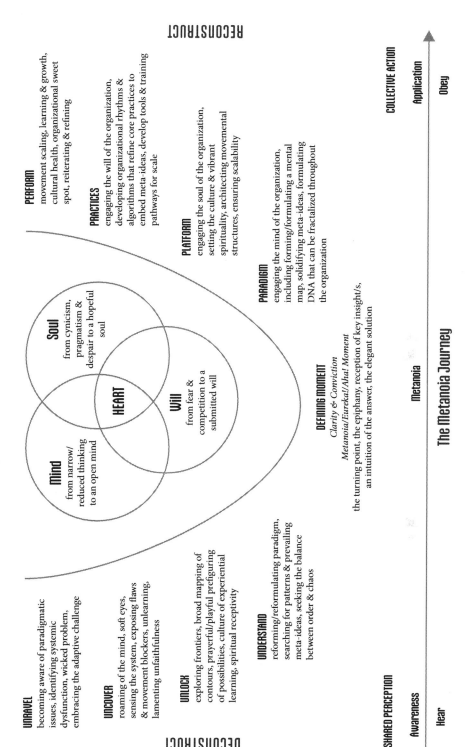

RECONSTRUCT

PERFORM
movement scaling, learning & growth, cultural health, organizational sweet spot, reiterating & refining

PRACTICES
engaging the will of the organization, developing organizational rhythms & algorithms that refine core practices to embed meta-ideas, develop tools & training pathways for scale

PLATFORM
engaging the soul of the organization, setting the culture & vibrant spirituality, architecting movemental structures, ensuring scalability

PARADIGM
engaging the mind of the organization, including forming/formulating a mental map, solidifying meta-ideas, formulating DNA that can be fractaled throughout the organization

Soul
from cynicism, pragmatism & despair to a hopeful soul

Mind
from narrow/ reduced thinking to an open mind

HEART

Will
from fear & competition to a submitted will

DEFINING MOMENT
Clarity & Conviction
Metanoia/Eureka!/Aha! Moment
the turning point, the epiphany, reception of key insight/s, an intuition of the answer, the elegant solution

UNRAVEL
becoming aware of paradigmatic issues, identifying systemic dysfunction, wicked problem, embracing the adaptive challenge

UNCOVER
roaming of the mind, soft eyes, sensing the system, exposing flaws & movement blockers, unlearning, lamenting unfaithfulness

UNLOCK
exploring frontiers, broad mapping of contours, prayerful/playful prefiguring of possibilities, culture of experiential learning, spiritual receptivity

UNDERSTAND
reforming/reformulating paradigm, searching for patterns & prevailing meta-ideas, seeking the balance between order & chaos

DECONSTRUCT

SHARED PERCEPTION
Awareness
Hear

Metanoia
The Metanoia Journey

COLLECTIVE ACTION
Application
Obey

changes the game entirely. The more clearly we can define the wicked problem in this phase of the Metanoia Journey, the better we can build a viable new platform on the upcurve of the journey.

To be generative, rather than destructive, a crisis needs to be engaged with the whole heart (mind, soul, will). It must not be avoided. It must be *felt* as a threat. Only in this way can it galvanize action and initiate a search for another way of thinking and acting. It must be experienced as something of a "coming apart at the seams" if it is to be proved fruitful.

At the Unraveling stage, it is critical to become aware of the anomalies inherent in the prevailing paradigm of the organization. In an earlier chapter, we explored why metanoia/paradigm shift is critical. Here we simply need to affirm that the paradigm is the largely unconscious *mental map* that orients the organization and determines meaningful action and ways of doing things. To unravel means to become conscious of ourselves, of our assumptions, and of the prevailing paradigm, in order to shed obsolete thinking and redundant practices. The crisis forces us to investigate the system, to become aware of hidden assumptions and to chart the contours of the predominant mental map—the map that is producing the problems in the first place.[5]

One of the tools MLC uses to help identify the crisis in the moment is what we call a "pre-mortem." Whereas a post-mortem happens after death, a pre-mortem is a mental exercise where participants imagine the future failure of a church or marketplace project in which they are currently investing all their energies. Participants visualize the death and anticipate all kinds of brokenness and loss. The challenge for the participants is to try to figure out *why* and *how* the project failed. What are they not doing now that led to that failure? What things could they now do to offset the danger? By imaginatively grappling with the demise of the organization they love and serve, we have found that leaders are compelled to explore possible ways in which the crisis can be averted by decisions made in the present. There is nothing like an existential encounter with death to bring clarity and focus to life!

At the Unravel stage, key questions to explore might be:

- What does this (or some future crisis) reveal about the fragilities and the vulnerabilities that are latent in our system, and in our own leadership of it?

- Are we willing to take a serious look under the hood of our system, to name the wicked problem we are now facing, and to become aware of how ill-prepared we might be for these conditions?

- As leaders, are we willing to take personal responsibility for our role in the crisis, as well as being willing to lead the organization out of it? If unable, are we willing to step aside and let others lead in this time?

- Are we resolved to embark on the difficult journey of un/learning that will almost definitely upset the status quo (including the financial model)?

Uncover

This stage follows closely that of Unraveling. Having faced (and named) the wicked problem, with all its associated threat and promise, this next stage ought to initiate a quest to both solve the problem and create new possibilities. This quest must be undertaken (as we mentioned in chapter three) with what we call "soft eyes":

> "You know what you need at a crime scene?... Soft eyes... If you got soft eyes, you can see the whole thing. If you got hard eyes—you staring at the same tree missing the forest... Soft eyes, grasshopper!" (Detective Bunk, *The Wire*)[6]

No one is sure of the exact origin of the phrase "soft eyes," but it was probably used by Native Americans when tracking and hunting animals. Having soft eyes is essential to hunting, detective work, medical diagnosis, and to all new discoveries and learning. In order to see something, we must be willing to "look again" and see it as if for the first time, choosing to defer judgment and remain open. So, for instance, if we look at a crime scene with hard, prejudiced eyes, we are likely to miss the details necessary to solve the crime. Having hard eyes means reaching a conclusion before really *seeing* the scene.[7] Therefore, as you initiate this Metanoic Journey, in which the destiny of your organization is at stake, it's important to ask yourself how much of your thinking and practice has been predetermined by historical processes you have uncritically inherited. The very fact that the Christendom paradigm is still overwhelmingly predominant, even though we have been living in a post-Christendom context for at least two hundred years, ought to be proof of how lacking in self-awareness most of us as church leaders really are. We are part of the system! We must have the courage to look again.

A critical aspect of becoming self-aware (for both individuals and organizations) starts with the recognition that all is not well with the status quo. There are serious threats not just from the changing cultural context but also from within the collective mind. There are *anomalies* in the system itself. An anomaly is that "splinter in the mind" (as it was called in the movie, *The Matrix*); the nagging sense that something somewhere is missing or wrong.[8] Coming to grips with the anomalies initiates the collective "roaming of the mind," the necessary intellectual curiosity that is the precursor to a new way of seeing the issues and solving the problems. For instance, Margaret Wheatley points out that, in science, the problem with the Newtonian understanding of the world was that it could not account for the behavior of the most basic structure of life—the atom. When scientists began to study atoms and what they were made of, they soon realized that they behaved quite differently from how standard cause-and-effect typology would predict. This fundamental anomaly finally led to the birth of a new paradigm called quantum physics, which operates on an entirely different rationality than the preceding paradigm.[9]

Sensing anomaly is one aspect of what we call *upstream processing*. If the river runs dry at the bottom of the mountain or it is polluted, you look upstream for the source of the problem. We need to untangle the knots in the system and set things right by going to the source of the issue. (See appendix six on upstream and downstream processing.) We engage soft eyes to see things afresh. We need to access the mind of Christ, to attend to God the Designer and what he wants to say, to sense the Spirit's correcting and leading. We must seek to attune ourselves to the distinctive features of our particular mission, calling, and design. We try to identify the ways in which we have drifted from our core purpose.

Even more specifically, we aim to uncover the meta-ideas—those foundational concepts on which subsequent thinking is built. (We introduced this concept in chapter five.) Think of a meta-idea as playing a role like that of a seminal thought-leader in a field of knowledge—for example Einstein in science, Kant or Kierkegaard in philosophy, or Bach or The Beatles in music. These persons deeply impacted the mindset and the trajectory of their various disciplines. Locating these foundational concepts is strategic in that they are potent cultural levers that enable us to impact the system with the least effort. But meta-ideas also help us gain needed clarity on identity and purpose because they go on to inform the DNA that will define every aspect of the organization going forward. This is what we call "fractal organizing,"—a concept we will explore more comprehensively in the upcurve process in the next few chapters.

As examples of powerful meta-ideas, consider those that frame MLC's vision and purpose to engender movemental forms of leadership and organization wherever and whenever we can. To do this we focus on movement DNA (what we refer to as mDNA) because, taken together, they ensure authentic movement in any context.[10] The mDNA are the vital elements that together make for a movemental understanding and practice. They are:

- *Jesus is Lord*—a radical and unwavering commitment to Jesus at the center of identity, mission, and purpose. As a meta-idea, this determines both the character and the content of the organization. Any move away from this defining center will inevitably distort the personality, nature, and purpose of the church in God's world.

- *Discipleship and Disciple-Making*—a clearly articulated understanding of what discipleship is, why it matters, along with clarity about the intentional processes that ensure disciple-making happens throughout the whole organization. As a meta-idea, this determines the focus of effort and thus *disciplines* the organization. Failure at this point undermines *everything* else we seek to do.

- *Missional-Incarnational Impulse*—a commitment based on the theological pattern of the *missio Dei* and the incarnation of Christ to extend the movement by crossing boundaries and incarnating the gospel and church into every context. Our greatest theology thus undergirds, characterizes, and informs our best methodology. As a meta-idea, this determines and shapes how the organization engages in different contexts. Failure here means we don't *go* anywhere and are stuck with one model of the church.

- *APEST Culture*—the ministry of Christ expressing itself in and through the body of Christ. APEST forms the latent intelligence and potential baked into the church. When unlocked, it brings needed healing, fullness, unity, and functional maturity to the body of Christ. As a meta-idea, this determines the key functions of the organization and the required competencies of its leadership. Meddle with the full APEST typology, and it will undermine our capacity to extend the mission of Christ in the world.

- *Organic Systems*—the decentralized organizational system that undergirds transformative movements. Here the organization is built on reproducibility and scalability and empowers everyone across the whole system, from center to edge. As a meta-idea, this determines the ability of the organization to prevent power and function from being centralized and will ensure reproducibility and scalability is built in from the get-go. Failure here means we opt for a high control, centralized, elitist, clerical system that leaves most people as passive attenders rather than active agents.

- *Liminality and Communitas*—the condition of risk, danger, and ordeal (liminality) that creates a much more vigorous form of community (communitas), and produces a willingness to regularly take risks together. Liminality is a catalyst for comradery, learning, and innovation. As a meta-idea, this determines the willingness of the organization to engage in, and grow through, risk and adventure. Failure here means we end up with church as a risk-averse, uncreative, boring Sunday gathering.

The core proposal of my (Alan) book *The Forgotten Ways* is that, although each of these is highly significant in themselves—and much is gained by improving even one of these in isolation from the others—it is when all six coalesce and inform each other they create an emergent system where transformative Jesus-movement becomes absolutely *inevitable*. Alignment or misalignment changes the nature of the whole system.

Because MLC's vision and purpose is to engender movemental forms of leadership and organization wherever and whenever we can, we ask leaders to assess whether their mindsets and praxis enhance or inhibit the movemental capacities in their system. By undergoing a force-field analysis, they can begin to see how their core meta-ideas are either activated or suppressed in the life and culture of their respective organizations. Other meta-ideas (for example, a leadership pipeline, microchurch, or forms of worship) can also be placed in the center, applying the same dynamic.

BOOSTERS	Movement Vision	BLOCKERS
Forces FOR Change		*Forces AGAINST Change*

Driving Force	JESUS IS LORD	Restraining Force
Driving Force	DISCIPLESHIP	Restraining Force
Driving Force	MISSIONAL-INCARNATIONAL	Restraining Force
Driving Force	APEST CULTURE	Restraining Force
Driving Force	ORGANIC SYSTEMS	Restraining Force
Driving Force	LIMINALITY-COMMUNITAS	Restraining Force

In the living-systems theory of organizations, all living systems are designed for health and flourishing. For example, when you consider your body, if you eat the right kinds of foods and maintain a healthy balance of exercise and rest—what we refer to as *boosters*—you are more likely to thrive and live a fruitful life. If, however, you do things that damage the health of the system—what we refer to as *blockers*—you are more likely to experience some form of disease. In a similar way, Jesus has designed his church for health and flourishing. There are inbuilt potentials lying dormant in the heart of every authentic group of believers. Therefore, if we simply remove the blockers, everything ought to naturally flourish. For example, if you want your church to be missional/sent ("go to them"), but most of the "mission" is centered on an attractional mindset and praxis ("come to us"), the focus on attractional forms of evangelism will always undermine your capacity to "go." In other words, the "come-to-us-ness" cancels out your "go-to-them-ness"—it effectively blocks genuine missional engagement. This is a significant problem in the majority of churches that operate largely from the inherited Christendom paradigm of church—a paradigm built squarely on the "come to us" forms of *ecclesia*. They might believe in sentness/mission, but they never really do it because everything in the system works against it. To see clear indicators of this, just look at the way churches tend to use their buildings and their programming. Everything about the building says, "come to us." Understood in this way, attractional forces are blockers to a genuinely missional paradigm.

A force-field analysis can be applied to any particular organizational vision to see what is either hindering or enhancing it. It ought to be relatively easy to see how metanoia comes into play in this situation. Helping participants sense the system and expose the forces hindering the achievement of the stated vision invites repentance and new thinking/acting.

Regarding the dynamics of blockers inherent in the system/paradigm, economist John Maynard Keynes wrote these startling words in the foreword of his seminal book on economic theory:

> The composition of this book has been for the author a long struggle of escape, and so must reading of it be for most readers if the author's assault upon them is to be successful—a struggle of escape from habitual modes of thought and expression. The ideas which are expressed so laboriously here are extremely simple and should be obvious. The difficulty lies, not in the new ideas, but in escaping from the old ones, which ramify into every corner of our minds.[11]

This escaping of old ideas is no small feat, especially in the case of the church where a deeply embedded Christendom ecclesiology controls the way we understand church and its role in the world. In this situation, profoundly obsolete ideas, developed in fundamentally different cultural contexts, penetrate every corner of the collective mind. We have a lot to unlearn if we are to return to our first love (Revelation 2:1–7).

> Only where the plow of God has tilled our lives can sowing bear fruit. An enduring deepening of the interior life can be brought about only through the plowing of repentance. *Therefore our main task is to work for that spiritual revolution and re-evaluation which leads to metanoia— the fundamental transformation of mind and heart.*[12]

We will also need to *feel* the pain of our intransigence and inability to be what Jesus originally designed us to be. Metanoia will occur when mind, soul, and will are engaged; and when people and collectives are willing to experience lament—what our mystics have called "the gift of tears." The tears of lament are part of the process of wholehearted change because when we cry, we engage both sides of the brain, and the mind is connected with the soul and the will. We should therefore not be afraid to cry. Imagine what corporate lament can do for a community of people who feel stuck and who seek some form of breakthrough. Have you noticed that almost all revivals and breakthroughs are accompanied with weeping as well as rejoicing?

Questions you might ask at the Uncover stage are:

- Having gone through the last few years of cultural upheaval, what anomalies have we uncovered in the culture and structures of our own organization and the world at large (key events, items, or observations that differ significantly from standard behaviors or patterns)? How do these glitches and incongruencies make us feel? What are these telling us about the problems inherent in our system?

- Where have we become aware of our unfaithfulness to God's mission and purpose for our organization? Are we willing to lament these before God and community?

- In our context, what are the ideas and principles (the meta-ideas) on which other principles are based? What cornerstone concepts, foundational ideas, or points of high leverage (change here brings change everywhere) can we name for our organization?

- In the force-field analysis, can we identify three to five "blockers" (practices, habits, or aspects of organizational culture) that are hindering us from achieving our purpose? What can we do to change them?

Unlock

As we have noted, this journey involves something of a spiritual quest for a holy grail of peak performance and transformational impact. Because it is a profoundly explorative process, we must ourselves become intrepid trailblazers in search of new frontiers, charting the way forward for others to follow. Apostolic leaders especially need to form a new mental map to help the organization move forward in a meaningful and integral way.

Make no mistake, this is challenging work, and we mostly choose to avoid it in the hope that more of the same will deliver different results. However, if we are to change and become more like Jesus intended in the first place, we will have to find a way to deal with the muscle memory, habits, ruts, and defaults that now entrap us. "Escaping" from these snares is critical if we are to find new forms and ways of doing things. This can be achieved through healthy practices and the creation of new habits and appropriate tools. (This will be more comprehensively explored in chapter nine on Practices.) But what is unlocked at this stage of the journey will be critical in the process of "discipling the organization" that comes into full operation in the upcurve stage of the Metanoic Journey. Our discoveries here will also inform the organizational DNA, which will in turn enable the development of the platform and the practices essential for metanoia to be embodied, whether individually or collectively.

In this Unlock stage, we will also need to start exploring new frontiers, comparing notes with other agencies facing similar challenges, and cultivating a culture open to learning new ways. This will also involve prayerfully and playfully dreaming up new possibilities, as well as embracing the spiritual receptivity that is characteristic of children in the mode of learning. And so, we suggest learning from children and how they approach play.[13]

> [We] begin to understand why the Christian Bible insists on believers becoming like children … Children do not act as if their mental map is complete and reliable; they are open to outside guidance. Adults, on the other hand, choose to live as if their mental map is the final word on everything, and this makes it impossible for them to live any longer in the world with a certain playfulness as children do.[14]

Use childlike imagination to explore alternative ways of doing things. You need to think like a beginner rather than an expert. Deliberately put yourself out of your comfort zone. Think like a hacker—try to figure out the frailties in the system and crack the code. Learn from opposites, from people with a different outlook and culture. Look at how other disciplines have gone about resolving wicked problems. Sometimes the answer comes from entirely out of left field—such as Alexander Fleming's accidental discovery of penicillin.

At the Unlock stage, the key questions to explore might be:

- What are some of the bad habits, or behavioral ruts, we always seem to fall into? How do these bind us to outdated thinking and practices?

- What other organizations are facing similar challenges? How can we engage with them and actively learn from, and perhaps help, them?

- How can we explore new and better ways of doing core tasks? For instance, worship is a core function of the church. To worship God, do we have to sing songs? Are there other ways to worship other than communal singing?

- If we could start all over again, would we do things the same way? And if not, what would we change?

- If we are trying to think like beginners rather than experts, how can we deliberately and regularly step out of our comfort zones, and how can we harvest the learning gained in such situations?

Understand

Here, towards the bottom of the downcurve, we should have gained sufficient (collective) self-awareness—through assessing the flaws in our system and by exploring possible solutions to the wicked problem—to be able to name some viable alternatives to our inherited ways of thinking and acting. Although we won't yet have formulated a coherent mental map that fully interprets our situation, we ought to be aware of some of the broad frameworks of a new paradigm, and sense the promise of movement, along with some pointers to viable ways forward.

For instance, in the MLC Movement Lab, as participants enter the Understand phase, they will seek to gain a better comprehension of the broader characteristics of a distinctly movemental form of organization. This clearer mental picture of movement provides a point of comparison to the inherited paradigm upon which most churches are currently founded. Having access to a viable and promising alternative vision of the church-as-movement in turn guides the selection of the core DNA, as well as the development of the platform and practices in the relearning side of the process. As a counterpoint to the standard ways of organizing, we learn that movements …

- have a dynamic world-changing vision and "can-do" culture;

- are held together by committed relationships of shared purpose (comrades on a significant journey) as opposed to transactional forms of relationship (employer–employee);

- are DNA-based organizations;

- push power and function to the outermost limit;

- are structured more as a decentralized network than a centralized hierarchy;

- are more like starfish than spiders—each part can reproduce the whole; [15]

- are inherently adaptive because they are designed to move;

- are reproducing, reproducible, and designed to scale; and

- spread like viruses.

A cursory comparison with the overwhelmingly non-movemental, more institutional forms of organization will quickly highlight areas of needed un/learning and subsequent development for the organization to solve its wicked problem and so get to the next level.

At this stage, participants should also be able to identify the possible meta-ideas latent in the system that are waiting to be leveraged. Once again, in the MLC Movement Lab, the six elements of mDNA are understood as the primary meta-ideas, but there are others, and these—together with the mDNA—should be becoming increasingly clear to the participants and the team.[16] Clarity here is important because these meta-ideas will form the core of the organization's DNA, which will eventually be replicated in its culture, tools, practices, and processes.

At the Understand stage, the key questions to explore might be:

- After extensive research, which organizations have we found that seem to have resolved their wicked problems? How can we engage with their leaders to compare notes and look for best practices?

- Can we articulate what a movement is, and how it might compare with the more conventional forms of organization? How does our organization compare?

- What are some specific thoughts and actions in the current organizational paradigm that either aid or hinder our organization in becoming more movemental?

The Turning Point (The Moment of Insight)

Here we arrive at the bottom of the U-shaped curve that is the Metanoia Journey. By this point, we have engaged with a huge amount of un/learning; we have become aware of the frailties in our current way of doing things; we have sought to examine our systems to see what hinders and what helps in terms of achieving our preferred future; and we have also looked at alternative ways of fulfilling our unique calling. This is the point of nakedness and openness to God, but this is precisely the place where God can impact us in a new way. The bottom of the curve is powerful because it is where God meets us ... in the valley. Like Israel in the desert for forty years or Jesus' passion on the cross before the resurrection, this is that point in the hero's journey—the abyss— where insight into how to resolve the wicked problem is finally given. This is the turning point.

> After a time of decay comes the turning point. The powerful light that has been banished returns. There is movement, but it is not brought about by force ... The movement is natural, arising spontaneously. The old is discarded and the new is introduced. Both measures accord with the time; therefore no harm results.[17]

Much has already been said about the power of insight gained through metanoia, but in terms of the Metanoia Journey, this is experienced as something of an "Aha!" moment, where we are able to see something in such a way that it cannot be unseen. With regard to our organization's core paradigm, it is a moment of clarity that is experienced as something of a revelation, and where we receive the elegant solution that makes complete sense. The early church mothers and fathers talked about the idea of "rectitude" or "fittingness"—the intuition that "this just feels so right" that no other conclusion seems possible. For instance, quantum scientist John Archibald Wheeler extols the discovery of an elegant solution:

> To my mind there must be, at the bottom of it all, not an equation, but an utterly simple idea. And to me that idea, when we finally discover it,

will be so compelling, so inevitable, that we will say to one another, "Oh, how beautiful. How could it have been otherwise?"[18]

This metanoic moment ought to be experienced for what it is: a conversion, something that involves the whole heart and not simply one dimension of it. This is where you should *feel* the pressure of the invisible church— that ancient archetypal template of the church that is latent in the core consciousness of God's people—surging inside of you, seeking to express itself through you. You should make every effort to attune yourselves to it. But the elegant solution does not reveal itself without the element of passionate search that has been underway in the un/learning dimension of the Metanoia Journey. As I (Alan) have already noted, if you love something long enough, it will reveal itself to you. Metanoia really does mean paradigm shift after all.

For us, as authors, as well as for the organizations that we are directly part of (MLC, NewThing, Forge, City Leaders Collective, Redeemer City to City, For Charlotte Network), the elegant solution presents itself in the paradigm of the church-as-missional-movement, with all this means in terms of its identity, nature, purpose, and practices. This understanding of the church makes perfect sense of the transformative Jesus movements in the New Testament, as well as those that have occurred as defining moments of history, including the early church, the Celtic movement, and the missionary orders (for example, the Jesuits, Franciscans, the early Methodists, and the early Pentecostals).

Depending on the nature and purpose of your organization, the solution might be somewhat different. But we suggest that if you see yourselves as a functioning expression of the kingdom of God, united to Christ as a member of his body, then the movemental paradigm ought to be somewhat present because it is the paradigm that is most consistent with the fluid, adaptive, always-extending, and transformative nature of God's mission in the world. It is, we believe, the truly *instinctive* form of Jesus' church.

The Journey Up (Inventing a New Future)

Because the next few chapters will explore the Metanoia Journey in more detail, we now wish to simply point out that the reconstructive design process that follows builds on the significant un/learning gained through the downcurve process. As we have noted time and again, it is absolutely critical to undergo this disassembling/unlearning phase and to become conscious of the system itself if we are to have any hope of guiding the organization to more hopeful and fruitful outcomes.

The main purpose for the upcurve, on the other hand, is to design a viable, integrated, organizational model and then to ensure that this is properly integrated in every aspect of the system going forward. This will involve articulating a clear mental model, along with the DNA that characterizes it, building a platform consisting of culture and structures, and then embedding these throughout the organization through *fractal organizing*—the process by which various ideas, values, and practices are experienced at every level of the organization.[19]

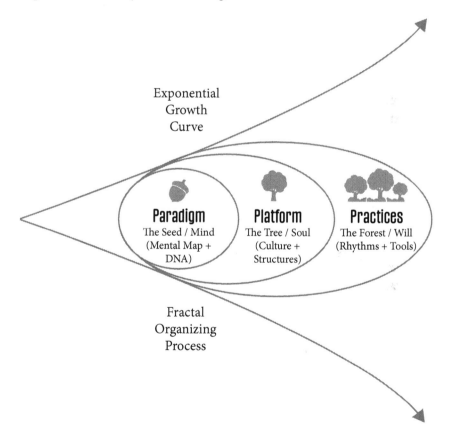

The upcurve therefore is about *repurposing* or, as we like to say, *discipling* the organization. And this is a critical process because failure here will mean that the system will simply revert to its prior path of least resistance *every time,* regardless of how much painful unlearning has taken place in the downcurve phase. Without new habits to replace the old ones, the organization will return to inherited ruts and routines. Institutional "muscle memory" pulls the organization back to the old and outworn modes of engagement. Attempts to change often fail because the organization hasn't been restructured in a way that is more consistent with the paradigm shift that has occurred. There can be no avoiding this renovation if we are to successfully solve the wicked problem and gain the prize that awaits at the end of the process. And because this process is so involved, we are dedicating the next three chapters to the three stages of the reconstruction upcurve of the Metanoia Journey. For now, here is a brief overview of each of these stages.

- *Paradigm:* Expressed in the form of a consciously articulated mental map, along with the DNA that defines and frames it, the paradigm informs and guides the organization (or individual) from deep within. It provides the inner logic or organizational mind. The key metaphor here is that of *the seed,* which contains the potential for the tree and the forest. Because of the conceptual component, the paradigm corresponds to the *mind* dimension of the heart.

- *Platform:* The paradigm must shape the explicit cultural *and* structural elements that together focus the organization toward certain, desired outcomes. The key metaphor here is that of *the tree,* which contains the potential for the forest. Because of the cultural component, the platform corresponds to the *soul* dimension of the heart.

- *Practices:* The cultural and structural elements need to be made accessible to all adherents through deliberate, observable practices that are consistent expressions of the organizational values. These common practices in turn effectively create a "rule of life," composed of regular rituals, repeatable patterns, and tools, which determine how actions are performed throughout. The key metaphor here is that of *the forest,* which has completely fulfilled the potential of the seed. Because of the practical component implied here, this corresponds to the *will* dimension of the heart.

It is important at this point to explicitly note how the design process itself (Paradigm > Platform > Practices) relates to how movements establish and grow. In the diagram on page 115, note the exponential "movement swoosh" that frames it. Movements start small, but if they are healthy, they end up growing big. This pattern shows us that movements come about through a paradigm shift that involves a catalytic idea whose time has come; an innovation that disrupts or changes reality; a new vision that brings about a conversion; and/or a highly personalized vocational call to participate in changing the world as we now experience it.

It is important to note here that each sequential phase of the process (Paradigm > Platform > Practices) is critical to the viability of the next phase, and therefore ultimately to the whole system. So, for instance, faulty or inadequate framing of the paradigm will undermine the movement's viability going forward (a bad seed); failure to create a viable/scalable platform will likewise undermine viability later on; failure to create accessible practices will mean that the movement will not be adopted, will not go to scale, and will inevitably flounder.[20]

As someone who has given their entire adult life to advancing what has been called "the missional movement", I (Alan) hate to admit that—apart from a few outstanding examples—all that great theology has not, in the end, really "changed the game" of the Western church. Many leaders now regularly use the term "missional" and affirm it in some way or another. (How could you *not* agree with Barth, Newbigin, Bosch, Guder, et al. on this topic?) Why then has it largely failed to impact our methods and our practice? Why has it not moved from our head to our heart and from there into our bodies? Why indeed? We believe that it did change the paradigm with a powerful idea whose time had come. However, it failed to move from the highly conceptual theological/paradigm level to impact the culture and structures (the platform) of local churches and organizations and was therefore never able to produce a way of life (practices) lived by all the adherents in these organizations. As a result, missional Presbyterianism remains, well, *Presbyterian*. The same of course is true for all the major denominations—their basic ecclesiology (platform and practice) has not changed to reflect the new paradigm. It largely remains a great paradigm that people bought into but that failed to produce the movement it promised to deliver. The missional seed did not become the great forest of a movement.

This challenge remains open-ended, and the task remains unfulfilled. And this is why we need to take charge in architecting the organizations we lead toward mature Jesus movements that *will* change the world because of the gospel of King Jesus that is at the heart of them.

Chapter Seven

Paradigm

Blowing the Collective Mind

---

*I still believe that reformation is a permanent
movement, that metanoia is the continuous
demand made upon us in historical life.*

H. RICHARD NIEBUHR

*Rather than blame things for being obscure, we should blame
ourselves for being biased and prisoners of self-induced
repetitiveness. One must forget many cliches in order to
behold a single image. Insight is the beginning of perceptions to come rather than the extension of perceptions gone
by. Conventional seeing, operating as it does with patterns
and coherences, is a way of seeing the present in the past
tense. Insight is an attempt to think in the present.*

ABRAHAM HESCHEL

*What is needed is not piecemeal reformation with minor adjust-
ments of character and conduct, but an alteration of the basis
of character and of the habitual way in which the mind works.*

JAMES LUTHER ADAMS

*It ain't what you don't know that gets you into trouble.
It's what you know for sure that just ain't so.*

MARK TWAIN

For years, I (Rob) have framed my own teaching, preaching, and church/ network consulting around what I referred to as "my three conversions." I used the word "conversion" because I didn't know of a better term to capture the power of these experiences—those once-you-see-you-cannot-unsee moments that occur at critical points in life, where a barrier is broken in our minds, and we know there is no going back. I now realize that what I had previously referred to as a conversion is more accurately described as *metanoia*.

My first conversion (or metanoia) centered on the theology of *union with Christ*. This specific doctrine was a game-changer for me. I have always found it helpful to state the obvious, so allow me to articulate this most beautiful of truths: Although we may have never met, all of us who believe in Jesus will spend forever together, perfectly united to God and each other, *in* the person of Christ Jesus. This is very good news!

My second conversion was to *the city*. In 2007, the human population crossed a remarkable threshold. For the first time in history, the world became majority urban.[1] Cities are the centers of commerce, culture, and power—and therefore should be the center of our mission. If the church can reach cities, we have the opportunity to transform every aspect of culture. In essence, cities have become the new 10/40 window of Christ's mission.[2] Or as my good friend Eric Swanson says, "If investing in Christ's mission in cities were a stock, I'm buying."

My third conversion centered on the concept of *platform*—the ideas and principles that show how decentralized, networked organizations are transforming the world. But to understand this notion in its fullness, you will need to stick around until chapter eight, where we examine this concept in greater depth.

I raise these personal metanoic experiences because they significantly shaped my life and ministry. They caused me to focus my calling on creating new paradigms that allow the church of the city to operate in the unity that our Lord Jesus both prayed for (John 17) and commanded (John 13). Experiencing metanoia has the power to completely shift the trajectory of your life and whatever organization you lead.

Beginning the Upward Journey

As discussed in previous chapters, a fully orbed biblical understanding of metanoia ushers in a new way of thinking, a new way of seeing and engaging with the world—a paradigm shift. For it is only by looking deeply within our own paradigms that we can make the needed changes that allow us to unleash our full kingdom potential. And even though this Metanoia Journey is one we choose to embark on, this work of shifting paradigms is far from easy, as experienced through the downward journey. As depicted in the U-curve diagram in the previous chapter, the Metanoia Journey is not simply climbing a mountain. It is far more akin to doing the rim-to-rim hike through the Grand Canyon. Think of the order—first going down, and then climbing. Those activities affect the body in different ways. Downhills are jarring. They pound the joints and ligaments and require keen awareness to avoid a fall. The uphill climb burns. The big muscles swell, the back aches, and extra endurance is required to make it to the top. Both directions involve pain, but knowing which pain comes at which stage is important. Whereas the journey down is full of unknowns and questions (Can I really do this? How long will it take?), the upward journey is full of hope. It is about building, creating, and charting a new way forward. But in this chapter we find ourselves at the bottom of the U-curve. We have reached the metaphorical Colorado River that carved out the Grand Canyon. It is here where we can stop and celebrate the progress we have made on our Metanoic Journey. At this point, having crossed the halfway mark, we can begin the upward journey with new confidence. From here on, endurance will be key. We will feel new muscles, and in short order they'll begin to burn— but take heart! When we experience these sensations, we're well on the way to an unimaginable vista.

As seen in the diagram on the following page, we begin the upcurve journey by articulating our internal organizational *paradigm*. This, as we will see, acts as the *mind* of the organization, with all its key DNA, mental models, and meta-ideas. The paradigm lays the foundation for the organizational platform and practices, addressed in the coming chapters, that will animate and propel the organization into the future.

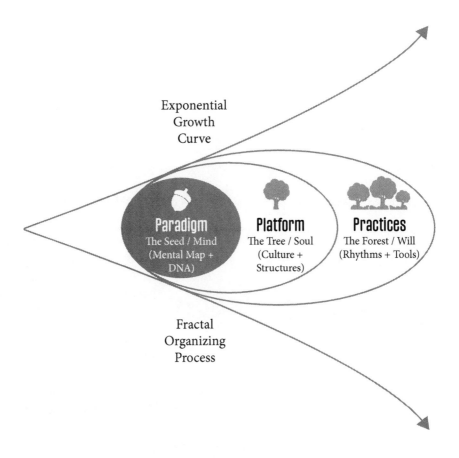

Exponential
Growth
Curve

Paradigm
The Seed / Mind
(Mental Map +
DNA)

Platform
The Tree / Soul
(Culture +
Structures)

Practices
The Forest / Will
(Rhythms + Tools)

Fractal
Organizing
Process

Once Upon a Paradigm

A paradigm is a way of perceiving and making sense of the complex world in which we live. Once established, paradigms in many ways do our thinking for us; that is their purpose.[3] Paradigms are largely shared realities—social constructs.[4] They are essentially the beliefs you share with those around you, such as your friends and family. These ideas, concepts, and beliefs that you and others have in common about religion, nationality, and other aspects of culture form a significant part of your individual and collective identities, but how often do you consider where they came from or how they might change? For example, you've no doubt heard the phrase "the American way." This is a paradigm because it refers to a collection of beliefs and ideas about what it means to be American, namely a pronounced individualistic and pragmatic way of life that adheres to the principles of life, liberty, and the pursuit of happiness.[5] For those who hold this paradigm, it will likely serve as the foundation of how they view or interact with the world around them. This example emphasizes one of the most important purposes of a paradigm, which is that it comprises beliefs and ideas that form a framework or a lens through which we approach and engage with other things or people.

Paradigm Blindness

However necessary paradigms are, everyone is subject to the limitations and distortions produced by their socially conditioned nature. Unless we undergo a disruptive event, or the deconstructive experience of the downcurve as described in the last chapter, the paradigm will remain largely unconscious and therefore unarticulated. Most of us generally assume that our paradigm is correct without ever having thought about it. In relation to organizations, a paradigm functions as the effective mind of the organization, controlling thinking and behavior without us being aware of how or why this might be the case. This is why the downcurve of the metanoia process is so vital and must not be bypassed. If we are to experience genuine metanoia, we must work to become conscious of the system itself, including its frailties and blind spots—what we called "anomalies" in the previous chapter.

You likely know the saying, "We don't know who discovered water, but it wasn't the fish." The fish simply swim in the water and take for granted that it is part of their reality. So, too, when we are fully immersed in a paradigm, we accept it as part of the real and natural world. Consider also the story of the woman who always cut off both ends of her ham roast before cooking it. When her husband asked her why she did this, she answered that she didn't really know, but she had learned it from her mother. The husband then approached his mother-in-law and asked her why she did it this way. She, too, replied that she didn't know why, but she had inherited the practice from her mother. When asked the same question, the grandma said she did it because her roasting pot was too small, so the meat needed to be trimmed to fit. In the same way, our churches and organizations have inherited certain ways of doing things, but we're not always sure why, and we repeat them endlessly even though we might have a sneaking suspicion there is a better way.

Although paradigms are essential and enable us to meaningfully negotiate the world, they can also create what is called "paradigm blindness"—an incapacity to see things from outside that particular perspective or paradigm. And this can account for why people fail to see certain things that might be glaringly obvious to others.[6] By selecting (or inheriting) a certain paradigm, we automatically deselect other alternatives. To illustrate how paradigms control what and how you see, consider the well-known image (shown below) that, depending on how you perceive it, looks like either a young woman or an older woman. We tend to see one at the exclusion of the other, even though both are there. We simultaneously see and are blinded.

This highlights just how important metanoia is in the equation of change. The steps of the downcurve of the Metanoia Journey (Unravel, Uncover, Unlock, Understand) reveal not only the fragilities in the prevailing system but also uncover the possibilities lying dormant in the threat. It is this point, at the moment in the curve when the fragilities and possibilities collide, that a "Eureka!" moment occurs. From there, we can actively design and construct a viable and meaningful mental map that will guide the organization toward achieving its greatly desired prize. We believe that this is the moment when organizations conceive of becoming a movement.

Paradigm as the "Seed of Metanoia"

As we begin the upcurve of the Metanoia Journey, we will examine the three distinct yet interconnected elements of an organizational paradigm, which we call the "the seed of metanoia." They are:

- paradigm as *organizational mind;*

- the associated *mental maps* that orient the organization in the world and guide choices and behaviors; and

- *organizational genetics* (something akin to *DNA*) that encode the core ideas of the paradigm and spread them through the system.

Because of how paradigm influences the genetics of the organization, we can think of no better illustration to show how these three key elements work together than the seed, shown below.

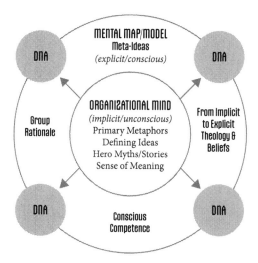

The Seed of Metanoia

Paradigm as Organizational Mind

Just as the apostle Paul commends the church to be transformed through the renewing of our minds (Romans 12:2), here we explore what it looks like to renew our organizational mind. To understand the organizational mind, we must examine the second part of the word metanoia (*–noia*), which, as we previously noted, is derived from the Greek word *nous*, meaning "mind." In the New Testament, this refers to a person or society's outlook or mindset. Just as your mind guides your choices and the way you see the world, your organizational mind serves as a guiding framework for the organization.

In order to change our mind, we need to become more aware of the nature of paradigms themselves—how they work and how they can change. In exploring corporate change, consider these elements of the organizational mind (paradigm).

Primary/Controlling Metaphors of Identity. The organizational mind reveals how we describe ourselves as a spiritual community, such as "the body of Christ," "church as organism," "the family of God," "network," "parachurch," or "mission agency." We might also use metaphors that describe our design or model for mission, such as a starfish (as opposed to a spider), a seed (which contains the potential for the whole forest), or a spark (which contains the potential for a forest fire).

The Heroic Story. The organizational mind is shaped by what and who the organization values. This is often revealed in the primary stories or origin stories that are central to their identity, such as what caused the founder/s to begin the organization in the first place, and the perseverance of the leaders, which allowed it to survive until now. Our sense of what we consider heroic is shaped by the stories of various transformative Jesus-movements throughout history. From Count Zinzendorf and the Moravian Movement to John Wesley and the Methodist Movement to the Great Welsh Revival to the Back to Jerusalem Movement happening today, Christian history is replete with amazing stories of men and women obediently pursuing God's mission despite overwhelming circumstances.

The Defining Idea. The defining idea acts as the core driver of the organization. For instance, the defining idea of MLC is that of an apostolic movement, as opposed to the less dynamic and more centralized ideas of organization.

Sense of Meaning. Most organizations have a sense of unique identity, purpose, and direction. Keeping with the example listed above, the core sense of meaning at the heart of MLC as an apostolic movement is the "sentness" of the church. When we understand that just as God the Father sent Jesus, Jesus has sent us (John 20:21), it allows us to see how we fit into God's cosmic plan of the redemption of all things.

All these come together to form the collective mind of the organization and its innate, ultimate sense of purpose (*telos*). They function as a worldview—a way of viewing reality for the community that shares them—and set the default of the organization.

Paradigm as Mental Map

From the organizational mind—the deepest dimension of the paradigm—we begin to develop a mental map. This aspect is usually more consciously held, even if it has not been fully considered. The mental map is often assumed to be legitimate until some event disrupts it and exposes its frailties and flaws. Consider, for instance, the assumptions on which most churches in the West operate—a Christendom paradigm in which the church is the primary or exclusive religion in culture and, as a result, churches operate almost completely in attractional mode. With this mindset, the expectation is that if the church offers services (whatever they might be), people will automatically come to the church (building) in order to find God. As a result, there is little understanding or practice of "sentness" in the standard Western church. Yet, when reading the Bible, it seems clear that having a unique outward-focused mission was an essential dimension of the early church's understanding and practice.

By this stage of the metanoia curve, the paradigm will have come out of the shadows of our collective unconscious and will be more concrete. We are now aware of its presence in both defining who we are (identity) and calling us forward to our unique purpose (mission). We will also be aware of the flaws of the prevailing paradigm and will begin to address them throughout the rest of the upcurve journey.

With this understanding of paradigms in mind, leaders must take responsibility for constructing the mental map that will guide the organization going forward. This process of creating a mental map is far more important than most people realize, and so we encourage you to proceed prayerfully and with the mind of Christ fully active and engaged. The mental map must appeal to the whole heart by awakening the mind, soul, and will of the organization.

Here are the key areas of the mental map to develop:

Meta-Ideas. Not all ideas are created equal. Some ideas are more important than others, as they have the power to shape and transform the whole system.[7] As opposed to defining ideas which act as the core driver of the organization, meta-ideas are the set of foundational concepts on which you begin to build the organization. For example, whereas the defining idea of MLC is that of apostolic movement, the meta-ideas of MLC are the six mDNA elements. Meta-ideas act like the cornerstone of an arch, a foundation on which other ideas are built. Meta-ideas help determine and frame other ideas. The stronger and bigger the meta-ideas, the more they make sense of the smaller ideas, providing leaders with points of high leverage which re/build the paradigm going forward. For instance, if a church held to mDNA as its meta-ideas and was approaching governance and structure issues, the mDNA of "organic systems" would guide the church away from a rigid hierarchical structure. When you have defined and refined your meta-ideas, they bring alignment to how you organize what you do, bringing clarity to how your organization works.

From Implicit to Explicit Belief System and Theology. A mental map includes the assumptions and beliefs that are largely implicit within the organization. Implied beliefs are often legacy ideas that are assumed to be true—much like the woman who trimmed the meat without realizing why—rather than people grappling with ideas in a way that is applicable and relevant to their current context. For instance, much of the way we think about church is assumed from an inherited denominational paradigm. This is the theological water in which the ecclesial fish swim. Redesigning a viable mental map requires a thorough theological audit to move us from our largely uncritical acceptance of consciously held beliefs to more explicit belief statements. Such beliefs have a significant impact on the culture of the organization, an aspect we will explore more deeply in the next chapter.

Conscious Competencies. A well-formed mental map will require the organization and its members to move from unconscious incompetence, built on assumptions inherited from the past, to consciously held competencies that can be passed on as patterns of behaviors. These will be further explained in chapter nine.

Group Rationale. A clearly re/designed mental map will provide an explicit rationale of *why* and *how* things are to be done within the organization. This will often mean addressing the we've-always-done-it-this-way things, which we repeat without knowing exactly why. To reframe the organization, we need to deliberately assess and redevelop what we do. We will further explore this in the following chapters.

One of the greatest benefits of a well-designed, conscious mental map is that it helps create a *clear and compelling vision* for where we are going. After all, this is the point of a map! For instance, our vision for MLC is to "shift the tracks of history" by helping authentic movements to scale. The mental map created by the combination of all the above points guides everything we do.

Recognizing the key issues in our current paradigm will help us recapture the core of the missional movement our Lord Jesus inaugurated two millennia ago. But we believe this necessary paradigm shift will not happen unless we effectively dislodge the predominant institutional paradigm, which is stifling Christ's mission, and replace it with a more movemental one.[8] The institutional paradigm has been entrenched as a direct result of centuries of Christendom in which the church adopted the practices of centralized authority, strict hierarchies, and power structures of broader society. Although the church in the last few decades has finally become more aware of this legacy, this implicit paradigm is still very much alive throughout the contemporary church.

In the table below, we juxtapose some of the key aspects of church/organizational leadership and decision-making in the *implicit* institutional paradigm (the most common paradigm we see in the Western church) with an *explicit* movemental paradigm. We hope this illustrates how a prevailing paradigm creates a mental map for navigating key organizational decisions. Note, we are not saying that institutions are a bad thing, in and of themselves. However, we are saying that we need healthy institutions that are rooted in a strong movemental paradigm. In this way, it is important that we delineate between healthy institutions (which are good) and rigid institutionalism (which almost never is).

Category	Implicit Institutional Paradigm	Explicit Movemental Paradigm
Organizational development	Building an organization	Growing a movement
Leadership focus	Authority & influence	Inspiration & sense of ultimate purpose (*telos*)
Leadership style	Command & control	Equip & engage
Leadership structure	Top down (management)	Distributed
Decision-making	Procedural & slow	Relational & rapid
Relational ethos	Transactional: what you can do for the institution	Relational: what the movement can do for you and the world
Organizational ethos	Conservative, protective of existing conventions	Innovative & entrepreneurial
Communication	Marketing	Storytelling
Change	Averse	Embracing
Values	Security, predictability	Risk, serendipity
Feels like	Siloes, departments	A unified whole

As you examine the key aspects of organizational leadership in this chart,[9] what does it tell you about your current paradigm?

Paradigm as Organizational Genetics (Elements of DNA)

In many ways, paradigms operate in a similar way to genetics in an organic system, thus we suggest the metaphor of *organizational genetics*. The DNA dictates both the uniformity as well as the uniqueness of the organism. For instance, if you're reading this, it's pretty likely you're a human, a member of a group of billions of other organisms called *homo sapiens*. But even though there are multiple billions of humans, you are an utterly unique expression of this group, with your own distinct characteristics and identity. The *Encyclopedia Britannica* defines DNA as an "organic chemical of complex molecular structure that is found in all organic, living, cells."[10] We can also say that DNA:

- codes genetic information for the transmission of inherited traits;

- is self-replicating;

- carries vital information for healthy reproduction; and

- when it mutates, affects the integrity of the whole system.

Functioning like organic DNA, organizational DNA is composed of the elements that make up the organizational mind (primary metaphors of identity, the heroic story, the defining idea, and the sense of meaning) but are now transformed into concentrated statements that become the determinative "genetics" of the organization. Each element of DNA ought to contain a big idea (or meta-idea) that frames the way we see things. For instance, seeing things through the lens of the five APEST functions of the church (Ephesians 4:11) changes how we see and do mission, leadership, and organization. As such, each strand of DNA can also be understood as a sub-paradigm within the overall meta-paradigm of movement.

So how do we formulate DNA in a way that it can exert its influence throughout the organization? Start by identifying and naming the meta-ideas, and from there find ways to embed and *fractalize* them throughout the organization (see page 133). The process might be something like this:

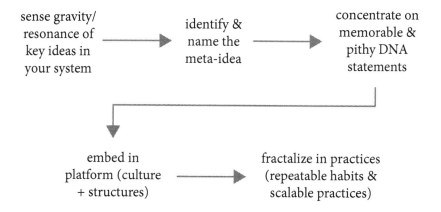

If I Had a Lever Long Enough

As a recap, a meta-idea is essentially an idea that determines and organizes other ideas. Think of it as a foundational idea that provides a platform on which to build a working theory or an organizing principle; or as a cornerstone concept around which other ideas are formed. A meta-idea is therefore not a "mere" idea among others; it is a doorway to the thinking of the organization. It is a primary idea that organizes other secondary ideas.[11] Meta-ideas provide a way of seeing better and working smarter because they help us make sense of lots of confusing experiences and seemingly isolated facts. As such, meta-ideas are critical in creating the right culture and behaviors in the organization.

Theology is loaded with meta-ideas. Consider, for example, the doctrine of the Trinity, or of the incarnation, crucifixion, and resurrection of Jesus. We know all too well that when someone seeks to distort or diminish any of these central theological tenets, it has ramifications across our entire theological system and, as a result, for our culture and behaviors.

Meta-ideas are not simply doctrinal; they have huge, practical implications. Take discipleship, for instance. To test whether discipleship is simply a good idea or a meta-idea, ask yourself, What problem in the church does discipleship not fix? Think hard about that, and you will soon discover that, if discipleship is done well, then everything in the organization changes. On the other hand, to fail in the task of discipleship and disciple-making means to fail everywhere. Right now, our assessment (and it is not ours alone) is that most contemporary churches are built squarely on non-discipleship. This accounts for many of our dysfunctions. Discipleship, it turns out, is a huge meta-idea.

Another way of seeing the importance of meta-ideas is to see them as levers for system-wide change. It was Archimedes, who once stated that if he had a lever long enough, and a fulcrum on which to place it, he would be able to move the entire world. And he's right! Meta-ideas are those ideas that act like levers that can change everything. For instance, consider again the impact of a robust APEST typology capacity in the life of the organization. Activating a fully orbed, fivefold understanding of ministry and leadership changes everything. Legitimizing and activating the apostolic function in the system will always bias the organization toward more *missional* outcomes. A mature prophetic ministry will ensure that the church remains faithful to being an alternative society in the world—worshipping the One God and renouncing idols, as well as seeking justice and holiness in all dimensions of life. Like a radar in an airplane, switch the prophetic function off, and you will more than likely crash into the mountain. APEST leverages the entire church/organization toward fulfilling what it was purposed to do. It turns out that APEST is a red-hot meta-idea!

All the mDNA are powerful meta-ideas, which is why we recommend them to leaders who want their organizations to become more movemental in form and expression. When all six elements of mDNA are activated, they will precipitate an emergent living system that will inevitably express itself in a movement … *every time*! The mDNA therefore are the basic genetics of all movements. (See appendix seven for how the six mDNA elements address key issues in the contemporary church paradigm.)

Name the Baby

Following the clues from living systems, and from what you have learned along the Metanoia Journey, you are now ready to identify and name the core DNA of your organization.

Once you have identified the meta-ideas that have high leverage in your organization and that are consistent with the organizational mind and mental model, naming DNA is relatively simple. It will require forming statements in the "love language" of your organization, which can be reflected at every level of the organization. Once again, let's use discipleship as an example. A DNA statement might well be expressed as follows: "We are committed to discipleship in all that we do, to ensure that every believer is involved in an observable process of becoming increasingly like Jesus." It is important that this not simply be a statement of intellectual belief but instead one that requires observable and measurable action. Another example of DNA might be a commitment to incarnational forms of ministry and mission. This can be measured in a consistent culture and practices that can be seen in the life of the community—for example, how the church contextualizes the gospel or its physical proximity to those the church is trying to reach.

The process of developing explicit DNA statements that encode the organizational paradigm must be a prayerful exercise, which takes place over time and with your core leadership team.

Fractalize It Y'all

To best understand how DNA scales, we must understand the fractal nature of movemental organizations. A fractal is an irregular or fragmented geometric shape that can be repeatedly subdivided into parts, each of which is a smaller copy of the whole. In other words, it's a pattern that recurs at every scale. Fractals can be found everywhere in the natural world. In trees, for example, the limbs, branches, and leaves reproduce in the exact same pattern. DNA is a powerful fractal in your body as well—it is in every one of your thirty-two trillion cells! You can also see fractals in snowflakes, lightning and electricity, plants, flowers, seashells, clouds, crystals, and in the circulatory systems of mammals. In other words, fractals represent how God designed the created order to scale.

In the diagram on the following page, the basic *fractal* is that of the simple triangle. This pattern in turn forms the foundational structure of the more complex patterns that build on it, while maintaining the core element intact. Organizational DNA fractalizes in the exact same way. The fact that the fractal recurs at every scale of the organization is crucial, because it means the idea will inevitably occur throughout. Thus, when DNA arises from deep within the paradigm, takes shape in the platform, and is infused into all the tools and practices of the organization, it will achieve scale. We will examine this in more depth in the next two chapters.

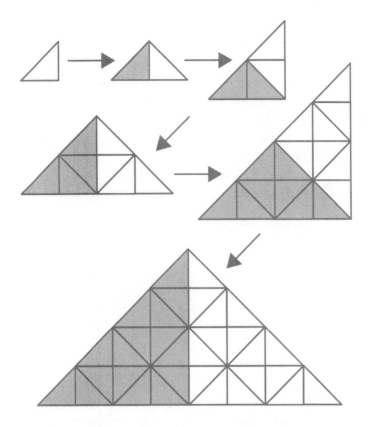

From Paradigm Set to Paradigm Shift

Now that we have examined the nature and power of paradigms and how they control the organization, we will move on to what must be in place to shift your organizational paradigm—to "blow your (organizational) mind." As you begin this upward journey, remember the following:

- A paradigm shift is a major change in how people think and act that upends and replaces a prior paradigm.

- A paradigm shift can result after the accumulation of anomalies or evidence that challenges the status quo; or due to some revolutionary innovation or discovery.

- Incumbents or organizational insiders often show resistance to a new paradigm.

Essentials for Shifting Paradigms

Several essential elements must be present if your organization is to experience paradigm shift (metanoia) and become a movement-ready organization.

Shifting Paradigms Requires Leadership Unity

It might seem obvious, but a disunified leadership team cannot unite a church or organization around a new paradigm. It is important to remember that shifting paradigms is an important part of organizational discipleship. This requires all the organization's leadership to be involved and on the same page. Below are a couple of common barriers to leadership unity that stifle paradigm shift:

Staff/Board Division. In our work with churches and ministries, one of the biggest barriers to metanoia we encounter is the divide between senior level staff (pastors/directors) and their board/elders. Sadly, in most organizations, this is not the exception but the rule. Part of organizational discipleship includes senior leaders bringing their boards along in addressing paradigm issues, while navigating internal politics and power structures.

Leadership Insecurity. Many senior leaders are afraid of shifting paradigms because of identity issues. They think when subordinates point out areas of dysfunction within the organization it will reflect negatively on them or, in some cases, is a direct attack on their leadership. This fear of "looking bad" stifles a lot of organizational change. Ironically, when senior leaders open themselves to this process and address paradigm issues within the organization, it both builds internal team unity and typically turns out well for them personally, in the following ways:

- Other staff and leaders respect the senior leader more for addressing organizational issues head on.

- Staff and leaders feel more trusted and are more inclined to help solve organizational problems, causing them to be more committed to the mission/vision.

- As a senior leader wrestles with areas of dysfunction and insecurity in their leadership, although it is hard, they experience personal and professional growth that will bear fruit for them and their future ministry.

We must not let leadership insecurity get in the way of the change that is needed. Too much is riding on it!

Shifting Paradigms Requires Apostolic Imagination

One of my (Alan) favorite sayings is that, as organizations, we are perfectly designed to produce what we are currently producing. In other words, most of the problems we face are because of the choices we (or others before us) have made that need to be corrected if we are to see change. This is clearly evident in the church as most of us know it, which has been formulated and primarily led by pastors and teachers, and thus is perfectly designed to produce pastoral and didactic outcomes. The problem of course is that the church is meant to be more than that. One of the biggest design faults in the church is that it lacks apostolic imagination and focus—the very thing the New Testament church had in abundance. So what do we mean by "apostolic" imagination? Technically, apostolic refers to the "sentness" of the church. The apostles were the ones sent by Jesus—the ones willing to take risks and innovate to create new structures and organizations.[12]

Most leadership within the Western context is dominated by left-brain thinking, focusing on logic, analytics, methodologies, and the like, all of which can be extremely positive. But left-brain thinking can only take us so far. For the church to chart new ways into the future, we must activate our collective right brain—the seat of creativity, intuition, and imagination. This doesn't mean leaving logic and reason in the past; instead, just as we are to become wholehearted organizations as examined earlier in this book, we must also become "wholebrained," leveraging all the creative gifts God has given us. We worship a creative God, who has given us his creative Spirit, so if we are to create new paradigms, both within our organizations and within our culture, it will require operating in the power of the Holy Spirit, allowing him to cultivate apostolic imagination within us. Imagination is soaked in possibility; it can see around corners and make the intuitive leaps that trigger paradigm shifts.

Unleashing apostolic imagination will require church leaders to be willing to take risks. As we mentioned in an earlier chapter, we must abandon the concept of "failure is not an option." Failure is not failure when you learn from it. Failure is simply "validated learning." And in this time of extreme liminality, if we cannot shift our paradigms, we should not be surprised when our churches and organizations die. This process of activating apostolic imagination is a way to foster joy and new life within your organization's leadership team—and the church as a whole needs joy now more than ever!

Shifting Paradigms Requires Perseverance

Perseverance is needed in shifting your organizational paradigm because:

Shifting Paradigms is Hard. Genuine paradigm transformation requires getting to the deepest parts of the organization. This is almost always a hard, painful process. In his book, *Systems Thinking for Social Change*, David Stroh uses an iceberg to illustrate how this unfolds.[13] Even though the majority of the issues lie under the surface, most leaders prefer to deal with what we see above the waterline. From our conversations with leaders who have engaged with the challenging work of shifting paradigms, the illustration of an iceberg seems only fitting. They often describe the process as a cold, dark, and lonely endeavor, in which it is often hard to breathe.

Shifting Paradigms is Incremental. There are no shortcuts on the journey of metanoia. No silver bullets. It takes time and patience. To see the change you hope for, you must play the long game—which is why we spend four chapters of this book on the journey of metanoia.

But take heart. Some of God's greatest work in conforming us into the likeness of Jesus, both personally and organizationally, comes through perseverance. We know this both experientially and through the Scriptures, which consistently refer to hardship as something that builds character, hope, and maturity (Romans 5:3–5; James 1:2–4).

Shifting Paradigms Requires Telling an Alternate Story

The late Austrian philosopher, Ivan Illich, was once asked about the most revolutionary way to change society. He responded by saying,

> Neither revolution nor reformation can ultimately change a society, rather you must tell a new powerful tale, one so persuasive that it sweeps away the old myths and becomes the preferred story, one so inclusive

that it gathers all the bits of our past and our present into a coherent whole, one that even shines some light into our future so that we can take the next step forward. If you want to change a society, then you have to tell an alternative story.[14]

Illich is right; the only way to upend an existing powerful story is with a better story. If we wish to move beyond the limitations of the prevailing paradigm that dominates our current approach to leadership and church, we need to reframe our paradigm through a different lens; an alternative and better story, a story that is unapologetically laser-focused on the person of Jesus and the establishment of his kingdom in every realm of our lives, organizations, and society. We must not allow our stories to get caught up in the prevailing church story, which promotes simplistic reductionism or false dichotomies, such as us/them, left/right, God/science, sacred/secular, and the like.

Once we write a new and compelling story, one that sets the hearts of God's people on fire, we must allow it to reframe us and seep into every part of our culture, systems, and practices. It is only through the reframing of the all-determining paradigm that our organizations experience the change, growth, and impact we desire. And unless the paradigm at the heart of the organization shifts, there can be no lasting change. Change must come from deep inside the paradigm (the bottom of the iceberg!). Anything less will simply be surface level.[15]

Shifting Paradigms Requires Letting Things Die

In part one of this book, we addressed the reality that if you fall in love with your system, you lose the capacity to change it. This love of the system can be tantamount to idolatry. People are formed by the things they love, which is why idolatry is so dangerous. It is misplaced love, and it blinds people to the only Person worthy of our affections. Perhaps the clearest picture of how idols affect us is the golden calf narrative in Exodus 32. When Moses came back down the mountain and saw the idol the people had created, he destroyed the golden calf, ground it into dust, and forced the Israelites to drink it. They literally consumed their idol. It became part of them. And from that point on in the story, the Israelites are often referred to as having the qualities of their idol. Just like the golden calf, they had eyes but could not see. They had ears but could not hear. They were hard-hearted and a stiff-necked (stubborn) people.

The church might be the chief of sinners when it comes to holding on to systems, paradigms, traditions, programs, and thinking that need to die. This process of letting things die is far from easy, but it is essential if we are to see lasting change. Management consultant Peter Drucker notes that organizations spend a lot of time teaching people what to do but don't spend enough time teaching people *what to stop doing*. He says that each organization needs to learn the skill of *systematic and purposeful abandonment.* He writes:

> The first measure is abandonment. Every three years, an organization should challenge every product, every service, every policy, every distribution channel with the question "If we were not in it already, would we be going into it now?" By questioning accepted policies and routines, the organization forces itself to think about its theory (or paradigm). It forces itself to test assumptions. It forces itself to ask, "Why didn't this work even though it looked promising when we went into it five years ago? Is it because we made mistakes? Is it because we did the wrong things? Or is it because the right things didn't work?" Without systematic and purposeful abandonment, an organization will be overtaken by events. It will squander its best resources on things it should never have been doing or should no longer do. As a result, it will lack the resources, especially capable people, needed to exploit the opportunities that arise when markets, technologies, and core competencies change.[16]

Shifting Paradigms Requires Seeing Reality for What It Is

The last element that must be in place to shift paradigms is the ability to see reality for what it is. Well-known businessman Max De Pree noted that the first responsibility of a leader is to *define reality*.[17] We fully understand that Jesus is the One who decisively shapes the movement that claims his name, but leaders need to take very seriously this task of delineating the parameters of how people think about his church. Allowing Jesus to guide us, leaders must manage how the organization sees itself and its function in the world. In other words, it's the job of leaders to define *ecclesia* for the people and organizations they lead. This puts a huge theological responsibility on leadership to ensure that they have a vision of the church that is consistent with the church Jesus built.[18]

Those of us who wear glasses understand the necessity of looking through clear lenses. Unfortunately, leaders tend to look at their paradigms through lenses that skew reality. Following are just a few of the most common "clouded" lenses leaders should be aware of when attempting to see reality for what it is:

Rose-Colored Glasses. Defining reality requires leaders to be honest about what is truly going on within their organizational paradigm, as opposed to diagnosing what they want it to look like. Leaders often diagnose their organizations with an overly optimistic and positive slant. This leads to seeing what they want to see rather than what actually is.

Confirmation Bias. Confirmation bias is incredibly common within our culture, especially in the church.[19] This is the tendency of leaders to interpret reality in such a way as to confirm their beliefs or paradigms. People display this bias when they favor information that supports their views, ignoring contrary information, or when they interpret ambiguous evidence as supporting their existing attitudes. Its effect is particularly potent among those who desire certain predetermined outcomes, in emotionally charged issues, and for those with deeply entrenched beliefs. It can also be seen in how leadership teams are formed—when senior leaders surround themselves with yes-people and sycophants rather than a team that allows for diverse types of thinking to thrive.

All Answers, No Questions. Leaders are expected to have all the answers people are looking for. Unfortunately, trying to be the source of all knowledge is both exhausting and can significantly hinder your pursuit of the unknown. Defining reality requires leaders to approach the task of shifting paradigms by having many more questions than answers—not resting on your past knowledge but fervently seeking to be attentive to the present and what is unknown. American philosopher and rabbi Abraham Heschel argues that people are kept from seeing reality because what they know is always getting in the way of what they don't know. He states, "The principle to be kept in mind is to know what we see rather than to see what we know."[20] He goes on to teach about the importance of being able to truly think and see things in the present. This ability is the basis of true insight … metanoia.

Becoming an Open-Minded Organization

As we seek to be transformed through the renewing of our minds, we close this chapter asking, What does it mean to be an open-minded organization? Through extensive experiments in the field of perso-nality psychology, it has been shown that open-minded people process information in different ways and may literally see the world differently from others. Open-minded people are more inclusive in their thinking and more expansive in how they process information. They tend to be intellectually curious, creative, and imaginative. They are interested in art and are voracious consumers of music, books, and other fruits of culture. According to personality theorists, this level of openness reflects a greater "breadth, depth, and permeability of consciousness" and propensity to "cognitively explore" both abstract information (ideas and arguments) and sensory information (sights and sounds). In other words, open-minded people are able to see and understand things that close-minded people can't.[21] The same is true for open-minded organizations. Becoming an open-minded organization is at the heart of metanoia. As explored in earlier chapters, our minds are in constant need of recalibration to the mind of Christ. As we look at the state of the contemporary paradigm of the church, we see that we have quite a challenge before us.

That said, changing the course of history will not require every Christian leader and organization to shift paradigms all at once. That simply isn't the way mass change works. In a standard bell curve of the diffusion of innovation, the first 2.5 percent of people are referred to as the *innovators*.[22] When they embrace a new paradigm—a new way of seeing the world—and shift their systems, the *early adopters* will take note. Early adopters make up the next 13.5 percent of the whole. When they embrace a new paradigm, the next 34 percent of leaders, called the *early majority*, will pay attention.

The question every leader and organization must wrestle with is what group they will be in. Will they be part of the 2.5 percent that are willing to take the risks, open their minds, and do the hard work of becoming wholehearted leaders and organizations for the sake of the future of the church and her mission in the world? Or will they leave it for whoever comes after them? If you are part of the 2.5 percent, you are ready to purposefully architect your organizational culture and structures so those you lead can begin to embody your new paradigm.

Chapter Eight

Plat*formed*

Shaping the Collective Soul

*The more I considered Christianity, the more I found that
while it has established a rule and order, the chief aim of
that order was to give room for good things to run wild.*

G. K. CHESTERTON

*If you have attempted change, improvement, advancement, and
growth, but have not changed the underlying structures that cause
the current tendencies for behavior, you are unlikely to succeed.*

ROBERT FRITZ

Every system is perfectly designed to get the result it gets.

W. EDWARDS DEMING

*The platform revolution is here, and the
world it is ushering in is here to stay.*

SANGEET PAUL CHOUDARY

As we continue our way up on the Metanoia Journey, it is now time to explore *Platform*. Between *the Seed* and *the Forest* is *the Tree*. Between *the Mind* and *the Will* of the organization is *the Soul*. Between the *Mental Map + DNA* and *Rhythms + Tools* is *Culture + Structures*, which brings us to the central premise of this present chapter: Platform is the indispensable hinge between Paradigm and Practices.

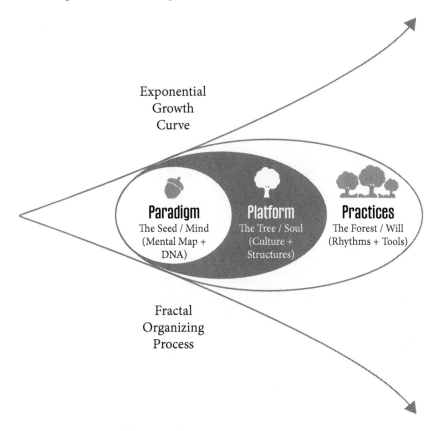

When the 2010 movie *Inception* was released, it became something of a cultural phenomenon with surprising staying power. At the center of this mind-bending story is Dom Cobb (played by Leonardo DiCaprio), a thief who steals corporate secrets by using a dream-sharing technology. However, instead of being hired to steal someone's thoughts, the protagonist is hired to implant a thought deep within the subconscious mind of a CEO, a process called *inception*. Through this inception technology, Cobb and his team enter into the dream world of their target, journeying so deeply into the subconscious that they are able to change the CEO's mind. And all this is achieved through architecture! Within this dream world, the architect has the power to create completely new realities, guided by systems and structures that change how all those who participate in them operate. For instance, while in this dream world, the city's streets and buildings look, move, and function in new and extraordinary ways, where the laws of gravity seem to be mere suggestions. But even in this dream world, the architect cannot change someone's mind *for* them. Rather, they architect the settings, surroundings, scenarios, and characters so purposefully that the idea simply "occurs" to the target. When the dreamer wakes, it is *their* idea—they know just what to do. And if the architect has done their job well, the subject will never know the architect was even there![1]

This is similar to the way *platforms* work. As leaders, our role is not to change the mind of the people we lead by force, but to create platforms that architect the organizational culture and structures so purposefully that those we lead subconsciously begin to embody the new paradigm. Because these platforms so clearly align with the paradigm itself, the practical implications become obvious.

Plat*formed*

In the previous chapter, I (Rob) referenced the first two metanoias that dramatically shaped my life and ministry—a conversion to "union with Christ" and a conversion to "the city." Working in, for, and with churches for more than two decades—and seeing and experiencing the brokenness of the system of the church—led to my third conversion: to the concept of platform.

Today, many use the word "platform" to describe either a technology (such as Airbnb, Uber, or Facebook), or someone's own personal platform (their public persona). However, the way *we* use the term refers specifically to the *movemental infrastructure* of an organization, which provides the basis for its various practices and rhythms—in a similar way to how the operating system in your smartphone provides the platform on which the various apps function. This platform infrastructure is made up of two essential aspects: 1) organizational *structures*, and 2) the distinct collective *culture*. The power of culture and structures cannot be underestimated. They impact how everyone experiences and moves within the organization.[2] For those that prefer formulas, here's a simple way to illustrate this:

Platform = Culture + Structures

Think of platform as one of the key components of movemental organization that must be in place for the church/organization to both move (structures) and to move in the same direction (culture). A healthy, movemental platform, based on the un/learning derived from the downcurve processes, deeply rooted in the mind of Christ, and focused on the mission of Jesus in the world, is the primary vehicle by which we can disciple the collective church/organization rather than only the individuals within it. We play on words in the term 'Plat*formed*' because platforms are so incredibly, well … *formative*. Platforms are how the vision of the movement expresses itself and takes *form*, while simultaneously *forming* each of the individuals within it. The platform embodies the hard-won paradigm, where concepts are experienced more concretely. Without creating a movemental culture and structures, we might have a great paradigm, but it will fail to have any real impact. It will be movemental sentiment without any movement.

The table below shows the key components of platform that we will review in this chapter. To facilitate a truly movemental infrastructure, both culture and structures must be fully architected and implemented.

Platform	
Culture	**Structures**
- Theological Distinctives - Core Values - Shared Vocabulary - Heroes to Emulate - Behavior to Celebrate - External Brand	- Relational Structures - Resource Structures - Result Structures

Platform Alignment

To understand how the different aspects of the organizational platform work together, consider a piece of furniture most of us have in our homes: a table. A table is a physical structure that has a purpose. It can bring people together; it can be a surface on which to place your coffee or food; or it can be a place on which to work, and so forth. Thus, a table is a *structure* (a literal, physical platform) on which people can perform certain functions. But that's not all there is to say about tables. The type of table (coffee table, dining room table, conference table, school desk), what it's made of (metal, plastic, wood), and the environment in which it exists (coffee shop, board room, office, kitchen) completely changes the working function—or the *culture*—of each particular table. Placing a kitchen table in a conference room would feel incongruous. But when a kitchen table is placed in a kitchen, or a conference table is placed in a conference room, both culture and structures are fully aligned. In the same way, healthy, movemental platforms are formed when culture and structures are aligned. But let's be clear: In this illustration, the focus is not on the table but rather on what is happening around that table—whether a deep conversation over a shared meal, or a team accomplishing an important project, the point is on architecting the table properly, with its purpose in mind, in order to accomplish the desired outcomes.

Unfortunately, in the majority of churches and organizations, a strong alignment between culture and structures is the exception rather than the rule. Often this is because leaders don't see the two dimensions as being two halves of a whole. Only when the two sides are working together does the platform work. To carry forward the table illustration, a misaligned culture and structures would be like placing a large conference table in a small coffee shop or, even worse, using that table as a chair. It would be clunky at best and would no doubt impact customers and sales.

In the field of psychology, family systems theory has much to teach us about the importance of culture-structures alignment. In her book, *Brain-Body Parenting*, Mona Delahooke examines the connection between the brain and the body in children, and the necessity for them to be functioning in alignment for the child to be physically and mentally healthy, regulated, and operating in homeostasis.[3] Whereas the brain (similar to *culture*), controls how the child acts, the body (similar to *structures*) is the visible and physical expression of the child acting. Ironically, the term Delahooke gives to the interconnectivity of the brain and body within the nervous system is called the "platform"! When the platform connection between the body and brain of the child is misaligned, the internal systems within the child break down. This can lead to severe physical and emotional consequences, such as outbursts, depression, anxiety, and a variety of illnesses; and the presence of these symptoms helps parents and health professionals diagnose the misalignment.

Organizations work in exactly the same way. When the platform (the interconnectivity between culture and structures) is not aligned, the whole organization is out of sync with itself. This inevitably leads to extensive internal conflict and dysfunction, frustrating everyone within the organization. And again, as with parenting, the evidence of the dysfunction helps us diagnose where the misalignment may be.

When I (Rob) was a child, my mother would often say to me, "Your actions are speaking so loudly, I can't hear a word you are saying." (I may have had a slight rebellious streak.) Similarly, in most churches, we can say with confidence that our systems are speaking so loudly that people can't hear a word we are preaching. This can often be seen in how most churches structure for mission. For instance, a church leader, considering themselves to be missional, may regularly preach about what it means to *go* (to make disciples or to plant churches), but everything about their system is saying *come* and *watch*. Similarly, if a pastor wears full clerical garb while trying to (genuinely) affirm the priesthood of all believers, church members will get the message that there are only one or two priests around, and it is certainly not them. It turns out that the famous quote by philosopher Marshall McLuhan really is correct: that the medium (of attractional church or clericalism) really is the message![4] What we win people *with* is what we win them *to*. This misalignment between culture and structures creates inevitable frustration and doubt.[5]

A Unique Opportunity

In addition to the concept of platform as we have just defined it (Culture + Structures), the notion of platform can also encapsulate a set of principles, rules, and processes for how platform-based organizations are governed. These principles and processes, which are deeply rooted in network science and theory, look very different from traditional, hierarchical, and institutional organizational operating systems and structures. Platform principles and practices have been proven to lead to far greater scale than traditional operating systems. These principles have been nearly perfected with the advent of the internet and global technology platforms, such as Facebook, Amazon, and Google—and have led to what many call the "platform revolution."[6]

But here is the beautiful thing about these platform principles. The more we study and understand the design principles that undergird them—which we will be doing later in this chapter—the more we realize they reflect how our Lord Jesus intended the church to operate in the first place. This presents the church with a unique opportunity. If churches and organizations can effectively architect and implement a new platform based on these principles, we have the opportunity to "double align" our organizations with reality. First, to align our organizations with Jesus' original design and ongoing intent for the church; and second, to come into alignment with the broader cultural platform revolution that is happening in our day—thus, developing a kingdom equivalent to the movie *Inception*. New churches and organizations will be more aligned to Jesus, while simultaneously aligning with a redeemed version of our cultural reality. Bring on this *inception*!

Having established that our platforms are the movemental infrastructure of our churches and organizations—and that we not only form them, but they ultimately form us—the remainder of the chapter will focus on the two major components of platform: culture and structures.

Culture: The Soul of the Organization

Just as the paradigm operates as the "mind" of the organization, the platform—and more specifically, the culture—is the functional "soul" of the organization. When you think of someone's soul, you think of their true self, their essence or ethos. The culture of your organization acts in exactly the same way. It embodies what is most true about the organization. Getting your culture right, therefore, cannot be left to chance.

As we noted earlier, Peter Drucker once famously quipped, "Culture eats strategy for breakfast." Was Drucker saying that strategy is unimportant? Certainly not. He was just saying that getting the culture of the organization right was of the utmost importance, and no matter how good your strategy is, if the culture is unhealthy, strategy won't make a difference. Culture is formed over time and is a complex, moving target. Unfortunately, toxic culture is all too often the norm, and maintaining a healthy culture is extremely difficult.

A healthy culture should begin to explicitly (and implicitly) bring to light what we truly value. In other words, we have to name the values that are important, make them concrete, and develop a living culture that will set the tone of the church or organization.

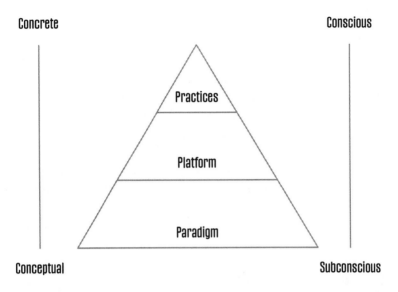

Below are the six key aspects of organizational culture, each of which is essential to discipling the organization:

Identify and Develop Theological Distinctives

As churches and organizations, we have all been given the gift and foundation of orthodoxy, as expressed in the Scriptures and the earliest creeds of the church, which should be nurtured and consciously rehearsed. However, as churches and organizations, we will all have core theological distinctives. Therefore, to be a leader within Christ's church requires us to be working theologians, helping people understand those theological distinctives. We are to share theology in a way that makes it contextually unique. This process of articulating explicit theological distinctives is directly tied to identifying our implicit beliefs (explored in the previous chapter).

Theological distinctives should clearly communicate to those stepping into the church or organization what you hold most dear. Members or participants should be able to read them and say, "Oh, that's why they defined it that way." We suggest forming only three to five theological distinctives, as too many can cause confusion. For instance, we have friends who have planted churches that frame their theology as *Sacramental, Communal, Missional.* These three words give their members and prospective members enough information to discern whether this is the right community for them. Theological distinctives might also reflect denominational background, such as charismatic, Spirit-filled, reformed, complementarian, egalitarian, and the like.

When I (Rob) was forming the For Charlotte Network, we were aware that we were working with a diverse, citywide network of churches from across racial, denominational, and socioeconomic lines. Therefore, our team took time to refine our explicit theological distinctives, which are: *the Centrality of Christ, the Unity of His Church,* and *the Flourishing of Our City.* Of course, we are orthodox in every way, which we acknowledge openly, but these three distinctives—which can be shortened to *Christ, Church, City*—frame what is core to us and are easily reproducible by the pastors that lead one of the many networks in the For Charlotte Network platform.

Formulate Core Values

In the process of creating culture, it is important to delineate between theological distinctives and values. Both are essential, but they are not synonymous.[7] Values are often implicit, but through a process of dialogue in community, these are made explicit and then must be categorized according to their relative weight and significance. In other words, the difference between general values and core values should be clear. Core values get us all passionate and worked up. In this way, they are tied to the meta-ideas and DNA statements articulated in your paradigm. Core values translate the DNA into and through the organization. This is at the heart of the fractal organizing process addressed in the previous chapter. When fully adopted and embodied, core values ensure the DNA is embedded as the organization scales. Leaders must take great care to articulate core values, since they impact every aspect of the organization.

As a best practice, we recommend creating six to eight core values. Once we are clear about what we truly value, we can then deliberately reorder our thinking and choices around them. In such a way, values become guides to thinking—shaping attitudes and behaviors. Core values act like road lines, which help us keep our car in the appropriate lane or from veering off the road altogether. But road lines only do this if they are clear and well lit, and if the person in the driver's seat is paying attention to them as a matter of course! So, take the time to craft value statements that capture the imagination. The best core values are typically a fun combination of honesty, creativity, stickiness, and most of all, are deeply personal and unique to the organization.

Develop Shared Vocabulary

As we addressed in the previous chapter, words define reality. If you can shape the various conversations in the community, you can shape the culture. If you can change the language, you can significantly restructure the way people process information and communicate. The Bible is very clear about verbal integrity and avoiding the sins of the tongue (see James 3:1–12; Matthew 15:11, for example), so we must be careful that the development of our vocabulary is not manipulative. At the same time, we must recognize that it's extremely important to shape the organizational discourse—to guide how members talk about church, mission, heroes, and so on. We suggest you define or redefine terms and create a commonly understood vocabulary consistent with the central paradigm of your church or organization. For example, because most people have a concrete perception of church, you might choose to use the word "movement" in place of the customary term "church" to describe who you are. If you start referring to your church as part of Jesus' movement in the world, it reshapes the consciousness of those you are leading, and in so doing helps them act like the movement of Jesus they are meant to become.

Identify Heroes

"Join together in following my example, brothers and sisters, and just as you have us as a model, keep your eyes on those who live as we do" (Philippians 3:17). "Remember your leaders, who spoke the word of God to you. Consider the outcome of their way of life and imitate their faith" (Hebrews 13:7). "And what more shall I say? I do not have time to tell about Gideon, Barak, Samson and Jephthah, about David and Samuel and the prophets" (Hebrews 11:32). The Bible clearly demonstrates, both by example and commands, that we should identify those who are worth following, and then imitate them. When we consider this in light of culture-making, we need to ask, Who are the organization's heroes? Who are the exemplars we wish to emulate? Can we name leaders, individuals, churches, and organizations who are doing things the way we want to do them? It's not enough to imagine Jesus in your mind, indispensable though that is; we need to see him lived out concretely in the lives of others. That is how the collective culture is shaped.

Our heroes ought to embody our values and live out what we all hope to become. In other words, show me your heroes, and I will show you who you are! Who an organization admires shows a lot about the type of organization they are or aspire to be. For instance, if your church's hero is a brilliant scholar and preacher, everyone gets the message that it is teaching, rhetoric, and scholarship that are most prized. If, on the other hand, the hero is the church planter or pioneer, people get the message that missional entrepreneurship is highly esteemed. Your heroes are living examples of what you are seeking to achieve.

Don't underestimate the importance of everyday heroes—they are embodiments of change, especially when empowered by the esteem of leadership. Conversely, an organization's heroes can also signal dysfunctions within an organization. For instance, if the senior leader is seen to be the hero and adopts a cultic stature ... beware!

Ask yourself, Who are the heroes of our organization—historically and currently? Are they the right heroes? Who should they be?

Celebrate Positive Behavior

"When Jesus heard this, he was amazed at him, and turning to the crowd following him, he said, 'I tell you, I have not found such great faith even in Israel'" (Luke 7:9). "She has done a beautiful thing to me ... Truly, I tell you, wherever the gospel is preached throughout the world, what she has done will also be told, in memory of her" (Mark 14:6, 9). Wow! Suffice it to say, Jesus celebrated positive behavior. This is not to say that negative behavior should go ignored. It's just that we often forget to promote good behavior.

Similar to the idea of identifying heroes, this means celebrating the actions of those who are living in a way that is consistent with the vision and culture of the church/organization—especially for those who are not in any formal leadership positions. Celebrating and affirming culturally consistent behavior has a profound effect on culture building. For example, think of the older couple faithfully serving behind the scenes year after year with no fanfare. What statement would it make to the rest of the community to acknowledge their servant leadership? What could it look like for those who lead well to be, as the Scriptures say, considered "worthy of double honor" (1 Timothy 5:17)? This shouldn't be seen as some sort of elitism, and certainly not as a manipulation of people, but rewarding individuals, publicly or otherwise, sends a profound message to those you are leading about what your church/organization values. This in turn has a major impact on your culture.

Individuals can be rewarded in multiple ways, but it can be particularly helpful to use rituals—regular and repeatable patterns and practices—in your gatherings. For example, affirm and commission members through the laying on of hands. Tell stories. Give gifts/awards. (Be sure to distinguish those who deserve to be singled out so the recognition has real value.) This is one area in which we can learn from technology platforms. Almost all successful platforms incorporate the concept of "gamification"—an embedded reward system that is central to their architecture. From the "like" button on Facebook to the "retweet" on Twitter to gaining points/credits on whatever game you are addicted to on your smartphone, gamification is foundational to successful platform architecture, as it shapes the culture and motivations of its participants. Let us be quite clear, however: the rewards we seek to incorporate into organizational culture are not for the sake of a hit of social dopamine—lest they "receive their reward in full" (Matthew 6:2). This is not about controlling or manipulating the motivations of those in our organizations. It's about leaders doing what is right for leaders to do. And it is right for leaders to celebrate positive behavior because such behavior significantly contributes to the culture we are seeking to create.

Brand the Organization

Once we do the hard work of renewing the organizational mind/paradigm internally, we are ready to brand the church or organization externally. We have to be careful when using this term, because advertisers and spin doctors profoundly manipulate branding. Nonetheless, it would be naive to think that managing the "brand" (how people perceive the movement) is irrelevant in creating a healthy missional culture in the church or organization. Because all organizations have a distinct identity through which they interact (even if it's just their name), we must steward how we externally communicate our distinctives and values. Think of a brand as *a promise kept*. A good brand keeps its promises, and a bad one doesn't—it disappoints. Your brand is your church or organization's public identity, and how you project your identity to the world has significant consequences. In other words, branding has to do with being intentional with our words for those encountering our church or organization. In many ways, the culture can automatically be incubated from within; but it would certainly not harm your cause to make sure the symbols, words, and ideas you project to the outside world are consistent with who you are and what you are about.

Final Thoughts on Culture

When you mix theological distinctives, values, vocabulary, heroes, reward systems, and your brand together, you create a distinct ethos and culture—and culture is what people interact with. The culture in turn creates an atmosphere—the "vibe"—that those encountering the organization can feel in the ether of the community. Or, as stated earlier, the culture is like the "soul" of the organization. This organizational soul affects people. In the same way a magnetic field has an influence on various metals, the aura of your movement will impact people coming into it.

For instance, a fast-food restaurant emits a different vibe (eat quickly, get out) than a fine steakhouse (stick around and work your way through the courses). Similarly, a megachurch in Southern California has a very different vibe (and invites different responses) than a Catholic chapel in New England. Different leaders and organizations create different emotive/cultural fields. Some are stern, some creative, and so on.

A culture thus communicates (verbally and nonverbally) through symbols, actions, and experiences what we really think and what we truly value. An explicit, well-developed culture is crucial in determining behavior, making the right choices, developing programming, allocating resources, and setting the overall direction of the organization.

In summary, then, among the ingredients for organizational culture formation, the following are most critical: 1) identify and develop theological distinctives—what makes the organization unique; 2) formulate core values—what drives the organization; 3) develop a shared vocabulary—how to talk about the organization with one another, and mean the same thing; 4) identify heroes—who to watch, pay attention to, whose examples to follow; 5) celebrate positive behavior—how to recognize when it's done well; and 6) brand the organization—how to summarize and talk about the organization with those outside the organization.

With these components of culture in place, we are ready to look at platform structures in depth. Although we are exploring the subjects separately, in practice we work on culture and structure at the same time. They are mutually informing—the two pedaling legs that give the platform its *movemental* quality, while also keeping the proverbial bike from falling over. Waiting to implement structure until the organization gets its culture "right" is not the best approach. Good structures make good culture possible—and vice versa. Culture and structure will offer correctives for one another when organizations work on them *concurrently*, and doing so is the most organic, expedient, and fruitful approach.

Now that we have looked at culture, we turn to focus on the practical components of architecting movemental structures.

Architecting Movemental Structures

"By the grace God has given me, I laid a foundation as a wise builder, and someone else is building on it. But each one should build with care. For no one can lay any foundation other than the one already laid, which is Jesus Christ" (1 Corinthians 3:10–11).

Because Jesus' kingdom operates differently from those of this world, the principles that govern architecting and building movemental churches and organizations differ from those of other organizations. Leaders should expect, therefore, that its structures—whether designed around people, resources, or the ways these are tested and measured—will look surprisingly different from what many will be accustomed to. Consider the difference between a farmer and carpenter. They are both laborers, but the *nature* of their labor is different. The principles that govern their work are different. The farmer thinks about rain and soil, sun and seasons, whereas the carpenter can afford to disregard much of that and instead is concerned with materials and tools. The farmer weighs their produce on a scale; the carpenter measures productivity and tracks progress. But this is not to say that the farmer can afford to disregard construction! Even a farmer must know how to mend a fence and build a trellis.

Consider that trellis. It is a modest structure that exists to raise and move the life of a vine across the length of a field. It is a piece of construction designed specifically to support and facilitate *movement* … and when it is working effectively, it is largely invisible. But somebody has to think about it. This is the nature of movemental architecture.

Before examining the specific structures for building movemental architecture, we must first consider the design principles that inform their creation. How do they differ from principles that people use to maintain the "status" of their institutional "quo"? Most of these principles will be things you are already familiar with, but we choose to state them as reminders, lest they get lost in the shuffle of this essential work.

Structure Determines Behavior

In the title of his innovative book *The Path of Least Resistance*, Robert Fritz expresses one of the most fundamental principles that shapes platform architecture and design. He states that once a structure exists, energy moves through that structure by the path of least resistance. In other words, energy moves where it is easiest for it to go. Thus, the *structure* of the organization *determines* the *behavior* of those that are part of the organization. Bear in mind, this is less a case of "ought" and more a matter of "fact." It is not that an organization or church's platform *should* operate according to the path of least resistance; it just usually does.

For example, consider the doors of a house versus the windows. Both doors and windows give people access into a home, but given the choice, people will nearly always choose to walk through the door instead of crawling through the window. It is the path of least resistance. When creating movemental structures, the same is true. As we will examine later, leaders must wrestle through how people, resources, and energy move through their structures. Do the structures facilitate the organizational mission, or do they constrain it?

The Primacy of Discipleship

"Therefore go and make disciples of all nations" (Matthew 28:19a). The central mission of the church of Jesus Christ is to make disciples. This should be the foundational design principle that informs all organizational structures. But for some reason, this overt disciple-making mission is often confused with "decisions for Christ," where initial conversion is a moment (or moments) in time. Discipleship, however, which includes ongoing metanoia, is a process. Evangelism is an essential component of our faith journey, and our part in the faith journey of others, but it is not nearly as comprehensive as the category of discipleship. Making un-discipled believers is a cataclysmic failure. And creating structures which only allow for "decisions for Christ" is a cataclysmic reduction of the call to make disciples. All mature disciples of Christ will experience conversion, but not all believers experience discipleship.

One of the most common issues competing for space with the central disciple-making mission of the church is *good programs*. As Jim Collins showed us in his best-selling book *Good to Great*, great organizations must be able to sacrifice good things for the sake of the most important thing.[8] It's very easy to fill our church calendars with weekly activities and events on campus that not only fail to equip our members for mission but also take time that could otherwise be spent living on mission. Cutting good programs for the sake of the greater disciple-making mission of the church requires honest and courageous leadership.

The Necessity of Unity and Collaboration

"Love one another ... *By this* everyone will know that you are my disciples" (John 13:34–35, italics ours); "I in them and you in me—so that they may be brought to complete unity. *Then* the world will know that you sent me and have loved them even as you loved me" (John 17:23, italics ours). When we read words and phrases like "by this" or "then," it should make us pay special attention. Even more so when the words come from the mouth of our Lord. In a church culture that is highly isolated, divided, and competitive, our next design principle as we structure our church or organization for movement, requires us to see other Christian leaders, churches, and organizations not as competitors but as allies—people and organizations with whom we may collaborate. The Scriptures are blatantly clear, both on the mission of the church (to make disciples) and the method for that mission (in unity and love). It is by our demonstrated unity that the world will see and experience the gospel. We must move past the stranglehold of competition that is so prevalent in the church today and begin to structure our organizations to tangibly live out both Jesus' command and prayer for the unity of his church, as expressed in the Upper Room Discourse, just hours before he would be betrayed, captured, tried, tortured, and crucified on our behalf.

The Responsibility of *All* Believers

"But you are a chosen people, a royal priesthood, a holy nation, God's special possession, that you may declare the praises of him who called you out of darkness into his wonderful light" (1 Peter 2:9). Our final design principle reminds us who is responsible for Christ's mission in the world. The principle of the priesthood of believers helps us to structure our organizations in a way that maximizes participation by everyone rather than leaving it to the so-called "experts." Peter is clear that all who are part of the royal priesthood are to proclaim the excellencies of Christ. Thus, effective platform structures help move all participants from consumers to contributors and, better yet, to leaders in the core mission of the organization. This is a fundamental principle of most modern platforms (such as Airbnb or Uber), and active participation for all was normative in the New Testament as well, from the apostolic authors to the countless names in the last chapter of almost every epistle they wrote. This highlights again a commitment to APEST culture—unleashing all the latent spiritual gifts within the community.[9]

When designing movemental structures, it's important that leaders help each disciple cultivate their unique, God-ordained vocation rather than simply thinking in terms of mass-scale volunteer mobilization for the next program or campaign. Every individual is looking for meaning in life, and it is simply not enough to plug them into a random space where you need a warm body. This can never replace a life fully committed to Jesus and his mission in the world.[10]

Frederick Buechner said, "The place God calls you to is the place where your deep gladness and the world's deep hunger meet."[11] Volunteerism only covers the latter part—"the world's deep hunger"—and the result is often passionless servitude. Structuring vocation around the former— the discovery of "deep gladness"—is usually the surest path to the latter. Was there a single disciple of Jesus who wasn't called vocationally first, discipled second, and sent third? Peter, Andrew, James, John, Levi ... none of these were picked from the crowds. Jesus walked over to their workplaces and selected them. "Don't ask yourself what the world needs," Howard Thurman said. "Ask yourself what makes you come alive, and go do that, because what the world needs is people who have come alive."[12] To say it plainly, if we want to see movement, we love people first, disciple them second, find out what they're good at as a subset of discipleship, and then set them free in their gifts and call—in that order. Movemental organizations do this even when the final result benefits the organization down the street. Hence the necessity of unity and collaboration.

Designing Structures for Scale

With our basic principles established, we now turn to the work of designing our three overarching types of organizational structures:

- Relationships: *People* Structures

- Resources: *Operational* Structures

- Results: *Measurement* Structures

Structures are the essential aspect of the platform because they facilitate our ultimate goal of scaling the mission. If the old axiom is true, that *healthy things grow*, what does that tell you about your structures?

Relationships: Designing *People* Structures

In designing and building people structures, leaders address how people will best connect, grow, and lead within the organization in order to most effectively accomplish its mission. Most traditional models of church and ministry, rooted in the church-growth paradigm, follow what can be described as a "pipeline," or industrial structure. Pipelines are based on one-directional flow. (Think Henry Ford and the assembly line making the Model-T.) Following the logic of pipeline structures, churches and ministries produce a program (or product) and deliver it to the people. This could be a sermon, a children's or outreach program, and the like. Although there can be benefits to these highly refined systems—such as high-quality products and efficiency—these structures tend to centralize authority and innovation, while constraining the flow of people and energy. In essence, they are designed more for product delivery than for people movement. Unfortunately, this both breeds and feeds the epidemic of consumerism within the contemporary church.

One of the key elements of the platform revolution our world is experiencing is a move from centralized to decentralized structures. Centralized, industrial systems tend to be larger with stricter hierarchies and more external laws that govern the hierarchy. Because these organizations are held together at the top, they are far more susceptible to failure, especially if there is a crisis with the senior leader/s (such as death or moral failure). Conversely, decentralized, networked organizations are held together by internal values, which makes them more resilient and adaptive when change or crisis hits.[13]

In networked structures, it is not just decentralization that occurs, but democratization,[14] as the influence, innovation, and intelligence of the people is pushed from the center to the outermost parts of the organization, leading to greater participation by all.[15] And because all are involved and responsible for the mission of the organization, networked churches and organizations have the potential for far greater scale than centralized structures. They tend to grow and reproduce in a far more viral, organic way.[16]

One of the most common ways churches decentralize and democratize their relational structures is through their primary discipleship vehicle. One example might be moving from on-site classes and small groups (or adult Sunday school) to small groups meeting in homes. Or, taking it further, moving from small groups to a missional community structure—which functions as the primary gathering of the church, and where community, discipleship, and mission occur. With this approach, Sunday's corporate worship gathering is focused on supporting and equipping those missional communities.

Perhaps one of the most pronounced shifts in how organic, networked organizations operate in relation to people is in the function of leadership. In decentralized systems, the focus of leadership is not on controlling a hierarchy but on influencing a community. In this way, leadership within organic systems reflects and promotes the inverse hierarchy of the kingdom of God; where the first are last and the last are first; where to live requires first dying to self; where we are called to take the lowly seat at the table. We are citizens of a kingdom whose King didn't come to be served, but to serve and give his life as a ransom for the many. We serve a Lord who washed the feet of his disciples, and then told them to go and do the same (John 13:1–17).[17]

This runs counter to contemporary, hierarchical church systems, where pastors and leaders are often put on a pedestal, leading to high levels of narcissism and a codependent relationship between leaders and congregations. We can combat this tendency by encouraging leaders to spend time working through their leadership structures—from board/elders, to staff, to key volunteers—examining their organizational chart and asking hard questions such as, How many layers does it have? How much access do "employees" have to the senior leaders? How does the structure impact how team members interact with one another?

We have seen some leaders flip their organizational chart upside down as a visual representation of this shift in emphasis and as a reminder of the role senior leaders should play in Christ's kingdom.

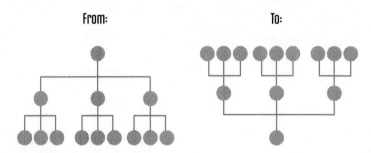

Finally, in thinking through the organization's relational structures, we encourage leadership teams to work through the following questions:

- How would you diagnose your overall relational structure? Is it a "pipeline" (industrial), or "platform" (organic) structure?

- Are your relational structures more passive (a program to be experienced) or active (participatory)? How easy is it for someone to be a part of your church or organization and not participate in anything?

- What are you doing for those you lead that they should be doing for themselves?

- How effective are your relational structures in accomplishing your stated mission? Are you seeing spiritual maturity and Christlikeness in those you are leading?

- Are your relational structures producing mature, well-equipped leaders? And if so, do your structures have room for them to lead as they grow?

- Do your relational structures enable people to be set free in their God-given vocation, or do they force people into a set program?

Resources: Designing *Operational* Structures

In designing and building resource structures, it is the task of leaders to answer how the key internal operations and physical structures of the organization will best facilitate its mission. In traditional, industrial structures, internal systems such as budgets, committees, accounting, and legal requirements can easily become overemphasized, which can lead to some of the clunky bureaucracies evident in the contemporary Western church. Conversely, the internal systems and structures in organic, networked organizations are all too often underdeveloped, making them fragile and vulnerable. All living systems need structure in order to survive and thrive. For instance, if your body didn't have a skeleton, it would just be a big, useless blob. So, we encourage leaders to pay special attention to creating what we call the *minimum viable structure*. Here, the responsibility of leadership is to navigate a dynamic tension of developing structures that will not lead to rigid institutionalism and bureaucracy but instead to build enough structure to ensure long-term organizational health and sustainability.

To carry forward the *seed, tree, forest* metaphor that undergirds the upcurve of the Metanoia Journey, where the organizational platform is the tree, think of your minimum viable structure as the trunk. We rarely focus on the trunk of the tree, but it plays an essential role. For one, it holds the tree upright. If it is too weak, the tree will simply fall over. But the purpose of the trunk runs much deeper, as it is the trunk that takes nutrients from the soil, through the roots, and pushes them up to the limbs, branches, and leaves. Similarly, these internal "trunk" systems pull from the paradigm and culture, and feed those "nutrients" through the organization.

Arguably the two most important internal operational structures that need consideration are the budget and calendar, "For where your treasure is, there your heart will be also" (Matthew 6:21). Apart from the Bible and the statement of faith, the calendar and budget are likely the two most theological documents in an organization. How organizations spend their time and money are tangible expressions of what they truly value and believe. Once budget and calendar are set, focus needs to be given to other basic systems and structures, such as business model, funding, communications, accounting, legal requirements, IT, and database.

The physical building and facilities of a church or organization are also a key indicator of its resource structure. In 1943, during the height of World War II, the UK Parliament's House of Commons Chamber was destroyed in a bombing. In discussing how they might rebuild this room that served as the seat of the British government, Prime Minister Winston Churchill famously said, "We shape our buildings, and then our buildings shape us."[18] Determining what physical structures an organization needs (if any) is an essential task of leadership. Facilities such as buildings tend to express what the organization truly believes. From a giant megachurch with an auditorium that seats thousands, to a coffee shop that happens to house a church gathering on a Sunday, the building speaks volumes and will determine the behavior of both members and visitors.

In thinking through the organization's physical structures, we encourage leadership teams to work through the following questions:

- What are the minimum viable structures needed to effectively accomplish the unique God-given mission of your church or organization?

- How do your structures help or constrain movement? For instance, do you meet in a big room with permanent rows, or do you have smaller rooms with circles of moveable chairs?

- Do your structures genuinely express the paradigm, DNA, and core values of the organization, or do they communicate something different? For instance, a large auditorium with lights and smoke machines invites mere attendance and suggests passive entertainment. Is this consistent with the stated missional (sending) purposes of the church/organization?

- How do the costs of your physical structures constrain your mission? For instance, do they redirect critical resources from missional efforts to a single-use building?

- Is your building designed for members of the community? Does it isolate you from your community, or help you serve it? How often will it be used? And by whom?

Results: Designing *Measurement* Structures

Finally, in designing measurement structures, it is the task of leaders to ensure the organization is measuring what most effectively accomplishes its mission. The fundamental purpose of platform principles and structures is scalability, so clearly defining and communicating key metrics and measurements allows everyone within the organization to know if the desired scale is being accomplished. As stated earlier, this must be done in tandem with culture development. Specifically, results structures should reflect the internal "shared language" and external "brand promise" of the organization. Additionally, in articulating the collective "win" of the organization, these structures encourage "behavior worth celebrating," and help build momentum and excitement within the organization.

What an organization measures indicates what it values and is a huge clue to the extent of its missionality. Failure to articulate measurement structures leads organizations to experience mission drift, causing confusion, frustration, and an overarching feeling of listlessness. For far too long in the contemporary Western church, which has been driven by the church growth paradigm, the primary issue hasn't been a lack of measurement but simply the measuring of the wrong things. Key measurements have primarily focused on attractional metrics, such as church attendance, budget size, and buildings (what many in the US affectionately call "nickels and noses" or "bucks, butts, and buildings").

The impetus behind the measurements in the church-growth paradigm look something like this:

- **Paradigm**: The purpose of a church is to grow large through constant addition of attendees.

- **Platform**: The culture and structures of the church are predominantly oriented toward attracting new people (which requires big budgets for nice buildings and great programs), while the internal systems are specifically designed to create comfort, enjoyment, and consumer experience.

- **Practices**: The strategies of the church are focused on the weekend service, attractional-ministry activity, and delivery of experiential enjoyment. What is celebrated is quantity in attendance (not necessarily discipleship).

Conversely, movemental metrics/measurements, require the organization to go beyond traditional, attractional metrics, and focus on how their relational and resource structures are changing how people live. Additionally, key movemental metrics will incorporate and reflect both the organizational paradigm examined in the previous chapter and the key design principles listed above. As an example, below are some common measurements we have seen used within highly movemental churches and organizations:

- The number of disciple-makers equipped and sent.

- The number of relationships built with those in the non-Christian community.

- The number of missional community (microchurch) leaders equipped and launched.

- The number of church planters equipped and launched.

- The number of community, city, or church partnerships created.

- The number of community organizations using the church building.

- The amount of money saved by local schools because of the church/organization.

- The number of small groups regularly serving with community partners.

- The reduction in crime in the surrounding community.

- The reduction in divorce rate in the surrounding community because of families/marriages served.

- The number of children receiving free or reduced-cost childcare in the community.

- The number of children and young people adopted or fostered by members.

- The number of people with additional needs engaged in the church.

Finally, in thinking through the organization's measurement structures, we encourage leadership teams to work through the following questions:

- Have you clearly defined the "win" for your organization? Do your measurement structures align with your win?

- What specifically in your stated mission are you trying to scale? Is it scaling?

- Are you measuring the right thing/s? How might you change your metrics and measurements to better reflect where you want to lead your church or organization?

- Do your measurement structures incorporate the core paradigm you want to see fractalized throughout your organization?

From the culture to structures, never underestimate the importance of getting the organizational platform right. It is the core infrastructure that both forms the people and scales the mission of the organization. A well-architected platform is where the Metanoia Journey becomes concrete and, just like the movie *Inception*, structures the organization to move people through their personal Metanoia Journeys.

Chapter Nine

Practice/s

Engaging the Collective Will

We shape our tools and then our tools shape us.

MARSHALL MCLUHAN

*In short, if you are what you love, and love is a habit,
then discipleship is a rehabituation of your loves. This
means that discipleship is more a matter of
reformation than of acquiring information.*

JAMES K. A. SMITH

*Sow a thought and you reap an action; sow an act
and you reap a habit; sow a habit and you reap a
character; sow a character and you reap a destiny.*

RALPH WALDO EMERSON

*If one of our orthodox beliefs has no corporeal value,
if we cannot come up with a single consequence it
has for our embodied life together, then there is good
reason to ask why we should bother with it at all.*

STANLEY HAUERWAS

As we continue our way up the Metanoia Journey, we now turn to *Practices*. With *the Seed* firmly planted, and *the Tree* established, we now seek to multiply into *the Forest*. And in our pursuit to become a whole-hearted organization, having addressed *the Mind* and *the Soul*, we now engage *the Will* of the organization, through the establishment of a set of *Rhythms and Tools*.

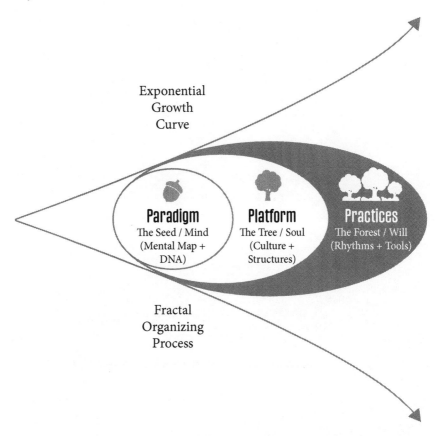

Strengthening the Willpower of the Organization

In the previous chapter, we addressed designing and building the organizational platform. One illustration for platform design that I (Rob) have appreciated over the years is that of hosting a dance. To host a dance, requires various structures—from the dance floor to the stage to the DJ booth to the sound system to the lighting. The emcee sets the culture of the dance by making announcements, choosing the music, and shining the spotlight on the best dancers. But once they have established all the essential elements of a successful dance party, the one thing the host has no control over is whether or not people actually dance.[1] Applying this metaphor to the church, we find ourselves with leaders constantly struggling to help people live out Christ's mission—to get involved in the proverbial "dance." Our churches often feel more like a seventh-grade dance, with the majority of attendees standing on the sidelines, segregated into their cliques and talking among themselves. As we look at the church in our current cultural moment, it is clear that the body of Christ is in serious need of help, and although we can't force participation, we can foster a love of "dancing" and teach people how to "dance."

When we're learning or teaching something new, there is only so far that theory can take us. In previous books I (Alan) sought to make a case that, from a distinctly biblical understanding of knowledge, it is not so much that we *think our way into a new way of acting* but that we *act our way into a new way of thinking.*[2] What this means is that we learn not simply by gaining a theoretical grasp on knowledge but also by *doing.* As always, this applies to both the individual as well as the organization. And as we will see, acting our way into a new way of thinking is a key aspect of discipling the organization.

As examined in chapter five, part of discipling the organization means becoming a *wholehearted* organization. This requires engaging the mind, soul, and will. And it is through consistent application of spiritual and missional practices that the will of the organization is fully engaged. These practices and disciplines don't just happen by accident. They must be learned and therefore teaching them is an essential function of leadership for the future of the church. Fortunately, we have the benefit of learning from many historic missional and monastic orders that gathered around a transformative vision (the paradigm/mind of the organization), were focused by a unifying culture and structure (the platform/soul of the organization), and were formed by a common set of practices. Whereas the paradigm (mind) is hidden, and the platform (soul) is experienced, the practices are visible to all because they are a conscious expression of the will. The organization will either choose to do them or not. It is through practices that organizational metanoia becomes tangible and embodied, both to those who are part of the organization as well as the surrounding community.

If we are to engage the will, we must be motivated and animated by love of God and people. People act on what they love, not just what they think.[3] To be a wholehearted person and organization therefore requires being rooted deeply in God's love. We are called to love the Lord our God with all our heart, soul, mind and strength, and to love our neighbor as ourself. In this context, "strength" can be understood as the will or willpower. Thus, common practices, when motivated by love, embody the values of the organization and are lived out through the lives of the members and the community. In other words, the practices are themselves specific expressions of our core DNA, which are fractalized throughout the organization.[4] This is the progression of the upcurve, as seen in the diagram on page 170. If the paradigm contains the DNA to be scaled, and the platform is designed for scale, it is through practices that scale is achieved. And this scale requires the organization to strengthen its willpower.

Movemental Rhythms

In addressing the practices of the organization, we will focus on the rhythms and tools needed to help people get off the sidelines and dance. We love the word *rhythm* because it refers to movement that occurs in a uniform and recurring pattern. And ultimately, what we are trying to do is both help catalyze and be a part of Jesus' movement in the world. To foster healthy rhythms that lead to movement, we will address the following:

- From *Core Values* to *Core Practices*

- From *Action* to *Habits*

- From *Rhythms* to *Algorithms*

From Core Values to Core Practices

In the previous chapter, we addressed the importance of core values, which is something most organizations and churches have already identified. Core values are often put on display on walls, in the literature, on the website and so on. So far so good. The problem arises in trying to actually live them out. One of the reasons for this is because we've mainly informed people's heads and not required anything of their behavior. When we talk about core values in a values-shaped community of believers, it's hard to disagree with them (there is a Bible verse associated with each value ... and who is going to argue with a verse of Scripture?). Because value statements appeal to what we *believe* and don't require much else, the common response for many is mere assent: Of course we *believe* in evangelism (though we hold back from it in most cases), and of course we *believe* we must care for the poor (even though we don't do much of it), and of course we *believe* in prayer (but seldom practice it). You get the idea. Stanley Hauerwas states:

> Christianity is not a set of beliefs or doctrines one believes in order to be a Christian, but rather Christianity is to have one's body shaped, one's habits determined, in such a way that the worship of God is unavoidable. In our embodied life together, the words of our doctrines take on flesh. If one of our orthodox beliefs has no corporeal value, if we cannot come up with a single consequence it has for our embodied life together, then there is good reason to ask why we should bother with it at all. The issue is not whether there is any such thing as purely spiritual holiness, but whether there is anything beside the body that can be sanctified.[5]

The problem is that simple value statements can easily become platitudes, which are preferred ideals rather than lived-out values. Without the development of practices based on the stated values, establishing core values simply becomes an intellectual process rather than a compelling way to live. People will rarely assimilate values into their lives by simply looking at a set of principles on paper or hearing them in a sermon. So, rather than simply writing, talking, teaching, and lecturing about culture and values, we suggest you develop common practices that will give people pathways to act their way into a new way of thinking.[6] Here are a few:

- *Formulate the Core Values.* If you haven't already formed your list of core values arising out of the development of the platform/culture, we suggest you do this. Again, for them to be effective, we recommend six to eight (and no more than ten).

- *Brainstorm the Core Practices.* Gather people from the broadest leadership group of the organization. Have them list out all the possible ways (practices) each value can be lived out and observed by others.

- *Distill and Refine the Core Practices.* Review the practices to make sure they have a connection to everyday life. Remember that core practices should be regular, everyday life rhythms, as opposed to an annual service day or a once-in-a-lifetime mission trip.

- *Formalize the Core Practices.* Select just one (no more than two) practices you feel best embody the associated core value. Try to ensure that these aren't seen as particularly "religious" or church-based activities but are as close to everyday life as possible. So, for instance, if the core value is hospitality, think about ways in which hospitality can be embodied outside the church walls (for example, a weekly shared meal, visiting the sick once a month, inviting others to stay in a spare room).

- *Name the Core Practices.* Develop an acronym that sums up your core practices. The key is to make it memorable.

- *Encourage and Expect the Core Practices.* Expect that members of the church/organization will do these things. Encourage the practices through regular incorporation into the calendar and communication rhythms, as well as spotlighting and rewarding positive behavior by those who are part of the organization. As you do this, core practices will both build and reinforce the culture of the organization addressed in the previous chapter.

- *Foster a Culture of Accountability.* Encourage accountability so the core practices lead to fruitful personal and organizational transformation.

See the diagram below for a summary of the flow of developing core practices.

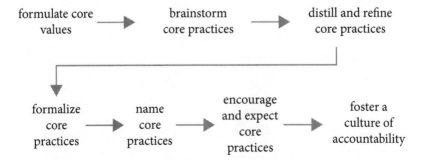

From *Action* to *Habits*

In a church culture characterized by constant action—much of which is good, but not necessarily fruitful—another way of establishing common practices is through the deliberate development of key habits. Habits are deeply ingrained rhythms in which culture becomes deposited in people in the form of dispositions, capacities, and inclinations that cause people to think, feel, and act in certain ways. These habits—which can either be positive or negative—can eventually become second nature. It's therefore crucial to recognize the organization as a habit-supporting institution that aims to help people replace bad habits with good ones. Deliberately deciding which habits to pursue will predetermine how the organization will act; it is another way of *discipling the organization*.

In his bestselling book on the topic, Charles Duhigg maintains that habits consist of three elements: a cue, a routine, and a reward. He suggests that to change the habit pattern requires understanding the cue (what prompts the habit) and reward (the benefit received), but the key is in changing the routine.[7] Similar to our concept of meta-ideas, he suggests that leaders ought to focus on the development of "keystone habits"; those habit patterns that are capable of triggering other habits in the lives of people and organizations. A simple example of this in a church setting would be rethinking small groups. People naturally feel the desire for human connection (the *cue*), so they attend a small group (the *routine*) to reap the *reward* of socializing (with a little Bible study tossed in for good measure). Knowing this need for human connection, leaders might shift the routine to a more missional form of discipleship, such as a missional community model. This model not only involves Bible study but other forms of intentional discipleship outside the walls of the church building, which provides the reward of human connection while simultaneously forming missional practices into the community.

Another way of thinking about building key habits (and thus practices) is through the metaphor of addressing old, as well as developing new, muscle memory. Muscle memory is a neurological process that allows us to remember certain motor skills and perform them without any conscious effort. Muscle memory is most associated with learning new motor skills such as playing a musical instrument or performing a physical activity.[8] Once you've established muscle memory, you can perform the task without consciously thinking about it. We all rely on this every day, even without knowing it. It is muscle memory and motor-skill learning that helps us master complex activities like typing on a keyboard where the fingers seem to be able to find each letter by themselves. The remarkable thing is that skill retention acquired from muscle memory can last forever, barring any neurological or physical ailments. In this sense, it is hardwired into the brain, ensuring that you do not need to relearn how to do something from zero. As the saying goes, *neurons that fire together, wire together*.

The power of habit, muscle memory, and engaging the will as foundational to our personal and corporate discipleship formation is an overt and frequent theme throughout the Scriptures. In 1 Timothy 4:7–16, the apostle Paul commends his young disciple to "train yourself to be godly" (v.7); "set an example" (v.12); "devote yourself" (v.13); "be diligent" (v.15); and "persevere" (v.16). In 1 Corinthians 9, Paul explains that we are to train in such a way as to "win the prize" (vv.24–27). Maybe the clearest example we see is in 2 Peter 1:3–11, where the apostle teaches that the regular and increasing practicing of central Christian virtues will keep us from being ineffective and unfruitful in our knowledge of our Lord Jesus Christ (v.8); help us to not forget our salvation (v.9); and confirm our calling and election, ensuring entrance into Jesus' eternal kingdom (vv.10–11). Simply stated, the biblical authors use incredibly clear and dynamic language to emphasize the importance of habit and practice for our spiritual formation.

Understanding the power of habit, we suggest leadership teams conduct a thorough evaluation of the key actions of the church or organization. Are they part of an intentional discipleship process? What habits already exist in the community? What fruit are the key actions or habits producing? How are they forming the community? What routines, if changed, would lead to the greatest spiritual formation within those who are part of the community?

From *Rhythms* to *Algorithms*

Have you ever wondered why Facebook beat MySpace, Google beat Yahoo, or Amazon beat, well … everyone? The answer: They had better algorithms. Although algorithms and rhythms are similar and highly connected, they are not synonymous. For the sake of clarity, let us explain. Rhythms are repetitive actions that are fundamentally connected to time intervals (such as two beats per second in music; or daily, weekly, or monthly actions in life). Similarly, algorithms are built on repetitive actions, but unlike rhythms, algorithms aren't required to be set to time (although they certainly can be). The one significant distinction algorithms have over rhythms is that algorithms are fundamentally about learning from the repetitive action in order to accomplish a purpose. For instance, in the early nineteenth century, French weaver and merchant, Joseph Marie Jacquard, learned that he could use algorithms to create one of the earliest programmable looms, allowing fabric manufacturers to create beautiful and complex products, such as clothing, rugs, and tapestries.[9] This invention played an important role in the development of subsequent programmable machines. And now we all live in a world controlled by computers.

The importance and power of algorithms cannot be overstated. Our world is dominated by them. Algorithms are central to the platform revolution we have experienced, as explored in the previous chapter. Below are some key reasons why algorithms are incredibly powerful when applied to your organizational practices and mission:

Algorithms posture the organization for ongoing metanoia. Because algorithms are fundamentally about learning, it makes them the perfect type of practice for achieving organizational metanoia, which is one of the most powerful forms of experiential learning. Through metanoia, we expand our minds. Algorithmic practices help organizations build the pursuit of metanoia into the everyday life of the organization, while simultaneously embedding the learnings of metanoia into its systems and structures.

Algorithms refine the organizational vision, mission, and strategy. Algorithms force leaders to paint a picture of what they are trying to accomplish (vision), before designing the steps to accomplish it (mission and strategy). The learnings that come through iterations of the algorithm will constantly inform and improve the mission that the organization is scaling. This is especially powerful when applied to the core disciple-making mission of the church or organization.

Algorithms help the organization learn and discern future decisions. As leadership teams collaboratively examine the learnings that come from algorithmic behavior, they are equipped to make better decisions for the organization. Whether discerning the launch of future programs or initiatives, or helping clarify the process as they step into new and unknown mission fields, algorithms strengthen leadership decision-making.

Algorithms help "what wants to happen." Effective algorithms help organizations understand people, allowing leaders to match them quickly and accurately to how they can best engage in the organization's mission. Where and how people serve and lead is invaluable data to an organization. It shows leaders "what wants to happen" within the people they lead, helping best unleash them into their God-given passions and giftings. As the For Charlotte Network has grown, my team and I (Rob) incorporated the algorithm Connect > Know > Match > Go, meaning we: 1) *Connect* with a new pastor or leader in our city, 2) Get to *Know* them through surveys and conversation, 3) *Match* them to the appropriate network, initiative, or tool we have in our platform, and 4) Equip and unleash them to *Go* and help other pastors and leaders in their sphere of influence to do the same.

   Algorithms are fundamentally movemental. Algorithms are about rhythmic action. They are about following specific steps in a set order and about accomplishing a purpose. Each of these require movement. In *The Rise and Fall of Movements,* Steve Addison shows how Jesus, and later Paul, used the following algorithm to train and send disciples, driving early church multiplication: Connect > Share > Train > Gather > Multiply, meaning, the early church would 1) *Connect* with people far from God, 2) *Share* the good news of Jesus with them, 3) *Train* them up to read God's Word and obey Jesus' commands, 4) *Gather* them into churches that reproduce, and 5) *Multiply* workers who take the gospel to the ends of the earth.[10]

Algorithms can change the game in how a church or organization learns and grows. Through consistent application and habituation, they have proven to lead to massive scale of the mission, while fractalizing DNA throughout the organization.[11]

Movemental Tools

Playing on Winston Churchill's famous quote about being shaped by our buildings, Marshall McLuhan, the man who predicted the internet some thirty years before it was made, once said, "We shape our tools and then our tools shape us." McLuhan and Churchill knew something we would be wise to take note of: the power of tools and architecture. Think of the smartphone sitting on the table right next to you as you read this book. Or maybe you are reading this book on your smartphone. It is an enormously powerful tool that has completely changed the way we live and operate. Monumental shifts in human history are often tied to the innovation of new tools. Consider how Gutenberg's printing press preceded the Reformation and Renaissance, or how the internet changed the way every person, church, and organization engages with the world around them.

Because tools are so powerful and ubiquitous, it is not a matter of *whether* leaders are going to use tools to advance their organizational mission but simply a matter of *which* ones. In the final three years of my (Rob) dad's life, God gave me a special grace. In the fall of 2015, my wife and I bought a house that we completely gutted and renovated. My dad was the ultimate weekend warrior, and together we spent countless hours working next to one another on project after project. While passing hammers and swapping drills, I received sage wisdom and warm affection that I treasure to this day. One of Dad's classic quotes to me was, "Rob, always get the right tool for the job." He was so right! Whether building a house or an organization, we must ensure we have the right tools for the job. To that end, let's look at what good movemental tools do, as well as the types of tools an organization must consider as they seek to scale their mission.

What Good Movemental Tools Do

Here is an overview of why good tools matter and how they empower an organization's practices, and thus scale their mission:

Tools build trust in the organization/platform. Trust is the currency of mission-based organizations. When selecting what tools will help best accomplish your mission, it is important to discern how the tool will reflect on your organization. What does the tool say about you?

Tools add value to members/participants. People join churches, networks, and organizations out of rational self-interest. They understand that they will connect with people, information, opportunities, and/or tools that help them grow and do the things they feel called to do. Good tools are adopted at scale because they add value to everyone that is connected to your organizational platform. Tools help people in the organization win in how they feel called to engage in the mission, and in turn, help the organization win.

Tools fractalize DNA and meta-ideas throughout the organization. As leaders constantly seek to embed the paradigm, DNA, and meta-ideas, tools will quickly become a leader's best friend. In this way, tools are highly formative. As McLuhan said, they shape the people within the organization.

Tools remove friction, enabling scale of your core mission. The most effective tools are simple, sticky, and scalable.[12] Simply stated, tools make it easier for people to do what they are trying to accomplish.

Tools add capacity to the church/organization. Tools allow leaders to equip and enable their people to accomplish the organizational mission on their own time and without the leader needing to be present.

Tools foster innovation and partnership. All tools exist to solve some type of problem. In gathering the tools that are needed to scale the mission, the organization may have to innovate. Sometimes, that means creating a tool internally. At other times it means partnering with others to borrow or create what is needed to solve the problem.

In my (Rob) own ministry, I have become increasingly aware of the power of good tools. In 2016, my team and I began to identify a major issue in Charlotte. Although we had a large and growing network of churches that desired to see Christ's mission advanced for the flourishing of our city, we didn't fully understand the city's needs. To address this issue, we created our first *State of the City Report*, a coffee table book to help pastors and leaders marry their biblical and missional convictions with the actual needs around them. The book was filled with research and data about the most pressing needs of the city, stories about those engaging them, and best practices from some of the most trusted Christian leaders in Charlotte. We couldn't have anticipated how deeply this tool would resonate. Over the next few years, we distributed over forty-thousand copies of the *State of the City Report*, and it quickly became one of the most used resources for the church of Greater Charlotte. We then went on to train more than fifty other city networks across the world in how to create their own report.

This tool overwhelmingly met the qualities listed above, as it 1) built trust in our network, helping us be known as a reliable source of data; 2) added value to all our network members, as they used the book to empower their missional activities; 3) fractalized our meta-ideas through story and theory about how the church can live out both Jesus' prayer and his command for unity, focused on collaborative mission for the flourishing of our city; 4) enabled scale by helping people join our network; 5) added capacity to our organization because people used it when and where they wanted it; and 6) fostered incredible innovation and partnership, both in the writing of the book (we had more than thirty contributors) as well as in how it was used by organizations to innovate new ways of engaging in Christ's mission together.

Types of Movemental Tools

It is not the purpose of this chapter to offer a comprehensive toolbox that can be used in developing a movemental church or organization. Our goal is to simply outline a few of the major types of tools that shape the collective behavior and practice of the organization. But first, here are a couple of key considerations when discerning which tools to adopt.

First, in thinking through which tool is right, leaders must consider *relational dynamics* and *social spaces*. In their excellent book *The Church as Movement*, our friends JR Woodward and Dan White Jr. point out that Jesus related to different groups of people in different ways. For instance, he regularly addressed, healed, and fed crowds; he mobilized the forty and the seventy for mission; he engaged in intense forms of training and discipleship with the twelve disciples; and shared more intimate experiences with the three (James, Peter, and John). Woodward and White point out that Jesus well understood what sociologists studying the science of proxemics have discovered: we all have the need to belong to public spaces (70+ people), social spaces (20–50 people), personal spaces (5–12 people) and intimate spaces (2–4 people). [13]

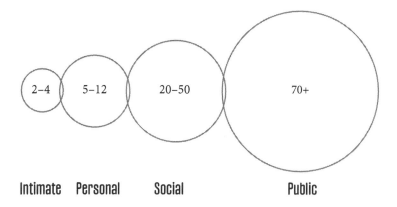

| Intimate | Personal | Social | Public |

Each of these spaces meets specific needs and operates differently from the other spaces. We can't meet our intimate needs in a public space, so it's not the best place to make disciples. But, since discipleship takes place through imitation, not just information and instruction, deep levels of discipleship *can* take place in personal spaces where individuals are close enough to see into each other's lives. We suggest careful consideration of what type of tool will most effectively work in each social space. It is worth noting that most churches tend to underuse and underestimate the importance of the intimate and social spaces, while leaning too heavily on public spaces (for example, worship gatherings) and personal spaces (for example, small groups).

A second consideration when thinking through which tools will best help accomplish the mission of the organization is how to most effectively leverage *technology*. We now live in a world where no matter what problem we might have, *there is an app for that*. Technology, with all its dangers and abuses, when redeemed, allows leaders to meet their people where they are at in their everyday lives, while giving far greater potential for scale than in an analog form. Each of the following types of tools can leverage technology for scale.

Physical Tools

Like hammers and screwdrivers, physical tools are things organizations can put in people's hands that make them more effective in accomplishing their mission. One of our favorite examples was created by our friends Dave Runyon and Jay Pathak, authors of *The Art of Neighboring*.[14] As a resource associated with their book, they created a refrigerator magnet that had a simple image of nine squares in a three-by-three pattern. The center square has an image of a house, titled "You Are Here." At the top of the magnet is the question, "Who is My Neighbor?" The goal of this magnet is to serve as a constant reminder (every time you open your fridge!) of your neighbors' names, and, if there are any blank spaces on it, as a prompt to learn your neighbor's name. The clear purpose of this wonderfully simple tool is to help people live out Jesus' great commandment to love their *literal* neighbor. It's impossible to do that if we don't even know our neighbor's name. This tool has become so effective that Dave Runyon will often say when speaking about starting a neighboring movement in a city, "If you have the refrigerator magnet, you don't need to read my book." (That said, we strongly recommend you use the magnet *and* read the book.) In 2019, our network mobilized over one hundred churches to participate in a neighboring movement that saw more than 62,000 people participate. This simple tool allowed the movement to scale numerically, but more importantly, it fractalized the DNA/meta-idea of "love thy neighbor" in a new and fresh way throughout the churches in our city.

Training Tools

As we are clearly taught in Ephesians 4, those that are leading a church or organization in their APEST gifting are called to equip the saints for the work of ministry. This makes it essential for leaders within Christ's church to be able to discern which type of training is best to enable those they lead to flourish in life and ministry, becoming mature disciple-makers. Training tools help leaders to find the right balance in the training processes they use. Cofounder of MLC, Rich Robinson suggests there are primarily three dimensions to learning—direct *experience*, which involves a personal engagement in some form of action; *equipping*, which comes in the form of apprenticeship, with learning passed on from one person to another; and *education*, which involves a theoretical grasp on ideas and is delivered in a classroom environment.

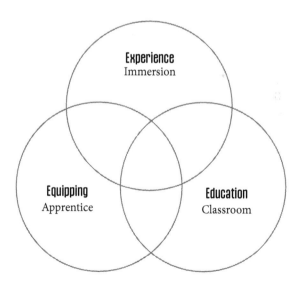

Training

We use the tool on the previous page, developed by Rich as part of MLC Movement Lab, to help churches and organizations develop a well-rounded way of discipling people and developing leaders.

Traditionally, churches lean strongly on education and offer very little in the way of experience and equipping, whereas best practices reverse that equation by emphasizing experience and equipping. For instance, over the course of a year, which do you think is going to lead to a more formed disciple: sitting in a classroom multiple weeks in a row, or, regularly meeting with a more mature follower of Jesus for incarnational discipleship, supplemented by occasional classroom learning and immersion? The irony is that we intuitively know the latter is more effective and apply it to other areas of our lives. Think of your house, for instance. Who would you rather hire to wire your house: an electrician that took a class and read a couple of books on wiring a house, or an electrician that was apprenticed by a master electrician for several years?

As churches and organizations consider how to train people, we strongly recommend creating discipleship frameworks that bring together all three dimensions of learning. Holistic discipleship frameworks that can be taught in classrooms, modeled in apprenticeships, and practiced individually or collectively in everyday life will make the ideas conveyed more memorable, leading to a more meaningful form of discipleship. For example, in his insightful and practical book *Surprise the World,* our friend Michael Frost puts forth a training framework of five essential habits for missional discipleship, summarized with the acronym BELLS, which stands for *Bless, Eat, Listen, Learn,* and *Sent.*[15]

Another helpful example of a discipleship framework created and implemented within a local church comes from Red Church in Melbourne, led by our friend Mark Sayers. They created the HUDDLE framework, which stands for *Home in the Fathers love, Usher ourselves into the presence of God, Dig into God's Word, Discern what God is saying through Scripture, Listen and pray,* and *Everyday life as the place where we live out Jesus' call.*[16] One of the things we like so much about this framework (as well as BELLS), is how each of the aspects of the framework has associated intentional and concrete practices.

Communication Tools

Different people respond to different forms of communication. Therefore, it is imperative for leaders to think through their various forms of communication and how they are received by a mixed audience. Using Rich Robinson's framework, we encourage leaders to leverage three primary forms of communication: *narrative*, *data*, and *theory*. Communicating in a narrative form is generally used by people who are good storytellers. About a third of listeners resonate highly with stories. Approximately another third of listeners will respond well to communication expressed in the form of theory. This tends to be people who prefer to see things in abstract ways (for example, scientists, who deal in theories and experiment based on them) and people who love wrestling through big concepts and how they apply to life. And then there is the third of people who love data and want proof (for example, statisticians) and resonate highly with statistical data, graphs, and tables. To reach a whole audience—be it through preaching, teaching, video, writing, or any other medium—leveraging all three dimensions of communication will allow everyone to engage both halves of their brain, leading to better adoption and engagement of the ideas being communicated.

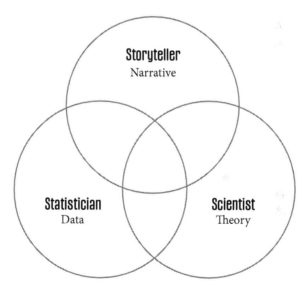

Communication

Joining the Dance

If you have never been to a Greek wedding reception, you are simply missing out. As opposed to the awkwardness of the seventh-grade dance referenced earlier, with all its wallflowers and insecurity, a Greek wedding dance is a joyful, unifying experience. In the dance, there are not just two dancers but at least three, who weave in and out in a wonderful circular motion. As they pick up speed, they stay in perfect synchrony with each other. Eventually they dance so quickly and effortlessly that it becomes a blur, yet each dancer maintains their individual identity. The sheer joy that the Greek wedding dance evokes raises the question, Why? Why does this dance resonate so deeply? It is because it is designed to reflect the divine dance of love within the Trinity.[17] We worship an all-loving God, who in his very nature is participating in a divine dance of interdependent persons, and through Christ, is inviting us to join his dance. What a gift!

The Greek wedding is a beautiful example to the broader church of getting the order of the Metanoia Journey right (which stands to reason since *metanoia* is a Greek word!). It starts with guests arriving at the wedding reception with a shared *paradigm* of celebration and love, which has been cultivated over time in community, and reflects the all-loving, movemental nature of God. Knowing this, the wedding planner builds the *platform*, with all the amazing food, music, and decorations (and don't forget the ouzo!). When the dancing starts, set *practices* dictate that the older participants teach the younger ones to dance in rhythm as a unified whole. And lo and behold, everyone experiences great joy (the joy of metanoia!).

As you have probably surmised by this point, the upcurve of the Metanoia Journey, although involving an incredible amount of work, is filled with hope and potential. From blowing the collective mind (*paradigm*), to shaping the collective soul (*platform*), to engaging the collective will (*practices*), when it all comes together, the church or organization you lead will be poised to change the world. With each aspect of the upcurve built and implemented, it is time to begin the dance and start experiencing the joy of metanoia.

Conclusion
Write Your Own Adventure

Do not call people back to where they were
(they never were there).
Do not call people to where you are, as
beautiful as it may seem to you.
But travel with them to a place neither of
you have been before.

VINCENT DONOVAN

Having reached the end of the book, observant readers might have noticed we have not yet elaborated on the "final" stage in the Metanoia Journey—Perform. This is where those who have successfully negotiated the dangerous hero's journey down into the valley and through the abyss finally climb to the rim and emerge to save the day. These heroes have solved the wicked problem that threatened their demise and have successfully negotiated the dangerous disruption by forming a more Christlike, intensely focused, integrated, high-performing, fruitful, and agile organization that can indeed achieve that for which it is intended.

Wash, Rinse, Repeat

The word "final" is in quotes in the previous paragraph because in many ways the journey of learning, of reaching for perfection, is never completed. Therefore, once you have gone through an arduous process of adaptive change in your life and organization, we suggest you will need to gather your energies and commit to another Metanoia Journey to the next peak! This is entirely consistent with the principle of ongoing metanoia.

Until God's kingdom comes, we will never experience perfection. Arriving at the current peak is the result of having taken the dangerous journey. It's a *genuine* prize and must be celebrated as an achievement, but it cannot be understood as the final destination. Without continued growth, obsolescence will eventually set it. All it will take is the next major disruptive event to highlight the problems inherent in the prevailing model, whatever they might be. If you become complacent and fall in love with your system (ideas, tools, practices), you will lose the capacity to change it.

We have already noted that all true learning (and innovation) is an iterative phenomenon. There are always new challenges to be faced, new crises to be overcome, new wicked problems to be solved. Therefore, we believe ongoing metanoia and un/learning ought to be factored into the very paradigm of the movement itself, inherent in the DNA—and therefore fractalized into the culture, the structures, and the practices—of a church committed to the way of Jesus. Movements are always moving; they are dynamic, adaptive, and innovative by nature because they are intrinsically *missional*, always pushing to the next frontier. And because of these factors they are what organizational theorists called "learning organizations." Organizations committed to the practice and discipline of metanoia will keep un/learning.[1]

As Simon Sinek says (see chapter four of this book), we are wise to remember that church is something of an "infinite game," where there is ultimately no such thing as "winning" because there's always a new set of challenges to deal with. We never stop learning and growing in life itself. This is what commits us to the ongoing discipleship journey of un/learning, maturing, and achieving. We are therefore not to get stuck in our most recent successes, or to rest on our laurels, but instead to always seek new ways to be more faithful and effective in our commitment to fulfill the mission that God has set out for us.

Regular metanoia is not a burden but is the root of ongoing fruitfulness. It is part of the joy of being a responsible human being (or organization) and is critical to maturity. It is a joy that is naturally associated with childlike wonder and awe. Lean into it.

Being Eternally Young

Childlikeness comes *highly* commended by Jesus, who says that the kingdom of God "belongs" to children, and unless we too become childlike, we have no hope of entering it (Mark 10:14–15). He goes further, saying, "Truly I say to you ... *unless you turn* and become like children, you will never enter the kingdom of heaven. Therefore, *whoever humbles himself like this child is the greatest in the kingdom of heaven*" (Matthew 18:3–4 ESV, italics ours). Jesus champions childlikeness because children are naturally humble and playful. They are often deep in un/learning mode, and frequently accept they have much more to discover.

Childlike thinking is essentially metanoic because it is invariably open to wonder and ongoing un/learning. Apparently what we all need is a "beginner's mind"—an approach to the world that is truly open and living in the present.[2] This is the most natural and simple path for all spiritual wisdom.[3] Although childlike reverence and awe is essential for grasping truths about God and the kingdom, it is similarly a prerequisite in any field of knowledge. Most people hesitate to ask what appear to be silly questions, fearing they might be humiliated. But Albert Einstein loved such questions. He never thought of things in terms of what was possible or not possible. Even as an adult, Einstein retained the playful curiosity of a child. He believed in the power of imagination, and this meant he always approached a problem creatively. In a letter to Carl Seelig, one of his biographers, Einstein claimed: "I have no special gifts. I am only passionately curious."[4] Understanding with other quantum physicians that observing something changes it, he retained a deep love for childlike curiosity: "The main source of all technological achievements is the divine curiosity and playful drive of the tinkering and thoughtful researcher, as much as it is the creative imagination of the inventor."[5]

The seminal philosopher Michael Polanyi also made direct links with childlikeness and metanoia, believing that "metanoia is a specialized, intensified adult form of the same world-view development found shaping the mind of the child."[6] He further noted that all creative thinking involves the same kind of thinking as a child, alongside the tools of logical structuring brought about by maturity. This combination, he said, is the key. Most rational structuring is bought at the price of this childlike thinking. And he's right; there remains a certain childlike quality in all great creative people. It is recovering this type of thinking that brings about the fundamental transformation of mind by which concepts are reorganized. In other words it enables metanoia, the "Eureka!" illumination behind all creative thinking.[7]

Thus we finally come to the end of this book. We hope the journey will have shown you what an incredible gift repentance really is and that it is a joy to undergo because it enables us to have a renewed experience of the living God, releases us from thralldom to obsolete ideas and practices, and opens us up to new and unforeseen possibilities.

If you long to see God radically transform you, your church, and your organization from the inside out, we pray you will have the courage to take the Metanoia Journey and the perseverance to continue when the challenges feel overwhelming, knowing that Christ is always present, and a great prize awaits. We pray you and your organization will receive metanoia as God's precious gift and that you and those you lead might have a greater understanding of the ever-greater God and the fruitfulness he longs to bear in his people.

Appendices

To read the appendices, go to www.themxplatform.com/onlineshop/p/metanoia-appendices-ebook.

Acknowledgments

Alan

I wish to make special mention to a new colleague and supporter, Tim Dunn. Thanks for believing in the work of the Movement Leaders Collective and for generously supporting our strategic mission to "shift the tracks of history."

Thanks also to all my colleagues throughout the Movement Leaders Collective with its one hundred Jesus movements and one thousand Christlike leaders and the amazing team that serves it. Grateful for your in/credible witness. It's my profound privilege to serve you.

Rob

Below are just a few people without whose support this book would not have been possible:

My beloved wife, Ani—Thank you for your undying love and support on this journey of life.

Addison and RJ—Thank you for the privilege of being your dad.

My mother, Jeanne Kelly; my sister, Sheila Kelly; and my mother-in-law, Janis Aghjayan—Thank you for your unending support.

My father, Bob Kelly, who went to be with Jesus in 2019, the man whose name I have the great honor to bear—Thank you for the example you gave me. Your fingerprints are all over this book.

The amazing board, team, and network leaders of the For Charlotte Network—It is such an honor to serve with you all as we pursue this vision of seeing the church united for the flourishing of our city. A special thanks to our core leadership team of Kevin Cobb, John Parker, Jessica Pierson, Andrew Weiler, and Casey Crimmins. I simply couldn't do this without you.

The amazing mentors who have shaped me and thus shaped this book—Leighton Ford, my spiritual father; Eric Swanson, who I have the honor of serving city network leaders with around the world; Alex Kennedy, who believed in me and helped launch me into this work; and my coauthor, Alan Hirsch. It has been such an incredible honor to learn from and serve with you through this project, my friend. Thank you for the opportunity.

Finally, my friend Justin Taylor—For your countless hours as a reader on this book, allowing me to verbally process through writer's block while pushing me to refine and shape my thoughts, I don't have the words to tell you how grateful I have been for your support.

Notes

A Briefing for the (Metanoic) Journey

1   Alan Hirsch and Mark Nelson, *Reframation: Seeing God, People, and Mission through Reenchanted Frames* (Cody, WY: 100 Movements Publishing, 2020).

2   Alan Hirsch, *The Forgotten Ways: Reactivating Apostolic Movements, 2nd Edition* (Grand Rapids: Baker, 2016); Alan Hirsch and Dave Ferguson, *On The Verge: A Journey into the Apostolic Future of the Church* (Grand Rapids: Zondervan, 2011); Alan Hirsch, *5Q: Reactivating the Original Intelligence and Capacity of the Body of Christ* (Cody, WY: 100 Movements Publishing, 2017).

3   It was Einstein who repeatedly insisted that the problems of the world cannot be resolved by the same kind of thinking that created the problems in the first place.

4   Another reason for the rather dense nature of this book is that the Western church suffers from a serious problem of pragmatism. We tend to shortcut the learning process, and to adopt someone else's plug-and-play app to achieve spiritual and missional renewal. Of course, the five-step miracle solution is a unicorn. It never works, and becomes mere patchwork that only further obscures the real problem at hand. We think that faulty pragmatism is more than half of the problem because, as we will see in chapter six, real transformational change requires us to first descend into the valley before being able to climb to the next peak. To engage the deepest paradigmatic issues we are facing, we must first address the underlying theological foundations on which our systems and structures are built. Otherwise, any changes made will be simply cosmetic and surface level.

5   "In systematically 'drawing out' the implications of revelation theology fulfills its 'function' within the Church as a corrective to any impulse, be it 'charismatic' or 'institutional,' that seeks to ground the Church in anything other than this faithful surrender to the Christ-form" Larry Scott Chapp, *The Theological Method of Hans Urs von Balthasar* (PhD diss., Fordham University, 1994), 306. Theology is not an ossified wall that signifies closure of a thought and conversation but rather a "point of departure" for a way of viewing the world that seeks to ground all things in Christ and to thereby "retrieve" its true meaning.

6   Henri J. M. Nouwen "Meditations," February 23, 2018, https://henrinouwen.org/meditations/what-is-most-personal-is-most-universal/. We are thankful to our friend John Chandler for making this point in his outstanding book *Uptick: A Blueprint for Finding and Forming the Next Generation of Pioneering Kingdom Leaders* (Cody, WY: 100 Movements Publishing, 2019), 27.

7   "The yearning for heaven which burns within us in prayer also has an effect on ordinary life and sears our actions with the glowing heat of eternal love." Hans Urs von Balthasar, *Prayer* (San Francisco: Ignatius Press, 1986), 286.

8   Henri J. M. Nouwen, "The Way of Change," *The Henri Nouwen Society*, July 12, 2022, https://henrinouwen.org/meditations/the-way-of-change/.

Part One: Why Metanoia (Introduction)

1   Witness the rise of the so-called "microchurch movement." This form of *ecclesia* is as old as the New Testament itself and has characterized all transformative Jesus movements in history, such as the early church, the Celtic movements, early Methodism, and the Chinese underground church. But this form has largely been ignored because it doesn't fit the paradigm or the metrics of Christendom churches and is ill-suited to serve the interests of hierarchy. In the current complex conditions, the microchurch form is being rediscovered as not only a more viable (and much less expensive) way of organizing, but also one that serves the dynamics of genuine movements much better than the unreproducible forms of the megachurch or the complex traditional forms of legacy churches.

1 The Apocalypse of the (Ecclesial) Soul

1   Andy Crouch and Dave Blanchard, "Designing for a Different Future: Pain & Possibility," *Praxis Labs*, May 2020, https://journal.praxislabs.org/designing-for-a-different-future-pain-possibility-1948352c738b.

2   Eric Hobsbawm, "War and Peace," *The Guardian*, February 23, 2002, https://www.theguardian.com/education/2002/feb/23/artsandhumanities.highereducation.

3   Catherine Keller and John J. Thatamanil, "Is this an Apocalypse? We certainly hope so—you should too," *ABC Religion & Ethics*, April 15, 2020, https://www.abc.net.au/religion/catherine-keller-and-john-thatamanil-why-we-hope-this-is-an-apo/12151922.

4   As believers, this should not be so strange to us. Jesus warned that when the powers in the heavens are shaken, there will be confusion, violence, and troubles on earth (Luke 21:24–31). Not only does the Bible contain a fair bit of apocalyptic literature of its own, but scholars also affirm that much of the New Testament is framed through a distinctly eschatological, apocalyptic lens and that it cannot be properly understood apart from this frame.

5   Hans Urs von Balthasar, *Spirit and Institution: Explorations in Theology, IV* (San Francisco: Ignatius Press, 1995), 465–8.

6   Hans Urs von Balthasar, *The Glory of the Lord, A Theological Aesthetics, III: Lay Styles* (San Francisco: Ignatius Press), 424, italics ours.

7   Then there are the genuinely apocalyptic (revelatory/unveiling) events related to the United States alone. In 2020, America experienced at least five category-five cultural tsunamis. Everything from the pandemic to the social unrest surrounding the death of George Floyd, to the political polarization, to the economic downturn—all of which contributed to the spike in mental health issues—had a transformative effect on the US, and in turn the world. The events of 2020 and following, along with the rise of China as the world's second

superpower, has historians saying that the so-called "American century" that began at the end of World War II is officially over. The deep political polarization in the US, which has been growing exponentially over the past two decades, reached its height with the election and presidency of Donald Trump and culminated with the riots at the US Capitol Building on January 6, 2021. No matter your particular political viewpoints, there is no denying that such events seriously damaged America's credibility and leadership on the world stage, and the role of apparent Christian leaders at the core of the polarization has had negative effects on the witness of believing Christians across the Western world but particularly in the US: "Ohh, so that's what Christians really believe and how they behave."

8   https://www.powerthesaurus.org/crisis/definitions (accessed February 28, 2023).

9   See the new edition of Alan Hirsch and Michael Frost, *ReJesus: Remaking the Church in Our Founder's Image* (Cody, WY: 100 Movements Publishing, 2022).

10 Harold Ramis, dir., *Groundhog Day*, 1993, Columbia Pictures.

11 In practice, the four terms are related. The more complex and volatile an industry is, for example, the harder to predict and therefore more uncertain it will be. Yet, all four represent distinct elements that make our world harder to grasp and control. See Jeroen Kraaijenbrink, "What Does VUCA Really Mean?" *Forbes*, December 19, 2018, https://www.forbes.com/sites/jeroenkraaijenbrink/2018/12/19/what-does-vuca-really-mean/. See also the useful article on VUCA in Wikipedia, https://en.wikipedia.org/wiki/Volatility,_uncertainty,_complexity_and_ambiguity.

12 Peter Drucker, *Managing in Turbulent Times* (New York: Harper Collins, 1980), 76.

13 Paul Evdokimov, *The Struggle with God* (New Jersey: Paulist Press, 1966), 57.

14 Karl Barth, "Letter to a Pastor in the German Democratic Republic," in *How to Serve God in a Marxist Land* (New York: Association Press, 1959), 45–80.

2 Metanoi-eh?

1   Pier Paolo Viazzo, Carlo A. Corsini, "The Decline of Infant Mortality in Europe, 1800–1950: Four National Case Studies," *UNICEF*, https://www.unicef-irc.org/publications/32-the-decline-of-infant-mortality-in-europe-1800-1950-four-national-case-studies.html (accessed February 28, 2023).

2   Ascribed to Henri Matisse. Source undetermined.

3   For instance, Tolstoy noted, "The most difficult subjects can be explained to the most slow-witted man if he has not formed any idea of them already, but the simplest thing cannot be made clear to the most intelligent man if he is firmly persuaded that he knows already, without a shadow of doubt, what is laid before him." Leo Tolstoy, *The Kingdom of God is Within You*, quoted in Matt Reimann, "Twelve of Leo Tolstoy's Most Brilliant Quotes," November 28, 2017, https://blog.bookstellyouwhy.com/twelve-of-leo-tolstoys-most-brilliant-quotes.

4   See David A. Lambert, *How Repentance Became Biblical: Judaism, Christianity, and the Interpretation of Scripture* (New York: Oxford University Press, 2016) and of course the standard biblical dictionaries (e.g., *Theological Dictionary of the New Testament, Dictionary of New Testament Theology*) for technical and grammatical details.

5   Insight derived from Bob Johansen, *The New Leadership Literacies* (Berrett-Koehler Publishers), Kindle edition, Kindle locations 19–20.

6   B. Kennedy, "Repentance," in *The Lexham Bible Dictionary*, eds. J. D. Barry, et al. (Bellingham, WA: Lexham Press, 2016).

7   *Te/shuva* is therefore capable of renewing a person from within as well as changing their relations to God and God's world. Martin Buber emphasizes the turning to God (*teshuva*) as an act that is done with your whole being, which can only mean with all your passion, and he identifies it with the return to the good. Still more clearly, he speaks of the *teshuva* as taking place "when man turns away from evil with that whole measure of power with which he is able to rebel against God." But Buber also speaks of the turning in a positive sense as turning from the way of man to that of God and perfecting God's image in oneself. "The fundamental way of encountering YHWH is through fear of God and through reversal, through a *turning* which brings ever new areas of the world into theophany and brings us ever closer to God." Maurice S. Friedman, *Martin Buber: Mystic, Existentialist, Social Prophet: A Study in the Redemption of Evil* (PhD. diss., University of Chicago, June 1950), 238.

8   (Pes. 54a[3]; Ned. 39b[4]; Gen. R. i.). "The Holy One, blessed be His name, said to Elijah, 'Behold, the precious gift which I have bestowed on my world: though a man sinneth again and again, but returneth in penitence, I will receive him'" (Yer. Sanh. 28b[5]). "Great is repentance: it brings healing into the world"; "it reaches to the throne of God" (comp. Hos. xiv. 2, 5); "it brings redemption" (comp. Isa. lix. 20); "it prolongs man's life" (comp. Ezek. xviii. 21; Yoma 86a[6], b). "Repentance and works of charity are man's intercessors before God's throne" (Shab. 32a[7]). Sincere repentance is equivalent to the rebuilding of the Temple, the restoration of the altar, and the offering of all the sacrifices (Pesi., ed. Buber, xxv. 158; Lev. R. vii). See article on repentance in the Jewish Encyclopaedia Sanh, https://www.jewishencyclopedia.com/articles/12680-repentance (accessed February 28, 2023).

9   Repentance has its subjective and psychological aspects, of course, but essentially it is "as little a 'spiritual' event as is a person's birth or death; [rather] it comes upon the whole person and is carried out by the whole person. The turning is something that happens in the immediacy of the reality between man and God. For the sake of the turning, the Hasidic masters have said, 'was the world created.'" Will Herberg, *The Writings of Martin Buber* (New York: Meridian Books, 1960), 28–9.

10 C. S. Lewis, *Mere Christianity* (New York: Harper Collins, 2017), 30.

11 Alister E. McGrath, *Re-Imagining Nature: The Promise of a Christian Natural Theology* (Wiley: Chichester, 2017), 51.

12 A. C. Thiselton, *The First Epistle to the Corinthians: A Commentary on the Greek Text* (Grand Rapids: Eerdmans, 2000), 19. For instance, Paul talks about the "the flesh" (e.g., Eph 2:3) as a way of describing a darkened perception, and in Rom 12:2 he talks about having our perception cleansed, "re/newing the nous." See also "Dianoia" in D. Mangum, *Lexham Theological Wordbook* (Bellingham: Lexham Press, 2014).

13 Treadwell Walden, *The Great Meaning of Metanoia: An Undeveloped Chapter in the Life and Teaching of Christ* (New York: Thomas Whittaker, 1896), 5–6. Remarkably, this book is over one hundred years old and is the *only* substantial one that we have found that is dedicated to an exploration of the idea of metanoia! This huge gap in our scholarship accounts in large part for our lack of understanding of the term and what it represents. Go figure!

14 He goes on to say that this new mind arrives directly as a form of self-contained truth derived from the biblical metanarrative. Stuart C. Devenish, *The Mind of Christ?: A Phenomenological Enquiry into Personal Transformation and Cosmic Revision in Christian Conversion* (PhD diss., Edith Cowan University, 200), 345–6.

15 "God's self-disclosure is that permanent revolution in our religious life by which all religious truths are painfully transformed and all religious behavior transfigured by repentance and new faith." H. Richard Niebuhr, *The Meaning of Revelation* (New York: MacMillan, 1941), 133. Also see Thomas Howard, *The "Moral Mythology" of C. S. Lewis*, https://marshillaudio. org/products/arp-26-m?_pos=1&_sid=81f2b51dd&_ss=r.

16 Birth from above (regeneration), a change of status before God (justification), as well as our evolving holiness (sanctification) are all ushered in through metanoia.

17 The Wachowskis, dir., *The Matrix*, 1999, Warner Bros.

18 Kallistos Ware, "Great Lent: The Season of Repentance," St Paul's Greek Orthodox Church, https://stpaulsirvine.org/great-lent-the-season-of-repentance/ (accessed February 28, 2023).

19 J. I. Packer similarly notes that the infusing of Hebrew understanding of *teshuva* and the Greek understanding of *metanoia* requires that we see change as comprehensive, involving all aspects of the human being. "The New Testament word for repentance means changing one's mind so that one's views, values, goals, and ways are changed and one's whole life is lived differently. The change is radical, both inwardly and outwardly; mind and judgment, will and affections, behavior and life-style, motives and purposes, are all involved. Repenting means starting to live a new life." J. I. Packer, *Concise Theology: A Guide to Historic Christian Beliefs* (Wheaton, IL: Tyndale, 1995), 162.

20 Devenish, *The Mind of Christ,* 345–6. For Devenish, the "keys" to the Christian worldview are its Christ-centeredness, its call for an exclusive commitment, and its rejection of a self- and world-centered concern in matters of morality and personal self-gratification, in favor of a life which is pleasing to God. He calls this aspect of metanoia, "the acquisition of mind." Ibid., 60.

21 "But let God transform you into a new person by changing the way you think. Then you will learn to know God's will for you, that which is good and pleasing and perfect" (Rom 12:2–3 NLT). The present-imperative form of the verb *metamorphous* indicates the ongoing dimension of transformation in the life of faith.

22 This knowledge is essential to understanding that conversion is really a response of love to the unconditional love poured out on the person while still a sinner (Rom 5:6–11). Comments by Daniel W. McQuire in his thesis, *Encounter–Call–Mission: Conversion in the writings of Hans urs Von Balthasar* (PhD diss., Marquette University, 2007), 43–4.

23 There may be momentous events or even several such events, but the conversion process is not often completed with speed. Peter is arguably the best example of a conversion moving forward in fits and starts. Despite his declaration of faith in the divinity of Christ (Mt 16:16) and the great reward promised for such faith (Mt 16:18), it is clear that Peter remained confused even to the shores of Tiberius (Jn 21:15ff). Peter's conversion was more labored in that he was drawn to Jesus earlier on but had a slower metanoic process where his mind struggled to catch up with what he was experiencing in walking alongside Jesus. As for existential encounter, consider Paul's conversion; not only what he radically reoriented but the shattering and reconstruction of his religious paradigms. Both event and process are two sides of the same coin.

24 Originally quoted by Nietzsche but popularised in recent years through Eugene H. Peterson's book of the same title. Eugene H. Peterson, *A Long Obedience in the Same Direction: Discipleship in an Instant Society* (Illinois: InterVarsity Press, 2000).

25 Olivia Fox Cabane, *The Net and the Butterfly: The Art and Practice of Breakthrough Thinking* (New York: Portfolio, 2017), 18.

26 Hirsch and Nelson, *Reframation*, 82.

27 This is almost certainly what the poet William Blake meant when he talked about "the doors of perception" being cleansed, enabling us to see things in their truer, more infinite, light. William Blake, *The Marriage of Heaven and Hell* (Oxford: Oxford University Press, 1975), verse 115.

28 Hirsch and Nelson, *Reframation*, 82. What is important to recognize at this point is that the New Testament builds on and develops the Old Testament teaching by adding a decidedly noetic element to the concept of repentance.

29 Joseph Chilton Pearce, *The Crack in the Cosmic Egg: New Constructs of Mind and Reality* (Rochester: Park Street Press, 2002), xi.

30 Similarly, my (Rob) experience in beginning the For Charlotte Network was like this. As a pastor in a church, I was deeply burdened by the division I was experiencing within my local church and between the churches of our city. It drove me to toward deeper study, prayer, and learning. It forced me to study new and different disciplines (technology, history, network science, etc.). I knew that this division wasn't God's plan for his church, but I didn't know what a healthy system could look like. I began traveling to other cities to see how God was moving. And finally, shaped by the overwhelming conviction of Jesus' prayer for the oneness of his church, I took the leap of faith to begin our network.

31 Abraham Heschel, *Man is Not Alone: A Philosophy of Religion* (New York: Farrar, Straus and Giroux, 1979), Kindle edition. Poet Gerard Manley Hopkins coined the term "inscape" to describe what is involved in becoming aware of the "manifold wisdom" made known in the church. Inscape is contrasted to the idea of a landscape, which is what we objectively see spread out before us against the horizon. It is relatively stable and can be described, painted, and cultivated. Inscape, on the other hand, sees the inner meaning of things; it is that intuitive sense that what we are seeing in a flash of insight is a living, organic form that strikes through the senses and into the mind with a feeling of novelty and discovery. Inscape involves becoming aware of what seems to be hidden and obscure and yet is so near at hand; that which—if only we had the eyes to see it—could be recognized through all dimensions of life. "Inscape is what something uniquely is, that which holds together whatever you are looking at or listening to, gives it distinction—proportions, shades of light, tints of color, shapes, relationships, sounds … Reading and reciting the poems of Hopkins is an immersion in inscape, a thorough and glorious apprenticeship in sensing the invisibles and inaudibles that give cohesion and wholeness to everything that we see and hear and taste, not just its superficial appearance but the inner core of individuality." See Eugene Peterson, *Practice Resurrection, A Conversation on Growing Up in Christ* (Grand Rapids, Eerdmans, 2013), 19, 139–140. To be sure, Heschel is here talking about what he calls "the ineffable" but also how it is accessed by way of immediate and personal insight.

32 David L. Schindler, "Living and Thinking Reality in Its Integrity: Originary Experience, God, and the Task of Education," *Communio* 37 (2010). This dimension of metanoia is by no means limited to the realms of religion; it occurs in all arenas of human knowledge. In

fact, there is a whole discipline of study dedicated to what is called "the eureka effect" or simply insight studies. See https://en.wikipedia.org/wiki/Eureka_effect (accessed February 28, 2023). Philosopher Martin Buber notes that "undergirding every scientific discovery is some moment of intuition or confrontation. Therefore, all essential knowledge begins with an I-Thou encounter, and is contained in an enduring concept." Martin Buber, "Replies to My Critics," in *The Philosophy of Martin Buber: The Library of Living Philosophers* (La Salle: Open Court, 1967), 692. Likewise, physicist Alan Lightman sees this as the critical dimension in the psychology of creative breakthroughs in art and science in his book *A Sense of the Mysterious: Science and the Human Spirit* (New York: Pantheon, 2005).

3 Why We Need to Repent

1   E. F. Schumacher, *A Guide for the Perplexed* (London: Abacus, 1978), 9–11.
2   See *The Forgotten Ways*, preface to second edition, and pages 1–73, as well as Hirsch and Ferguson, *On The Verge*, chapters one to three, for why paradigmatic change is fundamental.
3   Statistics from Protestant churches in The Netherlands and Great Britain, for instance, bear this out. See Hirsch, *The Forgotten Ways*, 174–6.
4   H. Richard Niebuhr, *The Responsibility of the Church for Society and Other Essays*, ed. Kristine A. Culp (Louisville: Westminster John Knox Press, 2008), 74–5. See also the papal encyclical, "Memory and Reconciliation: The Church and the Faults of the Past," December 1999, which deals brilliantly with the topic, https://www.vatican.va/roman_curia/congregations/cfaith/cti_documents/rc_con_cfaith_doc_20000307_memory-reconc-itc_en.html.
5   e.g., Ez 14:6; Zec 1:3; Mt 23:29–39; Mk 1:15, 4. Metanoia is absolutely necessary for what Norman Todd calls "godly organization"—a group determined to be ordered to God's will and intentions. Norman Todd, "Metanoia and Transformation: Godly Organization with Servant Leaders," http://www.modemuk.org/wp-content/uploads/2016/09/Metanoia-Part-2.pdf (accessed February 28, 2023).
6   It is interesting to note that what became known as The Confessing Church was the faithful response of German speakers to the decidedly nationalistic German Church. The word *confessing* here should not be lost, in that it involved confessing of sins and not just of statements of theology.
7   Prophetic ministry throughout human history would not make any sense if collective repentance and turning were not required by God. One of the signature terms of the prophet is "repent" for the kairos is upon us (as Jesus says in Mt 4:17). On the issue of the German church, Dietrich Bonhoeffer's work in calling it to account for the sins of racism and hatred is well documented. He was martyred for his effort.
8   One of the most remarkable examples of collective repentance and metanoia has emerged from the very churches that were complicit in apartheid. It's called the Confession of Belhar and can be read here: https://www.pcusa.org/site_media/media/uploads/theologyandworship/pdfs/belhar.pdf (accessed February 28, 2023).
9   Reinhold Niebuhr did a trenchant study on the nature of collective sins in his classic book *Moral Man and Immoral Society: A Study in Ethics and Politics* (Westminster: John Knox Press, 2012).
10 Ex 19:6; Lv 21:8; 1 Thes 4:7; 1 Pt 1:16.

11 David Liptay, *Beauty And/As Theology: The Theological Aesthetics of Hans Urs von Balthasar* (PhD diss., Syracuse University, 2010), 16.

12 Hirsch and Nelson, *Reframation*, 10.

13 "Images I must suppose, have their use or they would not have been so popular. (It makes little difference whether they are pictures and statues outside the mind or imaginative constructions within it.) To me their danger is more obvious. Images of the Holy easily become holy images—sacrosanct. My idea of God is not a divine idea. It has to be shattered time after time. He shatters it Himself. He is the great iconoclast. Could we not almost say that this shattering is one of the marks of His presence? The Incarnation is the supreme example; it leaves all previous ideas of the Messiah in ruins. And most are 'offended' by the iconoclasm; and blessed are those who are not. But the same thing happens in our private prayers. All reality is iconoclastic." C. S. Lewis, *A Grief Observed* (New York: Faber & Faber, 2015), 76–7.

14 In *Reframation*, we make the claim that all our problems are the result of reductionisms in our understanding of God, people, gospel, and mission. Reductionism happens when we take big ideas and reduce them down to containable god-in-a-box type formulas. This effectively fragments our knowledge of God and the things of God by breaking them down and reducing them to suit a limited human rationality. In fact, this is exactly what the New Testament labels as "heresy"; to grasp a fragment of truth and then make the claim that the fragment we have laid claim to is the *only* truth or the *whole* truth. Reductionism is problematic in any field of knowledge, but it is particularly problematic when it comes to the knowledge of the transcendent God. Hirsch and Nelson, *Reframation*, chapters one to three.

15 Quoted in Upton Sinclair, "I, Candidate for Governor and How I Got Licked," *Oakland Tribune*, December 11, 1934, page 19, column 3.

16 It is worth noting here that none less than Machiavelli commented that, "There is nothing more difficult and dangerous, or more doubtful of success, than an attempt to introduce a new order of things. For the innovator has for enemies all those who derived advantages from the old order of things, whilst those who expect to be benefited by the new institutions will be but lukewarm defenders. This indifference arises in part from fear of their adversaries who were favored by the existing laws, and partly from the incredulity of men who have no faith in anything new that is not the result of well-established experience. Hence it is that, whenever the opponents of the new order of things have the opportunity to attack it, they will do it with the zeal of partisans, whilst the others defend it but feebly, so that it is dangerous to rely upon the latter." Niccolò Machiavelli, *The Prince* (Random House, 2012), Kindle edition, Kindle locations 1026–31.

17 Von Balthasar, *Razing the Bastions: On the Church in this Age* (San Francisco: Ignatius Press, 1993), 38.

18 Lesslie Newbigin, *The Open Secret: An Introduction to the Theology of Mission* (Grand Rapids: Eerdmans Publishing Company, 1995), 110, 113, 150.

19 G. K. Chesterton, *Manalive* (Merchant Books, 2019), 19.

20 Richard Rohr, *Falling Upward: A Spirituality for the Two Halves of Life* (San Francisco: Jossey Bass, 2011), 37, italics ours.

21 Canadian philosopher Marshall McLuhan noted well how (and why) our organizations and our tools can captivate and blind us to their effects. McLuhan saw that technology and media

induce a "peculiar form of self-hypnosis" whereby people remain as unaware of the psychic and social effects of their new technology as a fish of the water it swims in. It is precisely at the point where a new media-induced environment becomes all pervasive that it also becomes invisible. For instance, notice how blind we now are to the ubiquitous presence of the internet. We assume its rightness even though it is a relatively new technology. It touches every aspect of our lives now without our even realizing it. See "Marshall McLuhan Explains Why We're Blind to How Technology Changes Us, Raising the Question: What Have the Internet & Social Media Done to Us?" *Open Culture,* August 8, 2007, https://www.openculture.com/2017/08/marshall-mcluhan-explains-why-were-blind-to-how-technology-changes-us.html.

22 Peter F. Drucker, "Drucker on Management: A Turnaround Primer," *The Wall Street Journal,* November 18, 2009, https://www.wsj.com/articles/SB10001424052748704204304574544302267861062.

23 I [Alan] have learned much about Catholic understandings of tradition and the role of the magisterium from dialogues with my friend and colleague, Catholic missiologist Fr. James Mallon. He notes that Catholics recognize a distinction between what they call "Sacred Tradition" and mere "traditions" (small t versus capital T). In Catholic thought especially, it's the capital "T" tradition that has authority in helping us interpret Scripture, not small "t" traditions. It's a fixation on small "t" traditions that give us traditionalism. In Roman Catholic understanding, "the magisterium" (from magister or "teacher") means the teaching office or function of the church. It serves Scripture and Tradition. Capital "T" tradition is not so much a collective canon but represents the historic memory of the church that includes the great theologians from the Apostolic and Post-Apostolic Age, as well as the church fathers, writings of the various saints and mystics over time—exactly what you get when you have babies and pass on the memory of how things have been believed and lived out in the past, a kind of living memory.

24 In fact, at its worst, traditionalism is associated with what the New Testament calls the *stoicheaia* ... the elemental spirits/principles that are part of the fallen power and principalities (Col 2:16–23; Gal 4:3). Traditionalism, precisely because it is an *-ism*, can be oppressive; we need only read the Gospels for evidence of that. Leaders know how resistant the church itself can become to the mission of God and what an impediment that is to the advancement of the gospel.

25 Seth Godin, "Tried and False," *Seth's Blog,* June 2, 2013, https://seths.blog/2013/06/tried-and-false/.

26 The MRS GREN acronym, for instance, is often used to help remember all the necessary features of living organisms: Movement, Respiration, Sensitivity, Growth, Reproduction, Excretion and Nutrition. Likewise, humans, and by extension human organizations, require all seven functions, including excretion, to be fully functional. See for instance, "MRS GREN," *Basic Biology,* https://basicbiology.net/biology-101/mrs-gren (accessed February 28, 2023).

27 And we ought not to be so shocked in using the term "crap" to refer to religious traditions: Paul references the same term (σκύβαλον—refuse, dregs, excrement, rubbish) when he says in Phil 3:8 that he considers all things as excrement in order that he may gain Christ.

28 Charles Taylor, *Modern Social Imaginaries* (Durham: Duke University Press, 2004); and *A Secular Age* (Cambridge, Massachusetts: Harvard University Press, 2007).

29 We don't think about these maps or decide if we want to use them; they become so much a part of our ingrained way of relating to the world in families, churches, and societies that we assume our internal understanding and practices of how the world works is precisely how the world works. Alan J. Roxburgh, *Missional Map Making: Skills for Leading in a Time of Transition* (San Francisco: Jossey Bass, 2010), xi–xii.

30 Peter M. Senge, *The Fifth Discipline: The Art and Practice of the Learning Organization: First Edition* (New York: Crown, 2006), 13–14.

31 Leonard Hjalmarson, *Introduction to a Missional Spirituality* (Leonard Hjalmarson, 2014), 11. Leonard quotes Leonard Sweet in saying that metaphors function in a similar way, as a kind of map, "When the root metaphors change, so does everything else."

32 Think about how the parish model in Britain was designed for people who were born, raised, and lived their whole lives in a certain region. There was a church assigned to that parish by decree of parliament. Now those lines don't exist, as everyone comes from everywhere and goes everywhere. And yet the Church of England adheres to these now very arbitrary mental boundaries to its great detriment. The parish system has been rightly called the condom of the Anglican church. Another example, as we have already noted, is that most seminaries train people for a role that no longer exists.

33 Adam Grant, *Think Again: The Power of Knowing What You Don't Know* (New York: Viking, 2021), 4.

34 See Hirsch and Frost, *ReJesus*.

35 Hirsch, *5Q*, xxiii.

36 Fritjof Capra, *The Web of Life: A New Synthesis of Mind and Matter* (London: Harper Collins, 1996).

37 Quoted in Morris Berman, *The Reenchantment of the World* (New York: Bantam Books, 1984), 101.

38 The quantum physicist Max Planck eulogizes childlike thinking in contributing to advances in science: "The feeling of wonderment is the source and inexhaustible fountainhead of [the child's] desire for knowledge. It drives the child irresistibly on to solve the mystery, and if in his attempt he encounters a causal relationship, he will not tire of repeating the same experiment ten times, a hundred times, in order to taste the thrill of discovery over and over again. The reason why the adult no longer wonders is not because he has solved the riddle of life, but because he has grown accustomed to the laws governing his world picture ... He who does not comprehend this situation, misconstrues its profound significance, and he who has reached the stage where he no longer wonders about anything, merely demonstrates that he has lost the art of reflective reasoning." Max Planck, *Scientific Autobiography* (New York: Citadel, 1949), 91–3. The nifty term "adultish" is used by author and friend Mandy Smith.

39 We recommend Mandy Smith's wonderful book *Unfettered: Imagining a Childlike Faith beyond the Baggage of Western Culture* (Downers Grove, IL: IVP, 2021) for an exploration of what it means to recover childlikeness in an overly-adultish church.

40 Ernst Käsemann, *The Testament of Jesus: A Study of the Gospel of John in the Light of Chapter 17* (Portland: Wipf & Stock, 2017), xii. Philosopher Martin Heidegger agrees: "We can learn only if we always unlearn at the same time ... we can learn thinking only if we radically unlearn what thinking has been traditionally." *Basic Writings: Martin Heidegger* (Krell: 2008), 374.

41 Barry O'Reilly, *Unlearn: Let Go of Past Success to Achieve Extraordinary Results* (New York: McGraw Hill, 2018), 3.

42 Grant, *Think Again*, 3.

43 Alvin Toffler, *Future Shock* (New York: Bantam, 1970), 211.

44 Susanne K. Langer, *Philosophy in a New Key: A Study in the Symbolism of Reason, Rite, and Art* (Boston: Harvard University Press, 1957), 5.

45 For instance, applied to the area of theology we can say that the task of theology is to read the Figure of Christ. "This means that theology can only perform its task by circular repetitions of that which is ever greater … He [Christ] is the perfect whole, and without him theology loses its necessary unity. He is the cornerstone of the whole theological edifice, being the holistic norm for theology. He is this to a degree we are not perhaps prepared to notice or admit." Bede McGregor and Thomas Norris (eds), *The Beauty of Christ: An Introduction to the Theology of Hans Urs von Balthasar* (Edinburgh: T&T Clark, 1994), 216–7.

46 O'Reilly, *Unlearn*.

47 "The assumption from now on has to be that individuals on their own will have to find, determine, and develop a number of 'careers' during their working lives." Peter F. Drucker, *Innovation and Entrepreneurship: Practice and Principles* (New York: Harper and Collins, 2009), 264.

48 Hirsch and Nelson, *Reframation*, 110.

49 Jack Gilbert, "Tear It Down," https://poets.org/poem/tear-it-down(accessed February 28, 2023).

ч Christo-Logic

1 John Howard Griffin, *Black Like Me, Third Edition* (Wings Press, 2011), preface.

2 Ibid., 69.

3 Sacramentality involves the ability to experience events with what Richard Kearney calls a "micro-eschatology" and "epiphanies of the everyday." He writes, "What if we were to return to epiphanies of the everyday? What if we could come back to the end in the here and now? … What if we could rediscover ourselves again face-to-face with the infinite in the infinitesimal? Touch the sacred enfolded in the seeds of ordinary things? Such a return would invite us to experience the ultimate in the mundane. The first in the last. The most in the least. It would bring us into dialogue with those who seek the divine in the pause between two breaths. Transcendence in a thornbush. The Eucharist in a morsel of madeleine. The Kingdom in a cup of cold water. San Marco in a cobblestone. God in a street cry." Richard Kearney, "Epiphanies of the Everyday: Toward a Micro-Eschatology," in John Panteleimon Manoussakis, *After God: Richard Kearney and the Religious Turn in Continental Philosophy, Perspectives in continental philosophy, no. 49* (New York: Fordham University Press, 1996), 3.

4 James E. Loder and Jim W. Neidhardt, *The Knight's Move: The Relational Logic of the Spirit in Theology and Science* (Colorado Springs: Helmers & Howard, 1992), quoted in Devenish, *The Mind of Christ*, 323.

5 Christmas Preface of the Gregorian Sacramentary.

6 Note the combination of re/turn and paradigm shift that together form the biblical basis of metanoia here. See McGrath, *Re-Imagining Nature*, 51. Likewise, John Calvin pointed to

the double derivation of the Hebrew and Greek words for "repentance": the Hebrew derives from conversion, or turning again, and the Greek means a change of mind and purpose. The meaning of the word, for Calvin, is appropriate to both derivations because repentance a) involves "withdrawing from ourselves," b) turning to God, c) "laying aside the old," and d) putting on "a new mind." John Calvin, *Institutes of the Christian Religion 3* (Grand Rapids: Eerdmans, 1995), 1–16. Loder and Neidhardt describe the mind of Christ as being endowed by the Holy Spirit, and, far from being something which is other-worldly and unrelated to a real assessment of this world, enables the religious actor to "behold this world as if for the first time" because it is knowing the world through the Logos, or the creative and redemptive personage of Christ. Calvin spoke of this vision as being imbibed from the Christian Scriptures in terms of the reception of "spectacles" which disclose the "pure knowledge of God." Loder and Neidhardt, *The Knight's Move*, quoted in Devenish, *The Mind of Christ*, 323.

7   Von Balthasar, *Prayer*, 270.
8   "Poor fool—he thought his mind was his own. Never his own until he makes it Christ's; up till then, merely a result of heredity, environment, and the state of his digestion. I became my own only when I gave myself to Another." C. S. Lewis, in *Letters of C. S. Lewis* (July 17, 1953), para. 2, 251.
9   Von Balthasar, *Prayer*, 71–3.
10 Devenish, *The Mind of Christ*, 62–3.
11 Von Balthasar, *Prayer*, 131. On the role of the Spirit in the knowledge of God we can say that if Jesus is the One who interprets God and makes him known in the world (John 1:18), then it is the purpose of indwelling Spirit to interpret Jesus to us—Spirit to spirit. Jesus himself said as much: "[The Spirit] will guide you into all truth ... it is from me that he will receive what he will make known to you" (Jn 16:13–14). "[T]he Holy Spirit can be recognized at work in a person by establishing in him the mind of Jesus and forming Christ in us. We have received this Spirit, that we might understand the gifts bestowed on us by God" (1 Cor 2:11f). Thus, access to this Jesus-Logic is a work of the Spirit of Christ in us who makes Jesus personal to us. Without the Spirit, the picture our spirit makes of Jesus is pale and flat, unable to embrace the tensions in which Jesus reveals the unity of God's innermost mind. This is sufficiently proved by the innumerable pictures of Jesus, drawn after the artist's own liking; pictures of a mild, dull Savior whose "solidarity" with the poor, oppressed, and sinners no longer glows red hot, and where nothing divine shines through. Paul dismisses all such "human, all-too-human" pictures painted "according to the flesh." Hans Urs von Balthasar, *Does Jesus Know Us? Do We Know Him?* (San Francisco: Ignatius Press, 1983), 34.
12 Von Balthasar, *Prayer*, 131.
13 Von Balthasar notes that, through the work of the Spirit in the believer, "[T]he whole profundity of God's truth is present, open and available to us ... however, the Spirit introduces believers to it progressively, by declaring and interpreting to them the revelation of the Word in Jesus, and incorporating them into it (Jn 16:13 f). The Spirit, who alone knows the 'hidden things of God', who 'searches everything, even the depths of God', has in principle opened up these depths to the 'spiritual', to 'those who possess the Spirit', who 'have the mind of Christ' ... The word of God, and all it involves, operates 'from Spirit to spirit'. The Holy Spirit of the prophets and the Incarnation carries the Father's word to us,

and the same Holy Spirit interprets it in a divine and spiritual sense in their souls, leading the human spirit back to the Father by means of God's word." Von Balthasar, *Prayer*, 71–73.

14 Jean Daniélou, *God and the Ways of Knowing* (San Francisco: Ignatius, 1957), 174–5. Paul employs the strongest image for this impressing of the knowledge of Jesus into the heart of the believer: he compares it to the original creation of light out of darkness: "For it is the God who said, 'Let light shine out of darkness,' who has shone in our hearts to give the light of the knowledge of the glory of God in the face of Christ" (2 Cor 4:6).

15 Hans Urs von Balthasar, *Spirit and Institution: Explorations in Theology, IV* (San Francisco: Ignatius Press, 1995), 443.

16 "Christ is the primary pattern of Christianity: in his face the glory of God shines and from there radiates into the heart of Christians (2 Corinthians 4:6) ... He is the one and only exposition of God (John 1:18), infinitely rich and of a paradoxical simplicity that integrates all the elements. He is absolute sovereignty and absolute humility; he is infinitely approachable who can be reached by everyone and infinitely inaccessible, ever beyond reach." Bede McGregor and Thomas Norris, *The Beauty of Christ*, 216.

17 To understand what Christoformity means, however, we need to understand this seemingly strange term "the form of Christ," and to do this, we need to in turn understand the term "form," upon which it is built. Essentially the form of something is the overall pattern, the design, a complete representation of a phenomenon that presents itself to us. The form is the figure, shape, or configuration of something; the particular way in which a thing exists or appears; its aesthetic impact. In German the word for form is *gestalt*, which in general psychology has come to mean the organized whole that is seen as more than the sum of its parts. This is important because it is the form that enables us to make sense of what we are seeing because it is knowing the whole that enables us to make sense of the parts. For instance, if someone showed you an apple core, you could, on the basis of your understanding of the total form of apples, "reconstruct" what the original apple might have looked like. This is because you know the form/pattern of apples. Similarly, this works with different styles of music. For instance, blues has a certain pattern that repeats itself throughout all forms of blues music. We can sense the genre by hearing a few chords—sensing its signature. Rock is the same, as is Celtic, Indian, African, and all other forms of music styles. Or, think about the competitions on music radio, where the listener has to recognize a song from a three-second sample of its chorus. So if we said "another brick in the wall" or hummed the famous Pink Floyd tune, you would no doubt recognize the entire song from just that line. Likewise, a doctor can recognize a disease by comparing it to the total pattern of health by which it is measured and assessed. It is by seeing the whole that we can make sense of the parts that we see.

18 "In the one Person of Christ, the individual's election, calling and justification become equally personal; the grace offered and communicated to him by the Father has a unique quality which arises from the Son's uniqueness and bears its mark; it is equally divine and supernatural as it is human and natural (because it comes from the grace of the God-Man, is permeated by it and is given in view of it). On the one hand it is made to man's measure, and on the other hand it has *per se* a Son-like and hence Word-like form. We say 'form' [Gestalt] in the absence of a better word to designate this mysterious reality, which is both the ideal archetype of redeemed and believing man in Christ and his own, authentic reality as the Father sees and judges him from now on, a reality according

to which, as a believer, he is challenged to live. In faith he enters into his 'christoform self'; Paul calls this 'putting on Christ' (Rom 13:14; Gal 3:27), 'putting on the new nature' (Eph 4:24; Col 3:10), 'Put on then, as God's chosen ones, holy and beloved, compassion, kindness, lowliness, meekness, and patience … as the Lord has forgiven you, so you also must forgive … And let the peace of Christ rule in your hearts, to which indeed you were called in the one body … Let the word of Christ dwell in you richly' (Col 3:12–16)." Von Balthasar, *Prayer*, 59.

19 In a video by N. T. Wright on what he would want to say to his children and grandchildren about Jesus. See "Look at Jesus featuring NT Wright," *The Work of the People*, https://www.theworkofthepeople.com/look-at-jesus (accessed February 28, 2023).

20 Søren Kierkegaard, *Journals*, November 26, 1834, quoted in David Gouwens, *Kierkegaard as Religious Thinker* (Cambridge: Cambridge University Press, 1996), 173.

21 Blaise Pascal, *Thoughts on Religion and Philosophy* (Glasgow: William Collins, 1838), 219.

22 Bonhoeffer understood this and called the church "the form of Christ in the world." The body/embodiment of Christ is meant to resonate with exemplary Christlikeness for the world to see what God is like. "The Church is nothing but a section of humanity in which Christ has truly taken form." See also John A. Phillips, *The Form of Christ in the World: A Study of Bonhoeffer's Christology* (London: Collins, 1967) and J. A. Woelfel, *Bonhoeffer's Theology: Classical and Revolutionary* (Nashville: Abingdon, 1970), 254.

23 Dietrich Bonhoeffer, *The Cost of Discipleship* (New York: Touchstone, 1995), 59, italics ours.

24 If a group claiming to be a *Christ*ian church fails to look/act/sound/think like Jesus, their Founder and Archetype, then we can only conclude that either it was a church sometime in the past and that it has the cultural forms of being a church but is on its way out, or that it's on its way to becoming a church, but in its current form, is not actually the body of Christ. How else will we recognize the authentic church? What other measure for the church do we have other than Jesus?

25 "In other words, all the events and turning points that together constitute Jesus' earthly ministry become, through the Holy Spirit, the dynamic framework within which every human life can come to fulfillment. It is not that the historical shape of the Incarnation is lost, in von Balthasar's view, by its ongoing inclusion of the redeemed, but rather the shape it attains through Jesus' historical ministry is the very pattern into which Christ's people come to participate." Mark A. McIntosh, *The Doctrine of the Incarnation in Hans Urs von Balthasar* (PhD diss., University of Chicago, 1993), 264.

26 In thinking through the mind of Christ, "the structure of human thought remains the same, but the stand-point of the whole person's being—from which one thinks, wills, and perceives—has been changed … The effects on the sphere of consciousness are indirect and successive, corresponding to the readiness with which the free person assents to this new inclination which has been bestowed upon him and made available to him, the readiness with which he allows this inclination to take root in him and permits it to have its effects on the clearly perceived and psychologically graspable personal sphere. Thus, no sharp line can be drawn where the infused virtues with their vital centre in caritas, begin to unfold consciously as the 'gifts of the Holy Spirit'. Ontologically, these gifts are already contained in the gift of grace itself and in the new inclination and readiness that are bestowed with it. But it is up to the believer and the lover to allow this inclination to gain an ever increasing ascendancy in his life of faith … The love which is infused in man by the Holy Spirit present

within him bestows on man the sensorium with which to perceive God, bestows also the taste for God and, so to speak, an understanding for God's own taste." Hans Urs von Balthasar, *The Glory of the Lord, A Theological Aesthetics, I: Seeing the Form* (Edinburgh: T & T Clark, 1982), 241–2.

27 "Since, then, you have been raised with Christ, set your hearts on things above, where Christ is, seated at the right hand of God. Set your minds on things above, not on earthly things. For you died, and your life is now hidden with Christ in God. When Christ, who is your life, appears, then you also will appear with him in glory" (Col 3:1–4). In his commentary on Colossians 3:2, Christopher Seitz notes that the term *zēteite* in 3:1 means "to seek," or "set your hearts on" is chosen to capture the sense of "orient yourself according to" and to parallel *phroneō* in 3:2, which is rendered as "set your minds on." The command is to "seek instead things above where Christ is." Paul is therefore saying that we must operate in this world with our attention firmly focussed on Christ at the right hand of God (cf. Rom 8:5; Phil 3:19). *Colossians: Brazos Theological Commentary on the Bible* (Grand Rapids: Brazos, 2014).

28 Stuart Devenish, *Seeing and Believing: The Eye of Faith in a Visual Culture* (Eugene: Wipf & Stock, 2012), 110–11.

29 The presence of the Spirit constantly "lifts" the individual believer into conformity with the mind of God. "Faith, the foundation of all our understanding of revelation, expands our created minds by making them participate in the mind of God, disclosing the inward divine meaning of the words through a kind of coworking with God; for this reason it is the saint, the person most open to the working of the Spirit, who arrives at the closest understanding. He will not do what the ordinary man, so dominated by original sin, does almost unawares, yet with such desperate persistence: confine the meaning of God's word within human bounds, admitting its truth only to the extent that it corresponds to human forms of thought and ways of life." Hans Urs von Balthasar, *Explorations in Theology, I: The Word, Scripture and Tradition* (San Francisco: Ignatius Press, 1989), 21.

30 Quoted by Steve Hawthorne in "Perspectives," *Mission Frontiers*, May 1, 2009, https://www.missionfrontiers.org/issue/article/perspectives.

31 Dante, *The Divine Comedy*, Canto xxxiii.

32 Quoted in Hans Urs von Balthasar, *The Glory of the Lord: A Theological Aesthetics, IV* (San Francisco: Ignatius Press, 1989), 394.

33 Even in the final heavenly state, where we will all possess the beatific vision, we will never fully comprehend God. In fact, the more we think we have grasped God, the more we realize that we have not grasped him—God is always the "ever greater" and cannot be fully grasped by the human mind. The Fourth Lateran Council in 1215 AD maintained that God's immanence and knowability is always qualified by an ever-greater transcendence and unknowability: It acknowledged an "ever-greater dissimilarity however great the similarity," which in effect teaches that between Creator and creature there can be noted no similarity so great that a greater dissimilarity cannot be seen between them.

34 Gregory of Nyssa, "The Life of Moses," quoted in Donald Haggerty, *Contemplative Provocations* (San Francisco: Ignatius Press, 2013), 19.

35 Eternity is to be understood as the proper horizon for those who have a thirst for the infinite. This is what poet-scientist Maria Popova means when she confesses her love of the mathematical calculus behind the concept of pi (π). For her, pi functions as both an anchor of

reality and a counterpoint to certainty. For her, pi provides a reminder that despite the rigor and devotion with which we may attempt to map reality, our maps remain what they are; incomplete, representational models that always leave more to map, more to fathom. And this, she suggests, should not surprise us because the same forces that made the universe also made the mind—what she calls the "figuring instrument"—with which we try to figure it all out. Maria Popova, "An Ode to the Number Pi by Nobel-Winning Polish Poet Wisława Szymborska," *Brain Pickings*, October 23, 2017, https://www.brainpickings.org/2017/10/23/wislawa-szymborska-pi/.

36 Simon Sinek, *The Infinite Game* (New York: Penguin, 2019), 8.

37 Ibid., 8–9.

38 Confirmation bias, also known as "myside bias," is the tendency to search for, interpret, favor, and recall information in a way that confirms or supports your prior beliefs or values. People display this bias when they select information that supports their views, ignoring contrary information, or when they interpret ambiguous evidence as supporting their existing attitudes. The effect is strongest for people who desire certain predetermined outcomes, in emotionally charged issues, and for those with deeply entrenched beliefs. Confirmation bias cannot be eliminated entirely, but it can be managed, for example, by education and training in critical thinking skills. See Raymond S. Nickerson, "Confirmation bias: A ubiquitous phenomenon in many guises," *Review of General Psychology*, 2 (1998): 175–220. A "self-sealing argument" likewise is an argument that is unfalsifiable in that it is set up in such a way that it is impossible to contradict or refute, so that no counter-arguments or evidence could possibly be used against it.

39 Nobody wants to admit to themselves that they're closed-minded, especially in relation to God, and particularly those closed-minded people who have developed a powerful religious rationale for their close-mindedness. God has always struggled with spiritual blindness in his people (e.g., Mk 8:18). In addition to asserting that most people think only once in their lives, usually when they are at college, Heschel notes that "After that their minds are made up, and their decisions, utterances are endless repetitions of views that have in the meantime become obsolete, outworn, unsound. This applies to politics, scholarship, the arts as well as to social service. Views, just as leaves, are bound to wither, because the world is in flux. But so many of us would rather be faithful to outworn views than to undergo the strain of re-examination and revision. Indeed, intellectual senility sets in long before physical infirmity. A human being can be assessed by how many times he was able to see the world from a new perspective [i.e., metanoia]." This is sadly very true. Abraham Heschel, *Moral Grandeur and Spiritual Audacity: Essays by Abraham Joshua Heschel* (New York: Farrar, Straus, Giroux, 1996), 53.

40 And as we have seen, closed-loop thinking is particularly problematic when it comes to God's people. According to Paul in 2 Cor 3, it led to the veiling/narrowing/closing of the Jewish mind when it came to recognizing what God was up to in the person of Jesus—who was the fulfilment of the messianic pattern.

41 N. T. Wright, *Acts for Everyone, Part 2* (London: Westminster, 2008), 137–8.

42 Lewis, *Mere Christianity*, 102.

43 Heresy/reductionism is clearly problematic in all arenas of human knowledge, but it is *particularly* problematic when it comes to the knowledge of the ever-greater, always transcendent God; the mystery of our own human natures; the incomprehensible grace of God in

the gospel; or the nature and purposes of the church—these are the things that are mysteries even to the angels and into which they themselves long to look (see 1 Pt 1:12).

44 Hans Urs von Balthasar, *Truth Is Symphonic: Aspects of Christian Pluralism* (San Francisco: Ignatius Press, 1987).

45 See Hirsch, *5Q*, chapter one. See von Balthasar, *Truth is Symphonic* and Daniel H. Pink, *A Whole New Mind: Why Right Brainers Will Rule the Future* (New York: Riverhead, 2005).

46 Hirsch and Nelson, *Reframation*, 135.

47 An understanding of spiritual instincts is further strengthened by adding the church's understanding of the *anima ecclesiastica,* which is the collective genius in the communion of saints.

48 For instance, Augustine extrapolated from these biblical teachings the idea of Christ as "the Inner Teacher." He understood this to be a manifestation of the indwelling truth of God, which illuminates the believer from the inside out. He suggested that the Inner Teacher is the presence of Christ in our inner being that guides the learner/disciple in their growth into maturity and Christlikeness. We can and must learn from, respond to, and actively rely on this presence. The Quakers chose to call this "the inner light," made available through the indwelling presence of God in the life of the believer. It is this mutual indwelling, this inner communion, that enables some form of ongoing internal dialogue with Jesus as our guide and teacher. (See Von Balthasar, *Prayer,* 63.) This in turn means that "prayer and worship are indispensable to the inner act of reason" because there is no other way in which we could sense and respond to this Inner Teacher or make sense of what he is saying. In describing this form of knowledge of God—and the role of prayer and reverence in accessing what he calls "the ineffable"—Heschel says, "It is not in a roundabout way, by analogy or inference, that we become aware of the ineffable; we do not think about it in absentia. It is rather sensed as something immediately given by way of an insight that is unending and underivable, logically and psychologically prior to judgment, to the assimilation of subject matter to mental categories; a universal insight into an objective aspect of reality, of which all men are at all times capable; not the froth of ignorance but the climax of thought, indigenous to the climate that prevails at the summit of intellectual endeavor, where such works as the last quartets of Beethoven come into being. It is a cognitive insight, since the awareness it evokes is a definite addition to the mind." Abraham Heschel, *Man is Not Alone,* 29. For an exploration of Augustinian epistemology and the idea of the Inner Teacher, see the article by Tapio Puolimatka, "Augustine and education in critical thinking," *Journal of Beliefs & Values,* Studies in Religion & Education, Volume 26, 2005, Issue 2, https://www.tandfonline.com/doi/figure/10.1080/13617670500164924?scroll=top&needAccess=true&role=tab.

49 Pearce reports experiencing this exact scenario. His instinctive "body-knowing" took over. Pearce, *The Crack in the Cosmic Egg,* 65.

50 Malcolm Gladwell, *Blink: The Power of Thinking Without Thinking* (New York: Penguin, 2006). Daniel Kahneman, *Thinking, Fast and Slow* (New York: Farrah, Straus and Giroux, 2015). For the idea of religious instinct, see Luigi Giussani, *The Religious Sense* (Toronto: McGill-Queen's University Press, 1997).

51 Seth Godin, "Intuition," *Seth's Blog,* February 26, 2016, https://seths.blog/2016/02/intuition/.

52 "It makes a great difference to the act of contemplation whether I see myself as an isolated subject, who, albeit assisted by God's grace, endeavors to understand something of the mysteries of revelation; or whether, in faith, I have the conviction that my inadequate attempt

to understand is supported by the wisdom of the Holy Spirit dwelling within me, that my acts of worship, petition and thanksgiving are borne along and remodeled by the Spirit's infinite and eternal acts, in that ineffable union by which all human doing and being has been lifted up and plunged into the river of eternal life and love." Von Balthasar, *Prayer*, 76.

53 Spiritual instinct is also an important aspect of APEST, which is part of the latent intelligences and capacities inherent in the body of Christ. See Hirsch, *5Q*. Perhaps another way of thinking about this body-instinct is through the traditional teaching of *anima ecclesiastica* (the soul of the church), which is understood as a dimension of the so-called communion of saints. I (Alan) and my colleagues have worked very hard to help the church understand the sheer power of APEST and have assessments, training, and coaching available globally. See https://www.5qcentral.com.

54 Karl Barth, *Church Dogmatics: The Doctrine of the Word of God, I, Part 2* (Edinburgh: T & T Clark, 1963), 696; and Markus Barth, *Ephesians: The Anchor Bible Translation and Commentary on Chapters 4–6, Vol. 2* (New York: Doubleday, 1974), 434.

55 Another example is what I (Alan) call "latent potential" in my book *The Forgotten Ways*. The name of the book itself says it all: the potential for transformative Jesus movement *always* lies "latent" in all genuine expressions of discipleship (individual and collective) and that, given the right conditions, they can be activated. In other words, I believe that apostolic movements are our most instinctive and primal (and by far and away the most transformative) forms of *ecclesia*. This latency accounts, for example, for the fact that even though separated by thousands of years as well as by radically different cultures and worldviews, the phenomenology of the Chinese underground church movement is precisely the same as that of the early post-apostolic church movement.

56 Devenish, *Seeing and Believing*, 24–5.

57 See Hirsch and Nelson *Reframation*, chapters nine to ten, for an extended exploration of the missional implications of the prevenient/preparatory evangelistic work of God in the world.

58 Von Balthasar, *Prayer*, 76.

5 Wholehearted Metanoia

1 Adam Ellwanger, *Metanoia, Rhetoric, Authenticity, and the Transformation of the Self* (University Park: Pennsylvania University Press, 2020), 1.

2 See Hirsch, *The Forgotten Ways*, chapter nine for a thorough socio-theological exploration of the process of institutionalization and a comparison with a more movemental understanding of the church.

3 See T. Sorg, "Heart/Kardia" in Colin Brown (ed.) *The Dictionary of New Testament Theology, Vol. 2* (Grand Rapids: Regency, 1976), 180–184. See also "Kardia" in the *Theological Dictionary of the New Testament* (TDNT), https://ref.ly/o/tdnt/16423375?length=775 (accessed February 28, 2023); and various articles and commentaries of biblical scholars but most notably Paul S. Minear's excellent overview, *A Theology of the Heart*, which is available at http://pmoser.sites.luc.edu/paulsmineararchive/MinearTheologyHeart.pdf (accessed February 28, 2023). The TDNT says, "The NT use of the word καρδία (*kardia*) agrees with the OT use as distinct from the Greek. Even more strongly than the LXX it concentrates on the heart as the main organ of psychic and spiritual life, the place in man at which God bears witness to Himself.

1. The thought of the heart as the central organ of the body and the seat of physical vitality is found only in Lk. 21:34 and the select poetic expressions of Ac 14:17: ἐμπιπλῶν τροφῆς … τὰς καρδίας ὑμῶν, and Jm. 5:5: ἐθρέψατε τὰς καρδίας ὑμῶν (cf. 1 K. 21:7; ψ 101:5; 103:15).
2. That the heart is the centre of the inner life of man and the source or seat of all the forces and functions of soul and spirit is attested in many different ways in the NT.
   a. In the heart dwell feelings and emotions, desires and passions.
   b. The heart is the seat of understanding, the source of thought and reflection
   c. The heart is the seat of the will, the source of resolutions
   d. Thus the heart is supremely the one centre in man to which God turns, in which the religious life is rooted, which determines moral conduct."

See G. Kittle, et al., *Theological Dictionary of the New Testament, Vol. 3* (Grand Rapids: Eerdmans, 1964), 612, https://ref.ly/o/tdnt/16423375?length=775 (accessed February 28, 2023).

4   Sorg, "Heart/Kardia," in *Dictionary of New Testament Theology, Vol. 2*, 180–184. The heart denotes "the thinking, feeling, willing ego of man, with particular regard to his responsibility to God. We can understand, then, how Paul can describe the heart as being 'without understanding' and recognize also how comprehensive is this description of fallen humanity. At the very center of every person, where the knowledge of God, if it is to have any positive effects, must be embraced, there has settled a darkness—a darkness that only the light of the gospel can penetrate." Douglas J. Moo, *The Epistle to the Romans*, ed. Gordon D. Fee, New International Commentary on the New Testament (Grand Rapids: Eerdmans, 1996), 107.

5   Henri Nouwen sums this all up pretty well when he talks of the heart as that place where body, soul, and spirit come together as one. "In our modern milieu, *heart* has become a soft word. It might refer to just feelings or the seat of the sentimental life. We think of the heart as the warm place where our emotions are located, in contrast to the cool intellect, where our thoughts find their home. But the word *heart* in Jewish-Christian tradition refers to the source of all physical, emotional, intellectual, volitional, and moral energies. It is the seat of the will; it makes plans and comes to good decisions. Thus the heart is the central unifying organ of our personal life. Our heart determines our personality, and the place where God dwells, but also the place to which the Evil One directs fierce attacks, causing us to doubt, fear, despair, resent, overconsume, and so on." Henri J. M. Nouwen, *Spiritual Formation: Following the Movements of the Spirit* (New York: HarperOne, 2015), Kindle edition, Kindle location 158 of 2697.

6   For instance, Paul Minear notes that, "If a person does not love the Lord with all their mind they do not thereby become a pure reason with no loves; they simply love something else with all their heart, soul, strength and mind. One's loves are always deeper than his reason; and reason is always in the employment of some love." Paul S. Minear, *Eyes of Faith: A Study in the Biblical Point of View* (Portland: Wipf & Stock, 2003), 72.

7   Metanoia activates the whole heart by integrating the mind, soul, and will. And it is this wholehearted devotion to something that tends to give power—for good or ill. You don't have to be a social psychologist to see that all ideologies are built on, and in fact require, the religious devotion of their adherents—just look at Trump's sycophants as well as the counter-Trump ones on the far left! Contending political ideologies fueled by fanatical devotion have brought America to what can only be called an "uncivil war." The reality is

that all false gods are jealous and demanding—they demand allegiance, and when given it, can prove themselves "productive" if they can take and "radicalize" the idolater.

8   Quoted in Jacob Immanuel Schochet, *Deep Calling Unto Deep: The Dynamics of Prayer and Teshuvah in the Perspective of Chassidism, The Mystical Dimension, Vol. 2*, (New York, Kehot Publications, 1990), 27.

9   So much so that, in the Bible, the words "heart," "soul," and "will" are sometimes used somewhat interchangeably but highlighting a particular dimension. The phenomenologist Dallas Willard rightly notes that these words point to the same thing, the same fundamental component of the person, but that they do so under different aspects. Dallas Willard, *Renovation of the Heart: Putting on the Character of Christ* (Colorado Springs: NavPress, 2002), 23.

10 Devenish, *The Mind of Christ?*, 89–90.

11 The "heart," as we have seen, is the central organ of the person, something which is not contrasted with the intellect, but which serves as the common foundation, both for the intellect and all other particular faculties. As with the other two dimensions of the heart (the soul and the will), there is no clear boundary between one and the other. They each infuse the other. And so, for instance, the New Testament understands the heart as a place where the most elaborate purposes and schemes are concocted, where complex reasoning takes place, and where critical understanding is required for genuine conversion (Mt 13:15). Paul Minear notes that the idea of a basic conflict between heart and head is entirely unbiblical; it relies on different metaphorical coefficients for both nouns. In fact, on a number of occasions the RSV translators felt compelled to translate *kardia* as "mind" rather than "heart" (Lk 21:14; Rom 1:21; 2 Cor 3:14, 15; 9:7). And this is also why there is no conflict between loving God with the heart and loving God with the mind (e.g., Mt 22:37). Minear, *A Theology of the Heart*, 251.

12 Richard Rohr, "Every Viewpoint Is a View from One Point," *Center for Action and Contemplation*, August 25, 2015, https://cac.org/every-viewpoint-view-one-point-2015-08-25/ (accessed February 28, 2023).

13 This is why Scripture says that to have an evil heart is to be double-minded; and that to purify the heart is to become single-minded (Jas 4:8). "It is in the 'reasonings' of people that this futility has taken place, showing that, whatever their initial knowledge of God might be, their natural capacity to reason accurately about God is quickly and permanently harmed. Parallel to, and descriptive of, this futility in thinking is the darkening of the 'un-understanding heart.' In the NT, 'heart' is broad in its meaning, denoting 'the thinking, feeling, willing ego of man, with particular regard to his responsibility to God. We can understand, then, how Paul can describe the heart as being 'without understanding' and recognize also how comprehensive is this description of fallen humanity. At the very center of every person, where the knowledge of God, if it is to have any positive effects, must be embraced, there has settled a darkness—a darkness that only the light of the gospel can penetrate." Moo, *The Epistle to the Romans*, 107. In the forming of a collective or individual mind, the notion of cognitive dissonance seems to be important. We make complex rationalizations in order to justify our actions in the world. No one does evil because it's evil; they do it because they think it is the right or even the good thing to do. Ponder the idea of slavery for instance. To justify slavery, the slave owner has to operate from a position that affirms slavery as not only possible, but as something that is in fact good. So much so that some people "made

a living" by hunting for slaves and selling them. There were many so-called "Christians" among these—think of Spain and Portugal, or the devout evangelical Southern states. Or apartheid South Africa. What kind of mind is the one that legitimizes and authorizes the idea of owning other human beings and doing to them as you see fit? Of dominating them totally? And slavery is only one of the possible narratives that we maintain to legitimize immoral actions. We can put all other endemic sins in here—pride, racism, sexism, greed, injustice, pornography, and patriarchy.

14 We have already noted that in Romans 12:1–2, something revolutionary has taken place at the core of a person's consciousness, their way of perceiving the world. The believer receives a whole new worldview in the act of conversion and begins to live from within that new orientation. "Since it is the mind that is being transformed, Paul is talking about a change in worldview, a Copernican revolution in one's thinking, not just an attitude adjustment. He is speaking about a new or 'renewed' and Christlike way of looking at the world. In the light of the previous verse, Paul must surely also mean that to offer proper and rational worship one must have a renewed mind. For one thing, one's concept of God, the one true God, must be renewed or transformed. Renewal of mind and presentation of body are two parts of what must happen if one is to offer true worship to God. But Paul also says that the renewal of the mind is the prerequisite to discerning the will of God, and so to behaving as well as believing in a way that worships and glorifies God ... Discernment of what is good and pleasing and perfect in God's will and eyes is possible only if the fallen person has had a transformation and renewal of his or her mind. Precisely because the believer is a new eschatological creation, though living in an old and obsolescent world, new modes of behavior are expected, indeed required. As Wright suggests, v.1 focuses on the body but with the mind involved, and v.2 focuses on the mind but with implications about what the body does. These two verses then together refer to the whole person dedicated to God in all things and orientations." Ben Witherington III, *Paul's Letter to the Romans: A Socio-Rhetorical Commentary* (Grand Rapids: Eerdmans, 2004), 287. The action of conversion is considered to be a "renewing of the mind" (Rom 12:2; Eph 4:23). In both cases the process is one whereby God takes control of the individual's mind through the Holy Spirit and leads the thoughts of that person into proper channels. Thus, they are given power to make proper value judgments. The convert has a new mind with which to make spiritual discernments. He or she has the mind of Christ (1 Cor 2:15–6). Thus, Paul can say that they therefore serve God with their mind (Rom 7:25).

15 Actually, the words "soul" and "spirit" both hint at the intangible quality of wind; both the Hebrew (*nephesh* and *ruach*) and Greek (*psyche*) words literally mean breath and living being and are synonymous with life itself. See Brown, *The Dictionary of New Testament Theology, Vol. 3*, 680, for a thorough lexical analysis of the terms used in Scripture.

16 The Catechism of the Catholic Church states that the term "soul" refers to "the innermost aspect of persons, that which is of greatest value in them, that by which they are most especially in God's image: 'soul' signifies the spiritual principle in humanity." https://www.vatican.va/archive/ENG0015/_INDEX.HTM (accessed February 28, 2023).

17 Jeffrey Ames Kay, *Theological Aesthetics: The Role of Aesthetics in the Theological Method of Hans Urs von Balthasar* (Frankfurt: Herbert Lang, 1975), 1–2.

18 He maintains that the soul 1) makes all meaning possible, 2) turns events into personal experience, 3) involves a deepening of experience, 4) is communicated and experienced

most profoundly in love, and 5) has a special relation with death, which highlights the pathos of life in the face of it. James Hillman, *Re-Visioning Psychology* (New York: HarperPerennial, 1977), xvi, and his *Suicide and the Soul* (New York: Harper Colophon 1976), 44–7. The mention of death here might be jarring, but death is significant for the soul because possibility (and hence imagination) derives from an existential recognition of our finitude: what is finite can imagine possibilities, some of which will be realized, others of which, owing to death, will not.

19 He adds "The holy Scriptures do everywhere place religion very much in the affection; things such as fear, hope, love, hatred, desire, joy, sorrow, gratitude, compassion, and zeal. It is evidence that true religion, or holiness of heart, lies very much in the affection of the heart, that the Scriptures place the sin of the heart very much in hardness of heart … Now by a hard heart, is plainly meant an unaffected heart, or a heart not easy to be moved with virtuous affections." Jonathan Edwards, *On the Religious Affections* (Carlisle, PA: Banner of Truth, 1961), 11.

20 It is fascinating that theologians believe that, before the fall, the first humans wore their souls on the outside of their bodies. In a sense they were clothed in their souls. They were "glorious" in that they literally glowed with vibrant and authentic life. This idea also accounts for the practice of portraying saints and holy people with a shining aura. They are people whose souls irradiate their bodies; they get to wear their souls on the outside. See for instance Hans Urs von Balthasar, *The Christian State of Life* (San Francisco: Ignatius, 1983), 97.

21 Boris Pasternak, "After the Storm," https://allpoetry.com/After-The-Storm (accessed February 28, 2023).

22 Willard, *Renovation of the Heart*, 60.

23 "From every deed an angel is born, a good angel or a bad one. But from half-hearted and confused deeds which are without meaning or without power, angels are born with twisted limbs or without a head or hands or feet." Martin Buber in Maurice Friedman, *Religion and Psychology: A Dialogical Approach* (New York: Paragon House, 1998), 6.

24 Martin Buber, *Between Man and Man* (Newark: Martino Fine Books, 2014), 46.

25 Both the Hebrew and Greek versions of Dt 6:4–5 describe a threefold response to God—heart, soul, and strength. Mark quotes Jesus adding a fourth element, the love of God with your whole mind or understanding. "Four times in Mark 9:30 the word 'all' is repeated, emphasizing the necessity of a total response of love to the lordship of God. God is the one and only Lord, not only of Israel but of every individual as well. God lays rightful claim to every facet of human personality: heart (affection), soul (spirit), mind (intelligence), and strength (will). Each of the four commandments is prefaced by the Greek preposition *ex*, meaning 'from the source of,' rather than 'by means of.' Thus, we are commanded to love God not simply *with* our whole heart, but *from* our heart." James Edwards, *The Gospel According to Mark: Pillar New Testament Commentaries* (Grand Rapids: Eerdmans, 2002), 771.

26 I (Alan) have done a fair bit of work on this dimension of discipleship and worship in previous writings, namely in *Untamed*, 65–8 and in *ReJesus*, 149–159. In this book we are focusing on the aspect of wholesale and systemic change that goes to the root of things. But we recommend exploring the material in *Untamed and ReJesus* to substantiate what is said here. See Alan Hirsch and Debra Hirsch, *Untamed: Reactivating a Missional Form of Discipleship* (Grand Rapids: Baker, 2010) and Frost and Hirsch, *ReJesus*.

27 "The word 'heart' connotes what is meant today by the term 'person' and 'center of the person'; From Pascal who understands 'heart' as the 'sensorium for the whole, for God,' we learn that it is in the heart that intellect, will and all the faculties have their common foundation. Thus faith, for Pascal, is defined as 'God perceived by the heart.' What in an older psychology is meant in Scripture by 'heart' was largely occupied by the will or love; but following Pascal, Peguy and others, von Balthasar goes beyond this understanding, suggesting that it is in the heart that reason and freedom, intellect and will attain their ultimate unity and integration. If one were to try to discern in von Balthasar's aesthetics a 'place of contact' in the human person between natural and supernatural orders, human and divine freedom, finite and infinite, it would have to be in the heart. There the light of God, the light of faith, is received by the human person if it is received (2 Cor. 4:5); there the substance of God touches the substance of the human soul; there the human person meets the personal God. The light of God shines in a heart that is open and ready to receive it. The prerequisite of a fundamental openness and receptivity on the part of the human subject in order for perception to take place applies on both natural and supernatural levels of seeing. This fundamental, free receptivity is the prerequisite, the precondition of all genuinely personal knowledge." Ann M. Callahan, *The Concept of Person in the Theology of Hans Urs von Balthasar* (PhD diss., Fordham University, 1993), 190–1.

28 Kallistos Ware, *The Orthodox Way* (St. Vladimir's Seminary Press, 2012), 154–5. We are reminded of Paul's exhortation in Rom 12:1–2: "By the mercies of God … present your bodies as a living sacrifice, holy and acceptable to God, which is your reasonable [*logikēn*] worship. Do not be conformed [*mē syschēmatizesthe*] to this world, but be transformed [*metamorphousthe*] by the renewing of your minds, so that you may discern what is the will of God." Douglas Harink, *I and II Peter: The Brazos Theological Commentary on the Bible* (Grand Rapids: Brazos, 2009), 56. See appendix three on the prayer of the heart.

29 To really *know* God we have to love him with all three dimensions of the heart. For instance, we cannot simply love God with our minds alone. Brute facticity and cold logic remain uncompelling for the human being when they are divorced from questions of meaning, beauty, and teleology. We need to love with all our soul-power as well as all of our will-power. In other words, we need orthodoxy, orthopraxy, and orthopathy to truly know God. Orthodoxy involves right belief and is a function of the nous/mind. Orthopraxy involves right acting as a way of knowing and loving God and is a function of will. And orthopathy involves an engagement of our affections and passions and aligning them with the One God. This is, of course, an engagement of the soul. See Hirsch and Frost, *ReJesus*, 143–53, and Hirsch and Hirsch, *Untamed*, 64–8 for a more thorough exploration of what we call a biblical epistemology, or way of knowing.

30 Willard, *Renovation of the Heart*, 47. That is why we have the biblical teaching that human good and evil are in the end matters of the heart. Freedom is therefore directly related to the human capacity for sin and rebellion. Response and responsibility, obedience and choice, are the basis of monotheistic religion.

31 Kay, *Theological Aesthetics*, 1–2. Kay goes on to say, "By rooting the senses in itself the heart makes all sensual activities into acts of the whole human. The senses are a person's opened heart. The eye, for instance, is the openness of the whole man to reality insofar as it is form and light. This integration of the mind's vision with the eye's vision is effected not only by their common agent, the heart, but also by their common object, Being."

32 Consider too that many Christians and churches go overboard on a theology of experience

that fails to integrate the intellect and the will. Von Balthasar notes that "Many aberrations of the theology of experience and of life throughout history derive in every case from the fact that feeling is too exclusively thought of as an isolated act alongside the intellect and the will, and too little understood as the integration of the person's whole life. Consequently, the criteria for the God-relationship are based too exclusively on individual emotional states and pay little attention to the event by which man's total constitution and disposition, which are the foundation for everything else, can be experienced in and through individual emotional states. The Scriptural arguments that oppose a pure theology of feeling lie ready to hand; but the very same arguments can equally be applied to defeat a theology that would attempt to establish man's rightful relationship to God simply on isolated acts of faith and love, instead of anchoring it within man's total disposition towards the living God." Von Balthasar, *The Glory of the Lord, I,* 237.

33 This example itself was suggested to me (Alan) by my friend Mandy Smith.

34 This paragraph is adapted from Richard Rohr, *Breathing Under Water: Spirituality and the Twelve Steps* (London: SPCK, 2016), 25.

35 A meta-idea is an idea that determines and shapes other ideas and thinking in the organization. In other words, it is what we might call a "primordial idea" or "cornerstone concept." Change here changes everything. Identifying these is critical in leveraging change throughout the organization. For those aware of Alan's mDNA model of movement, each of the mDNA are in effect meta-ideas. These are; Jesus is Lord (transcendent ideals that inform and motivate), Discipleship and Disciple-Making (system of recruitment and formation of adherents), Missional-Incarnational Impulse (how the organization extends and establishes itself onto new ground), APEST Culture (ministry and leadership typology and system), Organic Systems (movemental and scalable organization), and Liminality-Communitas (the capacity to take risks, innovate, and thrive in adaptive situations.) Each of these offers huge leverage throughout the organization.

36 In the church, core theology constitutes the meta-ideas that have significant scriptural weight/authority to be deemed necessary for faith.

37 Culture creates the environment where behaviors are legitimized, responsibilities are shared, and meaning and significance are transferred. This is clearly important because it involves reinforcing the motivational passions that keep people aligned to the communal cause. See Hirsch, *The Forgotten Ways,* 202.

38 See the article Ron Ashkenas, "Three Steps for Overcoming Passive Resistance," *Forbes,* December 17, 2012, https://www.forbes.com/sites/ronashkenas/2012/12/17/three-steps-for-overcoming-passive-resistance/?sh=6c18997f2f3e.

39 See Frost and Hirsch, *ReJesus,* chapter seven; and Hirsch and Hirsch, *Untamed.*

40 According to Strong's Concordance, the Greek word *horáō* means "to be able to see with the mind, to look upon, experience, perceive, discern."

Part Two: How Metanoia (Introduction)

1 See https://www.movementleaderscollective.com and https://www.themxplatform.com for details. Rob likewise has developed learning cohorts designed to bring about movements

across cities. He shares his insights in this book—especially in the next chapter on *platforms,* explaining why they are critical to changing the game. Rob's key role is with For Charlotte Network as well as the new City Leaders Collective. See https://www.forcharlotte.org.

2   Rohr, *Falling Upward,* 37.

3   "History amply shows, we prefer regularity and predictability and want to forgo the perils of adventure in exchange for a more manageable experience of life, especially in institutions. Here, at least in part, lies the psychology behind institutionalism: all institutions, religious or otherwise, are designed to provide the safety of predictability achieved through ritual, dogma, and control through regulations, policies, the promise of reward, or the threat of discipline. That is not necessarily a bad thing. In many ways, this is the boon that institutions confer on us: by providing regularity, recognizability, and ritual, they relieve us of having to incessantly develop new ways of doing things." Alan Hirsch and Tim Catchim, *The Permanent Revolution: Apostolic Imagination and Practice for the 21st Century Church* (San Francisco: Wiley, 2012), 185.

4   This insight is ascribed to British missiologist J. V. Taylor, but the reference cannot be properly sourced.

5   *Stoicheia* (the elemental spirits/elements in Gal 4:3, 9; Col 2:8, 20–22, etc.) are a category of spiritual powers that relate to religious tradition and ways of thinking and are a real issue in changing any organization—but especially religious ones!

6   The U-shaped journey is variously expressed in the New Testament in the doctrines of Christ's self-emptying (*kenosis*), the incarnation, recapitulation (*anakephalaiosis*), restoration of all things (*apocatastasis*), suffering (*pathos*) and the process of making divine through union with God (*theosis*). See chapter five of Hirsch, *5Q,* for elaboration of this idea in relation to Jesus.

7   See *Wikipedia,* "Hero's Journey," https://en.wikipedia.org/wiki/Hero%27s_journey (accessed February 28, 2023). The application of the hero's journey to organization is now well established. For instance, see Pat Purdue, "The Hero's Journey: How To Tell Your Personal Brand Story In A Captivating Way," *Forbes Magazine,* January 6, 2021, https://www.forbes.com/sites/forbesbusinesscouncil/2021/01/06/the-heros-journey-how-to-tell-your-personal-brand-story-in-a-captivating-way/.

8   All are built on the U-curve shaped experience. Otto Scharmer, *Essentials of Theory U, Core Principles and Applications* (San Francisco: Berrett Koehler, 2018).

9   Liminality is the quality of danger, disorientation, marginalizing, or threat that precipitates a learning journey. It means a threshold experience, in which we stand on the threshold or a transitional boundary.

10 Perhaps you should put yourself into the story where Jesus sends his apostles to do a liminal task: "And he called the twelve together and gave them power and authority over all demons and to cure diseases, and he sent them out to preach the kingdom of God and to heal. And he said to them, 'Take nothing for your journey, no staff, nor bag, nor bread, nor money; and do not have two tunics. And whatever house you enter, stay there, and from there depart. And wherever they do not receive you, when you leave that town shake off the dust from your feet as a testimony against them.' And they departed and went through the villages, preaching the gospel and healing everywhere" (Lk 6–9:1 RSV).

11 The slogan of the SWAT team just before they engage real danger in a raid. *S.W.A.T.* season 1, episode 4, "Radical," directed by Greg Beeman.

6 The Metanoia Journey

1 Robert Pirsig, *Zen and the Art of Motorcycle Maintenance: An Enquiry into Values* (New York: HarperCollins, 1999), 102.

2 Eddie Gibbs, himself one of the founders of church growth theory, once quipped that what emerged from all the management and marketing techniques applied to the church: "Oh, it's a pig with lipstick, but it's still a pig." He, of course, meant that the fundamental paradigm of (attractional) church remained intact.

3 In his brilliant book on the nature of prophetic consciousness, Abraham Heschel says that we must forget many clichés if we want to understand things in a new way. "Insight is a break-through, requiring much intellectual dismantling and dislocation. It begins with a mental interim, with the cultivation of a feeling for the unfamiliar, unparalleled, incredible. It is in being involved with a phenomenon, being intimately engaged to it, courting it, as it were, that after much perplexity and embarrassment we come upon insight—upon a way of seeing the phenomenon from within. Insight is accompanied by a sense of surprise. What has been closed is suddenly disclosed. It entails genuine perception, seeing anew. He who thinks that we can see the same object twice has never seen. Paradoxically, insight is knowledge at first sight." Abraham Heschel, *The Prophets, Vol. 1* (New York: HarperPerennial, 1962), xxiv-v.

4 We suggest that the VUCA conditions we now face require adaptive solutions, which by their nature call into question our established way of doing things. We must find new forms, or we will continue toward the precipitous decline associated with non-adaptive European Christianity.

5 Peter Drucker notes that all living organisms must have a functioning system of elimi-nation, or they will soon perish. He suggests therefore that a foundational principle for an adaptive organization is to "abandon yesterday" in order to free resources from being committed to maintaining what no longer contributes to performance, and no longer produces results. He suggests that "The *first* policy, therefore, throughout the entire insti-tution, has to be Organized Abandonment." Peter F. Drucker, *Management Challenges for the 21st Century* (New York: Harper Collins, 1999), 74.

6 *The Wire*, created by David Simon, Blown Deadline Productions HBO.

7 Most of us aren't homicide detectives, of course, but we all require soft eyes at numerous critical junctures of life. A doctor needs soft eyes in diagnosing a complex medical syndrome; a mechanic when repairing a motor vehicle; a political analyst in anticipating global trends; an economist tracking the invisible hand of the market; a scientist doing breakthrough research; a scriptwriter in a successful TV series; a business entrepreneur in seeking to exploit unantici-pated gaps in the market; and so on. This illustration is taken from Hirsch, *5Q*, xvii.

8 Coming to grips with the anomalies is a precondition for the turning, for the search of alternatives, and ultimately for paradigm change. In fact, it was the seminal philosopher of science, Thomas Kuhn, who noted that new paradigms begin when the very best theorists in their respective fields sense the anomalies in the prevailing paradigm—that the mental constructs of the predominant paradigm do not account for all aspects of reality—there are flaws at the core of the model. The anomaly initiates the unraveling of the system. It initiates the search for alternatives. Kuhn notes that the new paradigm begins to form when these people get together and begin to compare notes and collectively name the problem

and go in search for a solution. T. S. Kuhn, *The Structure of Scientific Revolutions* (Chicago: University of Chicago Press, 1962).

9   See Margaret J. Wheatley, *Leadership and the New Science: Discovering Order in a Chaotic World, 3rd ed.* (San Francisco: Barret-Koehler, 2018) for an extended discussion on the key implications of the paradigm shift.

10 Alan's book *The Forgotten Ways* is dedicated to an exploration of these six elements of mDNA (movement DNA).

11 John Maynard Keynes, *The General Theory of Employment, Interest and Money* (Harcourt, Brace & Company, New York, 1936), viii.

12 Eberhard Arnold quoted in Clare Stober, "Retooling the Plough," *Plough*, August 30, 2022, italics ours, https://www.plough.com/en/topics/community/retooling-the-plough.

13 An object that has one singular function for an adult (e.g., a chair) has many playful possibilities for the child. For an adult, it is "just a chair" whereas for the child it can be a house, a horse, an anti-aircraft gun, etc. This is also called "divergent thinking" by creativity experts—a thought process or method used to generate creative ideas by exploring many possible solutions. The alternative to divergent thinking is *convergent* thinking, which is more focused, systematic, and linear, arriving at one solution. Divergent thinking is non-linear logic that expands outwards by generating multiple ideas and using familiar materials in unfamiliar ways. (For more on the dynamics of imaginative thinking, see appendix five on a whole new mind.)

14 Willem H. Vanderburg, ed. *Perspectives on Our Age: Jacques Ellul Speaks on His Life and Work* (Toronto, ON: Anansi Press, 2004), 129.

15 See Rob Wegner, Lance Ford, Alan Hirsch, *The Starfish and the Spirit: Unleashing the Leadership Potential of Churches and Organizations* (Grand Rapids: Zondervan, 2021) for a thorough exploration of these ideas.

16 See appendix six on upstream and downstream processing.

17 I Ching, "Hexagram 24. Fu / Return (The Turning Point)," *I Ching Online*, https://www.iching-online.com/hexagrams/iching-hexagram-000001.html (accessed February 28, 2023).

18 Quoted in Wheatley, *Leadership and the New Science*, 2.

19 Thankfully not all members of the organization need to be involved at all stages of this process. We suggest that those working at the level of paradigm and mental mapping ought to bring key leaders (around 5 percent of people) into this process early as they are, in effect, the keepers of the paradigm. If they do not change then neither will the system. Broader leadership (around 15 percent) needs to be engaged in the culture-creation aspects of the platform. By the time we get to practices, everyone in the organization (the remaining 80 percent) becomes involved because everyone is affected.

20 This correlation between the design process and the movement that emerges from it is like a seed, which contains in itself the potential for a whole forest. The seed, is of course the paradigm and the DNA that provides the seminal code for what follows. However, if the seed is to not just survive but to thrive, it must germinate, take root, and develop into a tree. By doing this it creates a viable organism, which is the living expression of the potential life contained in the seed (platform). From there, the individual tree, if it is healthy and operates according to its inbuilt purpose, must go on to produce fruit in which the potential for the whole forest is contained (practices). But it is correct to say that the potential for the forest was already contained in the seed.

7 Paradigm

1 UNICEF, "World Urbanization Prospects 2018," https://population.un.org/wup/publications/Files/WUP2018-Highlights.pdf, 5 (accessed February 28, 2023).

2 "The 10/40 Window is the rectangular area of North Africa, the Middle East and Asia approximately between 10 degrees north and 40 degrees north latitude. The 10/40 Window is often called 'The Resistant Belt' and includes the majority of the world's Muslims, Hindus, and Buddhists. The original 10/40 Window included only countries with at least 50% of their land mass within 10 and 40 degrees north latitude. The revised 10/40 Window includes several additional countries that are close to 10 or 40 degrees north latitude and have high concentrations of unreached peoples." "What is the 10/40 Window?" https://joshuaproject.net/resources/articles/10_40_window (accessed February 28, 2023).

3 Hirsch and Catchim, *The Permanent Revolution,* xxxii.

4 Peter Senge notes that paradigms are deeply ingrained assumptions, generalizations, or even pictures or images that influence how we understand the world and how we take action. Very often, we are not consciously aware of our own paradigms or the effects they have on our behavior. He notes that in the world of commerce, "many insights into new markets or outmoded organizational practices fail to get put into practice because they conflict with powerful, tacit mental models." Peter Senge, *The Fifth Discipline: The Art and Practice of the Learning Organization* (New York: Currency Doubleday, 1990), 11.

5 "American way," *Wikipedia,* https://en.wikipedia.org/wiki/American_way (accessed February 28, 2023).

6 Hirsch and Catchim, *The Permanent Revolution,* xxxii.

7 Hirsch, *5Q,* 19.

8 Adapted from Hirsch and Ferguson, *On the Verge,* 122–3.

9 Adapted from Kn Moy presentation on "Social Movements: A Powerful Force for Change in Our Cities"; and Tim Keller, *Center Church: Doing Balanced Gospel-Centered Ministry in Your City* (Grand Rapids: Zondervan, 2012), 341.

10 *Encyclopedia Britannica, standard ed.,* CD-ROM, s.v. "DNA."

11 For instance, the American Association for the Advancement of Science recognizes that "Some important themes pervade science, mathematics, and technology and appear over and over again, whether we are looking at an ancient civilization, the human body, or a comet. They are ideas that transcend disciplinary boundaries and prove fruitful in explanation, in theory, in observation, and in design." To locate meta-ideas, scientists focus on

- Patterns—attributes that appear in a regular sequence over and over
- Cause and Effect—what happens when we....
- Scale Proportion and Quantity—which one is bigger/longer/higher
- Systems and Systems Models—parts make up the whole
- Structure and Function—things are arranged for a purpose
- Stability and Change—some things are always the same but almost everything changes.

National Academies Press, *A Framework for K-12 Science Education: Practices, Crosscutting Concepts, and Core Ideas,* chapter eight, https://www.nap.edu/read/13165/chapter/8 (accessed February 28, 2023).

12 See Hirsch and Catchim, *The Permanent Revolution* for an extensive look into the nature and functions of the apostolic person.

13 David Peter Stroh, *Systems Thinking for Social Change: A Practical Guide to Solving Complex Problems, Avoiding Unintended Consequences, and Achieving Lasting Results* (White River Junction, VT: Chelsea Green Publishing, 2015), 57.

14 Hirsch and Ferguson, *On the Verge*, 57.

15 Quoted in Scott Nelson, *Mission: Living for the Purposes of God* (Downers Grove, IL: IVP, 2013), 39.

16 Peter F. Drucker "The Theory of the Business," *Harvard Business Review*, September, 1994, https://hbr.org/1994/09/the-theory-of-the-business.

17 Hirsch and Ferguson, *On the Verge*, 54.

18 Adapted from Hirsch and Ferguson, *On the Verge*, 54–5.

19 See Nickerson, "Confirmation bias."

20 Heschel, *The Prophets*, xxxiv–v.

21 Adapted from Luke Smilli, "Openness to Experience: The Gates of the Mind: People who are 'open to experience' literally see the world differently," *Scientific American*, August 15, 2017, https://www.scientificamerican.com/article/openness-to-experience-the-gates-of-the-mind/?WT.mc_id=SA_MB_20170816.

22 "Diffusion of Innovation Theory," *Behavioral Change Models*, https://sphweb.bumc.bu.edu/otlt/mph-modules/sb/behavioralchangetheories/behavioralchangetheories4.html (accessed February 28, 2023).

8 Plat*formed*

1 Christopher Nolan, dir., *Inception*, 2010, Warner Bros. Pictures.

2 As we were writing this book, we heard Lucas Pulley, a friend and colleague of ours from the amazing Tampa Underground Network share: "We often rely solely on communication (our words) to shift a community or organization in a new direction. Those words are no match for a decades-formed *culture* and *structure* hell-bent on preventing any change. This dynamic is what's happening when megachurches do a sermon series on microchurch or on releasing the priesthood of all believers." We could not agree more with Lucas. Preachers, take note!

3 Mona Delahooke, *Brain-Body Parenting: How to Stop Managing Behavior and Start Raising Joyful, Resilient Kids* (Harper Wave, 2022), 19.

4 Marshall McLuhan, *Understanding Media: The Extensions of Man* (Cambridge, MA: MIT Press, 1994), chapter one.

5 A helpful exercise in diagnosing the misalignment between culture and structure is to write your "systems story." You do this by asking and answering the question, What story is your system telling? (See appendix eight for instructions.)

6 See Geoffrey G. Parker, Marshall W. Van Alstyne, and Sangeet Paul Choudary, *Platform Revolution: How Networked Markets are Transforming the Economy—and How to Make Them Work for You, Reprint Edition* (New York: W. W. Norton & Company, 2017).

7 As a great example of clearly articulating and delineating between theological distinctives and values, we encourage you to check out our friends at Creo Collective, https://www.creocollective.org/about (accessed February 28, 2023).

8 Jim Collins, *Good to Great: Why Some Companies Make the Leap and Others Don't* (New York: HarperCollins, 2005).

9 One of the remarkable, and often-overlooked, dimensions of New Testament ecclesiology is that Jesus has given us everything we need to get the job done. One of the ways that this is factored into the agency of the church is in the area of the APEST typology of Ephesians 4:1–16 which I (Alan) in my book *5Q* call the latent intelligence and capacities of the body of Christ. The Ephesians 4 typology of ministry and leadership is as good as any that can be found in best thinking from leadership and organizational studies. All the functions of ministry and organization are covered in this system from the missional/entrepreneurial (apostolic); the aligning function (prophetic); the capacity to recruit and get buy-in (evangelistic); to the human resourcing functions that are key to the functions of the shepherd and the teacher. The remarkable thing is that this is not just a leadership capacity but is "given" to all believers ("to each one of us," Eph 4:7) thus distributing a particular agency and function to all.

10 Not to mention, volunteerism is in massive decline in our culture. Most pastors or church leaders can verify this. Because the church in the West is in such steep decline, local churches are struggling to get people to fill volunteer roles—this alone should force us to examine our missional structures.

11 Frederick Buechner, *Wishful Thinking: A Seeker's ABC* (New York: Harper & Row, 1973), 95.

12 Quoted in Gil Bailie, *Violence Unveiled: Humanity at the Crossroads* (New York: The Crossroad Publishing, 1997), xv.

13 In his book, *The New Leadership Literacies*, Bob Johansen, shares that to thrive in times of extreme disruption, will require organizations to shapeshift from centralized to decentralized structures. In doing so, he emphasizes the necessity of distributing authority in and through their new decentralized form, ensuring each leader be given the authority needed to accomplish the role they have responsibility for (*New Leadership Literacies: Thriving in a Future of Extreme Disruption and Distributed Everything* [Barrett-Koehler Publishers, 2017], chapter 6). Also we refer you to Wegner, Ford, and Hirsch, *The Starfish and the Spirit* for a thorough exploration of "starfish" principles for movements.

14 We use the word democratize, not in its political sense but in its literal sense: to push out through all the people of the organization.

15 The move from centralization to democratization is a dynamic tension that can be seen in the Scriptures. Humankind's constant default is the elevation of self versus God's desire to democratize his Spirit and mission through all people. This tension is clear when juxtaposing the Tower of Babel narrative in Genesis 11 with Pentecost in Acts 2. In Babel, we see people building a tower up to God, and God confuses the languages, leading to humankind being scattered and divided; whereas, at Pentecost, God comes down to us, we are given the Holy Spirit, the gospel is unleashed around the world, and the many ethnicities present experience a miraculous unity.

16 This is why the mDNA of Organic Systems becomes an essential platform design principle. Another massive benefit of this structure is how it combats the hyper-individualism of our world. Organic systems, held together by common DNA, create a foundation for a deeper experience of authentic community, reflecting another mDNA element of Liminality and Communitas.

17 Healthy, networked organizations not only reflect Jesus' design for how the church should interact with itself but actually reflect the nature of the God we worship; the God in whose

image we have been created; the God in whom we have been united to in Christ; one God in three persons: Father, Son, and Holy Spirit. Many of the central characteristics of organic networks are Trinitarian (*perichoretic*) by nature: love, unity in diversity, mutual submission, common purpose, and the like.

18 "Churchill and the Commons Chamber," *UK Parliament*, https://www.parliament.uk/about/ living-heritage/building/palace/architecture/palacestructure/churchill/#:~:text= Churchill%20insisted%20that%20the%20shape (accessed February 28, 2023).

9 Practices

1 Adapted from an illustration I (Rob) heard years ago from my friend and leading mission network strategist Eldon Porter.

2 Hirsch, *The Forgotten Ways*, chapter five; Hirsch and Ferguson, *On The Verge*, chapter five.

3 James K. A. Smith, says, "What if, instead of starting from the assumption that human beings are thinking things, we started from the conviction that human beings are first and foremost *lovers?* What if you are defined not by what you *know* but by what you desire? What if the center of and seat of the human person is found not in the heady regions of the intellect but in the gut-level regions of the heart? How would that change our approach to discipleship and Christian formation?" James K. A. Smith, *You Are What You Love: The Spiritual Power of Habit* (Grand Rapids: Brazos Press, 2016), 7.

4 An example of a fractalized meta-idea is in what is often called Up-In-Out which refers to the three dimensions of biblical spirituality—upward toward God, inward toward community/people, and outward in mission in the world. This fractal can be applied at the level of the individual disciple all the way to the largest gathering. See chapter seven of this book to recall the definition and significance of fractals for viable expressions of movement.

5 Stanley Hauerwas, "The Sanctified Body," in *Embodied Holiness*, ed. Samuel M. Powell and Michael E. Lodahl (Downers Grove, IL: InterVarsity Press, 1999), 22.

6 Our practices don't arise in a vacuum; they are outward and visible expressions of what we think are important. They are formulated out of what we believe and are given their true meaning and significance from the way we perceive the world and our place within it. In other words, our practices are both expressions of our paradigm/s and embodiments of our culture.

7 The Golden Rule of Habit Change expresses the most effective way to stop addictive habits and replaces them with new ones. It states that if you keep the initial cue, replace the routine, and keep the reward, change will eventually occur, although individuals who do not believe in what they are doing will likely fall short of the expectations and give up. See Charles Duhigg, *The Power of Habit: Why We Do What We Do in Life and Business* (New York: Random House, 2012).

8 Performing an action repeatedly activates neurons in certain parts of the brain, particularly the cerebellum and basal ganglia, and creates a new neural pathway between the central nervous system and the muscles you're moving. Muscle memory is a form of procedural memory that involves consolidating a specific motor task into memory through repetition, which has been used synonymously with motor learning. When a movement is repeated over time, the brain creates a long-term muscle memory for that task, eventually allowing

it to be performed with little to no conscious effort. This process decreases the need for attention and creates maximum efficiency within the motor and memory systems. Muscle memory is found in many everyday activities that become automatic and improve with practice, such as riding bicycles, driving motor vehicles, playing ball sports, typing on keyboards, entering PINs, playing musical instruments, throwing a ball, martial arts, and dancing.

9   Marek Kowalkiewicz "How did we get here? The story of algorithms," *Medium*, October 10, 2019, https://towardsdatascience.com/how-did-we-get-here-the-story-of-algorithms-9ee186ba2a07.

10   Steve Addison, *The Rise and Fall of Movements: A Roadmap for Leaders* (Cody, WY: 100 Movements Publishing, 2019), 47.

11   Although the process of designing a unique organizational algorithm is beyond the scope of this book, we address the topic to emphasize the power of algorithms and to encourage organizational leaders to develop an algorithm. We have been highly influenced by the best of design thinking on the subject. Resources such as Stanford D. School's design-thinking process (https://web.stanford.edu/~mshanks/MichaelShanks/files/509554.pdf, accessed February 28, 2023;) and Eric Ries's Lean Startup Methodology (https://theleanstartup.com/principles, accessed February 28, 2023) are excellent places to begin this process.

12   JR Woodward and Dan White Jr., *The Church as Movement: Starting and Sustaining Missional-Incarnational Communities* (Downers Grove, IL: IVP, 2016), 38–40.

13   Ibid., 154–7. The model originated with the sociologist Edward T. Hall but was elaborated on for church settings by Joseph Myers in his book *The Search to Belong: Rethinking Intimacy, Community, and Small Groups* (New York: Harper Collins, 2003).

14   Dave Runyon and Jay Pathak, *The Art of Neighboring: Building Genuine Relationships Right Outside Your Door* (Grand Rapids: Baker, 2012).

15   Michael Frost, *Surprise the World: The Five Habits of Highly Missional People* (Colorado: NavPress, 2015).

16   Red Church, Melbourne, Austrailia, https://redchurchau-my.sharepoint.com/personal/red_redchurch_org_au/_layouts/15/onedrive.aspx?id=%2Fpersonal%2Fred%5Fredchurch%5Forg%5Fau%2FDocuments%2FDiscipleship%2FA%5FGuide%5Ffor%5FHuddles%2Epdf&parent=%2Fpersonal%2Fred%5Fredchurch%5Forg%5Fau%2FDocuments%2FDiscipleship&ga=1 (accessed February 28, 2023).

17   Adapted from: Katarína Pavelová "Perichoresis—The Divine Dance of the Trinity," *Vivat Deus*, June 5, 2022, https://vivatdeus.org/library/blog0065/, accessed February 28, 2023). The author goes on to write: "The Trinity is, so, an eternal dance of the Father, Son, and Spirit sharing mutual love, honor, happiness, joy, and respect, and living an eternal relationship of self-giving. In this dance, the three divine persons of the One God have loved one another and been in a relationship with one another for all eternity. They, also, deeply and intimately know one another and there is no fear, shame, or insecurity in their knowledge of one another. Father and Son dwell in a face-to-face relationship with the Spirit as the bond of love that unites them. The profoundly complete and pure relationship and free, full, and overflowing love is the central quality of God. Through this never-ending dance, the divine persons exist so intimately with one another, for one another, and in one another, that they constitute a single, unique, and complete unity by themselves."

Conclusion: Write Your Own Adventure

1   One of the best "formulas" to emerge from the Reformation was *semper reformanda*, which maintains that the church cannot rest on its current formulations and expressions; that we never arrive at the perfected form of *ecclesia*; that we must always be re-*form*-ing. This commits the church to constant adaptation—something we have all-too-seldom done, despite it being formulated over five hundred years ago. Most denominational expressions are deeply entrenched in now outdated paradigms and formulations.

2   Willem Vanderburg says, "Western culture tells us we should be complete and independent. It tempts us to believe we can escape our ordinary, human limitations—weakness, sickness, incapacity, ignorance. We swim in water that is toxic to humans. The more we bring that toxic culture into our Christian practices, the more we strip our faith of every way God wants to redeem us as ordinary, limited humans." Quoted in Mandy Smith, *Unfettered: Imagining a Childlike Faith beyond the Baggage of Western Culture* (Downers Grove, IL: IVP, 2021), 17.

3   For instance, "But just as love is not overcome by the everyday routine, but uses its imagination in a thousand ways to transfigure it, fashioning each day anew in small details, so it is with contemplation. Every day I am privileged to appear before the God who is eternally young, who never ages; God's meadows bloom as brightly and in as many colors as ever, and man's inner receptivity is renewed every day, provided that he makes use of it. His tiredness, listlessness, discouragement and bitterness are his alone, and he cannot complain about anything, since God has everything ready to refresh him, bowed down as he is under his burdens. He only has to pull himself together and shake off whatever is oppressing him and dragging him down. All he has to do is give it over and begin again." Von Balthasar, *Prayer*, 139.

4   Albert Einstein, *Wish I'd Said That*, https://wist.info/einstein-albert/6414/ (accessed February 28, 2023).

5   From a radio broadcast in Berlin opening the German Radio Exhibition, August 22, 1930. Transcribed by Friedrich Herneck in *Die Naturwissenschaften* 48 (1961), 33. Einstein Archives 4–044.

6   Pearce, *The Crack in the Cosmic Egg*, 8.

7   Ibid., 21.

CATALYZING JESUS MOVEMENTS TO SHIFT THE TRACKS OF HISTORY.

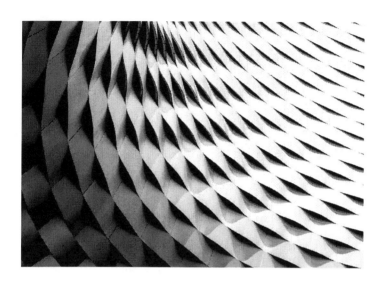

DYNAMIC. COLLABORATIVE. INNOVATIVE. CREATIVE.

Movement Leaders Collective exists to identify, train, and empower 100 Jesus-movements and 1,000 Christlike leaders using the mDNA framework to become dynamic, innovative, and generative movements able to shift the tracks of history.

Hybrid Publisher | Training Ecosystem | Leaders Collective

MOVEMENTLEADERSCOLLECTIVE.COM

Made in USA - Crawfordsville, IN
35193_9781955142373
06.13.2023 1842